# The INFORMANT Files

**The FBI's most valuable snitch**

ROBERT JAMES

Electronic Media Publishing Co., Inc.
A Nevada Corporation



Cover designed by Jack Holiday
Photos furnished by
The Cleveland Library, Daniel Dzina,
& Cleveland State University.
Manufactured in the United States

Library of Congress Card Catalog # 93-074941

ISBN 0-916067-06-8

This book is dedicated to the working men and women who toil with the indignities of a corrupt legal system. The crime and corruption detailed throughout this book would not have been possible without the sanctioned support of those serving in a public trust capacity.

— *Robert James*

# TABLE OF CONTENTS

# acknowledgments

A special thanks goes to Daniel Dzina, who provided documentation, photos and other records. Without his enthusiastic support, feedback and assistance, the quality of this three-year project would not have been possible.

The author also wishes to acknowledge Bari Lynn Presser for her cooperation in providing access to her private journals, artifacts, forged will, and general background information on her private conversations with other family members, especially those between herself and Big Bill, and her father. In addition, the author recognizes Harvey Friedman for his views, corrections and verification of material facts.

Both former undercover agent George Simmons, who served on the Strike Force on Organized Crime, and Special Agent Arthur Ventura with the U.S. Treasury, were provided with advanced copies of the author's manuscript for accuracy. They offered invaluable insight and leads as well as critical suggestions.

Throughout the preparation of this project, there were numerous individuals who provided key information and technical assistance. Some of these individuals are affiliated with the U.S. Marshal's Service, the Department of Labor, the Pentagon, the Secret Service and private industry. For obvious reasons, their names cannot be listed, but without their collective assistance, insight and leads, much of this material would have remained secret.

In addition to information gleaned from Bari Lynn's private journals, it should also be pointed out that the majority of the events appearing in this book were generated from material released by the National Archives, DOL reports and FBI files. The author makes no claim that the information contained in these records is totally accurate, but in absence of contradictory evidence, it appears to be the best information available.

Finally, the author would like to extend a very special thanks to Tony. He was most cooperative in correcting and verifying critical details, facts and conversations pertaining to many of the events appearing throughout in this material.

Not everyone chose to cooperate, although many individuals were contacted. The informant's attorney, John Climaco, his private secretary, Gail George, his fifth wife, Cynthia Ann Presser, Mafia member, Anthony Liberatore and the Ronald W. Reagan Library were contacted, but declined comment. The U.S. Treasury Department was officially contacted under the Freedom of Information Act (FOIA). Upon filing an appeal and review, The U.S. Treasury proclaimed that its official position is that all their records on the subject matter covered in this material have been either lost or destroyed.

# Forward

ALL EMPLOYMENT is a political issue. Nothing illustrates this better than the life and assassination of James Hoffa. Once designated an enemy of the state, he was subjected to relative justice, and law enforcement throughout the country was overjoyed, for it helped legitimize their existence.

The behind-the-scene actions were taken in the name of moral justification to maintain power, initiate change and promote stability. Hoffa's assassination, however, did not occur in a vacuum. The coverup that followed was well choreographed, leaving the public with the impression that his demise was an unsolvable mystery. To divert public attention, Hoffa's assassination became shrouded in rumors and carefully orchestrated media cover stories. In time, those rumors become the acceptable truth and new reality.

As a self-made celebrity, Hoffa's perceived power was that he could influence the electorate. He championed his own universe, comprised within a salad of working-class voters. He started on the ground floor, and with one member at a time, he built the country's largest labor organization before being nominated president of the International Brotherhood of Teamsters by Syndicate boss, Big Bill Presser.

For ten years, Hoffa's presidency was plagued with internal corruption and Syndicate interference. Throughout his presidency, the Director of the FBI and U.S. Attorney General accused him of an assortment of capital crimes.

But the closer one begins to pragmatically examine his life in terms of his accusers' participation, the cloudier his guilt becomes. Today, many questions about his guilt remain, even though his arrest, conviction and incarceration were heralded as a major victory against organized crime.

At center stage to this event was the Central States Pension, a $1.6 billion trust fund under the control of Big Bill Presser. With Hoffa's removal, Big Bill could now use these funds to finance discretionary projects. Hoffa's imprisonment eliminated the external problem with the government, as well as his internal interference with organized crime's access to the pension money.

Ironically, jail made Hoffa more popular, and the media-savvy Nixon administration took notice. Hoffa's popularity posed a serious threat to Nixon's reelection efforts, and Hoffa's political confinement was merely serving as a perverted moral victory.

The news of his release from federal prison triggered an unanticipated chain of maneuvers that would alter the course of history. During the process, an unknown individual emerged to the forefront of national power and White House influence. In less than four years, Hoffa's fate would help to serve this obscure individual's private interest as well as legitimize the FBI's nefarious law enforcement mission.

The FBI knew the assassination was scheduled for late July. The Bureau knew in advance who was involved, who was given the hit contract and approximately where the event would take place. Of peculiar interest, is how and why his assassination was covered up. What behind-the-scenes events were so important that it necessitated the FBI, IRS, Justice Department, U.S. Marshall's Service, Secret Service and U.S. Treasury Department to separately participate in one of the largest cover-ups in U.S. history?

Most people believe that it is impossible to successfully conceal truth in a democratic society. But that begs the questions. The tactic of invoking the National Secrecy Act nullified the equation as far as truth is concerned. Once a government agency invokes the Secrecy Act, no other Constitutional laws apply, leaving truth to struggle and twist in the wind.

To appreciate the circumstances surrounding Hoffa's assassination, it is necessary to consider the socio-economic and political agendas involved. To the world-at-large, we were professing constitutional structure fraught with the finest judicial system operating within a free and open society. Maintaining the illusion grew more difficult as Americans began losing faith in their leaders, government, laws, institutions and the economy. Eventually, many would begin losing confidence in themselves.

Depression did not happen overnight. It evolved through a prolonged effort to change social and economic fabric. Hardly a man or woman is now alive who remembers when it began during the closing years of the Victorian era. President Theodore Roosevelt created a small bureaucratic agency that employed 60 men of good character, a least to the extent he understood the term, which meant they shared his values and political beliefs.

During the closing years of his presidency, Theodore saw the change in America's social and economic conditions as a threat to his way of life. His newly created agency, the Bureau of Investigation, was an effort to hold back change. The agency was charged with the responsibility of safeguarding a proper social order, which Theodore viewed as more important than Constitutional laws that often conflicted with the rights of industrial ownership.

Once out of office, Theodore's agency floundered in its mission. Without form or substantive power, there was little the agency could do until World War I. The agency found its first important mission, which was to monitor the activities of undesirable aliens. A young man fresh out of law school was placed in charge of supervising Enemy Alien Status. The unelected bureaucrat discovered the power of holding an administrative pen. With one stroke, he was authorized to deny civil liberties to anyone he suspected of having committed any act of labor disloyalty.

Having a suspicious mind and an awesome amount of power, meant that he could correct or rectify social problems created by technicalities of the U.S. Constitution. The young attorney quickly realized that having unaccountable authority instilled great fear with those who valued their jobs and freedoms. He combined fear with ignorance to create an unique employment weapon.

Labor strikes had been expressly outlawed by Congress during the war, but those rights were restored when hostilities ended. An onslaught of post-war labor protests followed, demanding better working conditions.

At the time, the young attorney thought this was unconscionable. If employers gave into their demands today, tomorrow the working classes would only want more. Someone had to put a stop to it. Nonetheless, the end of hostilities forced the country to shift to a peace-time economy, which resulted in fewer jobs, and as a result, the popularity of labor unions increased.

By 1920, the 25-year-old attorney was reassigned to the General Intelligence Division within the agency. He was given a special mission, which was to squelch the labor-movement hysteria sweeping across the American landscape. The new assignment included the administrative authority to investigate anyone associated with the labor movement and to maintain secret dossiers on private and social behavior.

With many of the government's agencies scaling back, the young attorney realized it was critical to show his superiors that the Bureau was actively involved in an important mission. For this young bureaucrat, this meant finding and identifying an important crusade. He found such a crusade residing in the labor movement, and he persuaded superiors that behind every waving picket sign and strike poster there hid the Communist banner. Although President Wilson's administration did not take this postulation seriously, the same was not the case when his scandalous predecessor took office.

He moved quickly to establish himself with the new Warren Harding administration. Harding appointed his close friend Harry Daugherty to be the U.S. Attorney General. The young bureaucrat presented himself to Daugherty as someone who possessed moral values in the Victorian tradition—someone who could keep savory secrets while drowning out the wailing sirens of labor discontent.

Aside from his reproachable and interpersonal abnormalities, the young bureaucrat was no ordinary man. Daugherty saw valuable potential in J. Edgar Hoover, who was willing to use the Bureau of Investigation as a political hit squad against perceived enemies of the state.

For services rendered to the Harding administration, J. Edgar was promoted to Assistant Director. The promotion carried with it a new covert mission, which was to develop a cadre of black-tie loyalists who would enthusiastically carryout the Attorney General's political desires.

One of the Attorney General's wishes was for J. Edgar to use his agents to spy on prominent individuals and perhaps discover their deviant passions and sexual fetishes. To accomplish this objective, J. Edgar was to use his cadre of loyal agents to spy on the complaining civil rights activists, as well as develop a morass of informants that could infiltrate the labor movement.

The initially recruited informants proved highly unreliable. Although he wasn't necessarily interested in truth, J. Edgar realized that their access to important information was greatly restricted to fourth-hand rumors. He believed that eventually the Bureau would have to target individuals who participated in the decision-making process if the agency was ever going to be an effective spy network.

President Harding's unexpected death on August 2, 1923 ended Daugherty's ambitions. President Coolidge immediately replaced him with Harlan Stone. Preoccupied with Prohibition, the new Attorney General paid little attention to the Bureau. Without fanfare or approval from Congress, J. Edgar Hoover was quietly elevated to Director of the agency, a position he would bureaucratically hold like a Russian Commissar for more than 48 years.

For a nation gripped in a post-war recession, the clapper-banging era of Prohibition offered new employment and economic opportunities, but it was no panacea for the average worker. Employment outside of bootlegging became increasingly more difficult to secure, and the nation seemed caught in a boundless economic malaise. With the nation's labor force on the verge of revolt, it found no sympathy at the national level, and labor unions offered the only viable alternative to employment tyranny.

Those in power saw this labor unrest as history repeating itself; for only a few years earlier the vulgar masses had risen up and toppled the lawfully recognized throne of Russian's czarist monarchy. In the face of this ominous threat, J. Edgar suggested that the Bureau of Investigation's name be changed to include the word *Federal*. He reasoned that it was their collective responsibility to uphold a proper social order, and if the working masses should attempt a similar *coup d'état*, the nation had to be prepared.

Surprisingly, the simple change in the agency's name immediately improved its poor public image. The young director of the Federal Bureau of Investigation quickly realized the value of perception over reality. During the agency's name-changing process, J. Edgar discovered he had created a new reality, not unlike the one implemented during the war years.

It was his first significant success with the U.S. Congress, which he viewed as little more than populous renegades, more interested in getting reelected than serving the public good. He reasoned that such self-serving interests might be their Achilles' heel. He believed Congress could be controlled by fear and ignorance, just as he had controlled aliens during the war. Like foreign aliens, members of Congress would have to be carefully watched. Perhaps, they too might have dark passions and deviant desires.

Meanwhile, the nation's economy was headed for a day of reckoning as president-elect Herbert Clark Hoover was preparing to move into the White House. Major institutions were overextended, and the average American worker's future—tenuous as it was—hung in the balance.

The crash of '29 was the official starting date. And the day the stock market collapsed, Jimmy Hoffa lost his meager job at Frank & Cedars Department Store in Detroit. He, along with a host of others, experienced private employment devastation as employers turned ugly in the wake of economic disaster.

Employers turned the economic disaster to their advantage. While wages dropped, the standard work week grew to 75 hours. Anyone who complained about their tyranny found himself joining the hordes of the unemployed, and fear motivated workers to fall in line.

These years of unemployment brought a rise in criminal statistics totally unrelated to the $2 billion industry of bootlegging. Hollywood's motion picture industry responded to this change in the social order by offering more than 50 gangster movies, and for the first time, the public was treated to the stereotype images of a make-believe underworld. For a dime, moviegoers could watch *The Big House* or an up-and-coming star like Edward G. Robinson in his portrayal of *Little Caesar*. But it was James Cagney's starring role in the pistol-popping cinema of *Public Enemy* that captured public attention, including that of J. Edgar.

The shift in public interest toward law and order encouraged J. Edgar to expand his agency's mission and incorporate a law enforcement image. To merchandise this perception, the FBI would have to be involved in some type of law-enforcement activity. He began recruiting young accountants and newly licensed attorneys to serve as special agents. J. Edgar realized that to develop an effective spy network of reliable informants, he needed a better educated cadre who could apply more persuasive techniques.

With the full range of federal crimes already under some other government agency's jurisdiction, he was desperate for a mission: Something that would justify increasing the Bureau's budget, manpower and informational gathering resources.

IF ONE COULD REACH BACK IN TIME and touch the magic moment that ensured J. Edgar Hoover's place in history, it occurred on March 1, 1932. That day, a small-time thief by the name of Isadore Fisch supposedly entered the second-floor to Charles Lindbergh's home and kidnapped his infant son for ransom.

Many of the facts involving the case have long been destroyed or altered, but we do know that the public's outcry for justice was enormous enough to capture President Hoover's attention. J. Edgar stepped forward. This provided an excellent opportunity to have his agency officially recognized as a national crime-fighting organization. Kidnapping, however, was not a federal crime. Nonetheless, J. Edgar pleaded with the administration to enter the case in order to test the Bureau's network of informants and its newly constructed laboratory facilities.

To remedy jurisdictional issue, Congress enacted the Federal Kidnapping Statute, which would later become known as the Lindbergh Law. J. Edgar immediately threw the weight of his newly acquired federal authority behind a popular cause. He personally took charge of the Lindbergh investigation. During his investigation, his network of spies discovered that Isadore Fisch had fled the country to Germany. Before the government could arrange for extradition, Isadore died, leaving J. Edgar without a plausible culprit to arrest and convict.

One element that would prove itself significant in the Lindbergh case was that it served as the FBI's genesis for conducting future investigations. Time and again, the real outlaw would slip away, and someone with stained virtues would be tagged so that the interests of relative justice could be served.

With another war fomenting in Europe, and the economy still in malaise, Franklin D. Roosevelt captured the White House. The president-elect, designated Senator Tom Walsh to be J. Edgar's new boss. Walsh made it known that he was not impressed with J. Edgar's foot-dragging performance in the Lindbergh case. It came as no surprise when the designated Attorney General announced that his first order of business would be to replace J. Edgar when he took office. En route to the inauguration, however, Walsh suffered a fatal heart attack.

This fortuitous reprieve motivated him to take decisive action. Rather than reveal the questionable circumstances involving the Lindberghs themselves, national security was invoked. J. Edgar countered criticism by launching a massive public relations campaign. His efforts took him to Hollywood, where he recruited the services of Walter Winchell. Down the road, a cast of others would follow, including a newspaper columnist, Ed Sullivan, a cartoonist, Walt Disney, and a movie actor, Ronald Reagan.

Events such as Machine Gun Kelly's unceremonious surrender in Memphis, was choreographed and orchestrated, leaving the public with the impression that the FBI had single-handedly cracked the case. In the fanfare, J. Edgar publicly proclaimed he had eliminated organized crime in America. Although merely a social columnist, Winchell declared that Kelly pleaded with FBI agents as he surrendered, *"Don't shoot, G-men! Don't shoot!"* It was all pretext, but it captured headlines around the world.

By the time Prohibition ended in 1933, the term *G-man* had become a popular euphemism generically applied to the Treasury, Secret Service and FBI agents. J. Edgar's popularity was resounding, and an uncontested public relations success.

Continued media exposure prompted J. Edgar to hire scriptwriters to enhance his image as crime-fighter and gang-busting crusader. Rex Collier and Courtney Cooper offered Warner Brother Studios a few low-budget, black-and-white movie scripts that promoted the G-man theme. The studio quickly flooded the silver screen with gangbuster films, transforming the puffy bureaucrat into a living icon.

His new *he-man* of G-men image made him the spokesman for American justice. No one questioned his authority when he ordered the arrest of Bruno Richard Hauptmann for kidnapping the Lindbergh baby. J. Edgar had designated Hauptmann as the guilty party, and to ensure a verdict, he branded Hauptmann a Communist. That rumor, along with a persuadable witness and a few pieces of questionable evidence supplied by the FBI resulted in Hauptmann's conviction and subsequent execution.

J. Edgar's scriptwriters continued to develop an assortment of engaging movie scenarios that wove like a chain-link fence around gullible minds. The public began to believe that J. Edgar and his band of undercover agents were the only atoning force that stood between justice and unpunished evil, which the Bureau amorphously referred to as *the mob*.

Such terminology could then be selectively assigned to designated undesirables, such as striking labor unions, their labor leaders and marching civil-rights protesters. Once the FBI's portrait of organized crime permeated American psyche, anyone attired in mob-style regalia or driving a black sedan was automatically perceived to be mob connected. The carefully written G-man series began shifting scripts toward the labor movement, and attributed underworld activities to their motives.

In cities like Detroit, the Teamsters and individuals like Walter Ruther, Dave Beck and Jimmy Hoffa were becoming a general nuisance. In retaliation, The Employers' Association banded together to retain the services of the dreaded *Purple Gang* and hit men like Leo 'Lips' Moceri. Together, the two groups joined ranks with local law enforcement officials to collectively battle the troublesome Teamsters and beat their recalcitrant members into submission. J. Edgar assigned extra agents to Detroit, not for the purpose of protecting civil liberties of mistreated workers from the excesses of sanctioned criminal behavior, but rather to watch, record and report back interesting developments.

By 1936, J. Edgar had survived five administrations, outlasting friends and foes alike. That year, he portrayed himself in the starring role of *You Can't Get Away With It.* Disquietly, for the first time the film revealed a Big Brother theme and the FBI's ability to pry into the personal and private affairs of everyone. It was a prophetic revelation to discover that the Bureau's director had implemented a set of secret policies and procedures that voided Civil Rights.

One of the secret policies involved the granting of special FBI privileges to select individuals who cooperated with the agency's spying operations. The first two recipients to receive such privileges were a newspaper journalist, Ed Sullivan, and the other was master story-teller and social commentator, Walter Winchell. Their syndicated broadcasts put J. Edgar into every corner of society.

At five-foot four inches and still in his twenties, Jimmy Hoffa was delivering a different message to the American worker. Annoyed by Hoffa's behavior, J. Edgar ordered his agents to focus their attention on his labor activities. The Bureau would devote 39 years of its time and resources to watch and record his every move. In time, Hoffa would receive more FBI attention than the entire universe of organized crime.

On August 25, 1936, J. Edgar's career took a quantum leap. He received a top-secret directive from President Franklin Roosevelt, authorizing him to conduct extraordinary intelligence and spy operations on the entire population. He was now authorized to perform what he had been secretly doing since Prohibition. Now, however, he would be shielded from Congressional scrutiny.

As the nation began gearing up for another war, J. Edgar had established the Bureau's spy network throughout the western hemisphere. His hand-picked, all-white male force totaled 3,000 special agents. In June 1939, the President ordered him to use his influence with Hollywood film makers to create effective propaganda for the war effort.

By the spring of 1944, the end of the war was in sight when Germany ran out supplies. That summer, the Russian Army collapsed Germany's entire Eastern front. J. Edgar's intelligence gathering network had confirmed that hostilities in Europe would be over in less than nine months. He grew alarmed and moved quickly to expand his spy network to 4,900 agents, hoping to have a full contingency of loyal agents in place before the apocalypse prematurely ended.

With the war coming to a close, J. Edgar took to the CBS airwaves on the evening of October 7, 1944. Like a general returning from the front, he proclaimed that the Bureau had uprooted and defeated the non-existent Axis Fifth Column in the western hemisphere. The broadcast and its timing was a masterpiece of deception. J. Edgar Hoover, disguised as the new law-and-order messiah had arrived.

Roosevelt's death positioned J. Edgar as the most popular man in America, and he could have won the presidency, but his interests were long term. His authority was already greater than any elected official, and he made the decision to hold onto that power.

Against the fading backdrop of dwindling postwar celebrations, the bloom of employment began falling off the petals of prosperity as the country slipped back into recession. J. Edgar had likewise fallen on hard times. President Truman was not impressed with J. Edgar's dismal performance in conducting off-shore spy operations, and he was suspicious about J. Edgar's unaccountable power. To curtail the Bureau's adventurous escapades, Truman created the Central Intelligence Agency to replace some of the Bureau's spying activity. That same year, when an unexplained incident occurred in New Mexico, better known as *The Roswell Incident*, President Harry Truman assigned the top-secret UFO project to Army Air Force Intelligence. And, by the fall of 1947, the FBI found itself without a foe to fight—neither domestically, internationally, and in the Roswell matter, not even extraterrestrially.

President Truman compounded the assault by clamping a lid on J. Edgar hiring any new agents, leaving Washington insiders with the notion that the FBI was little more than rebels without a cause.

The House on Un-American Activities Committee came to J. Edgar's rescue. The creation of the Committee was viewed by many in Congress as an exercise in buffoonery, and few veteran politicians vied for a Committee seat. The lack of interest created an opportunity for men like Joe McCarthy and a 33-year-old freshmen congressman from Whitaker, California. By August of '48, the spotlight began to focus on the freshman when the FBI began investigating Alger Hiss for un-American activities as part of an elaborate communist conspiracy. When the Committee began holding televised hearings, Richard Milhous Nixon's name became nationally known.

With the Committee on Un-American Activities capturing the national limelight and upstaging him for media attention, J. Edgar created the FBI's *Ten Most Wanted* list. As a media stunt, it was a stroke of genius: As a crime-fighting tool, however, it was pure Hooverism. All serious criminals were excluded from the list, such Nazi war fugitives, Klu Klux Klan members, or known Mafia hit men. The list would never include such prolific hit men like Leo 'Lips' Moceri from Detroit, Joe Valachi from New York or Jimmy 'The Weasel' Fratianno from Los Angeles.

The Cold War that followed the Korean conflict brought General Dwight Eisenhower to the While House. He reluctantly accepted the 39-year-old Nixon as his running mate after the young attorney appealed to the American public on television in his now-famous Checker's speech.

The Cold War postponed the inevitable postwar recession and the job spigot was left on. The economy blossomed and the average American worker started to pursue *the American dream*: A secure job, an affordable mortgage and a new car was on every middle-class American's mind.

Eager to capitalize on this euphoric American dream was Jimmy Hoffa, who had been rising through Teamster ranks. He remembered the lean years, the years when life was not so good and the country's future not so bright. He knew the good economic times were merely an endorphin high that would eventually run its course before catching up with reality, and he wanted to protect his union members.

The world marketplace wanted everything America could produce, and there was no talk about balance of trade or national debt. The golden age of television had also arrived, along with a rapidly growing new industry of mass-media advertising. It provided the perfect ambiance for selling new thinking to the consumer-oriented public eager to improve its standard of living.

The Teamsters represented a dilemma. The Republicans wanted their endorsement, financial support and union-member votes, but not their philosophies on labor management. At the 1956 Democratic National Convention, Hoffa wanted the Teamsters to support Estes Kefauver as Adlai Stevenson's running mate. Dave Beck, the General President of the Teamsters, however, mysteriously threw the endorsement to Eisenhower and the anti-labor running mate, Richard Nixon.

When the Senate reconvened in '57, Senator John Kennedy appointed his younger brother Bobby to serve as general counsel to represent the Senate Rackets Committee, headed by Senator John L. McClellan. The Committee's investigation quickly focused on the Teamsters' illogical endorsement. How could the largest labor union in the country support an anti-labor enthusiast like Richard Nixon?

When Jimmy Hoffa was nominated by Big Bill Presser and subsequently elected general president in 1957, the Kennedy brothers zeroed in on the new man at the helm. Hoffa made the mistake of publicly voicing his perception of Bobby Kennedy, and the two immediately squared off in what would become a life-long blood feud.

Aside from their philosophical differences, Bobby Kennedy and Jimmy Hoffa had been raised in different realities. One had a fine legal education and could eloquently discuss abstract social issues, while the other had been educated in the streets. One had had access to the best of everything, while the other had struggled up the employment ladder, surrounded by smelly men who had toiled too long from backbreaking labor. Each man viewed labor issues from a different vista. While each man struggled to convince the public that the other was out of step with reality, serious crime was out of control. Such criminal activity could no longer be vaguely attributed to the mob. The public had grown too sophisticated for buying into this scenario. The finger was pointed at J. Edgar, and he was hard pressed to explain how he had let the social order deteriorate. J. Edgar's 25-year claim that he had eradicated organized crime no longer squared with reality.

J. Edgar reasoned that if television created the problem, it could also provide the solution. All that was necessary was to reprogram the viewing audience. J. Edgar Hoover's 1965 brainchild was a program called *The FBI*. He picked Efrem Zimbalist, Jr. to star in the leading role of Lou Erskin. The FBI pre-approved each program before airing to ensure that the mythical character projected a psychologically normal image. Rather than reveal the FBI's real mission, Special Agent Erskin spent his days and nights fighting crime. Despite the program's success with viewers, not a single word of the mythical role portrayed was true.

## *Chapter 1*

## Assassination

*"— Clear!"*

Sal lifted the switch and hit the button. With a *bang* the cylinders popped and rotated and triggered a blast of air. Effortless motion settled in.

Sal scouted the available sky that stretched out over the Atlantic. "Well guys, the weather looks pretty good."

He set the altimeter and gyrocompass then nudged the throttles to check the magnetos. *Fuel—check.* Punching the throttles to full thrust caused the rubber to play a low drum roll pounding over the runway, gradually building faster during acceleration. With one eye carefully monitoring the speed, Sal then pulled back to rotate the controls, "Here we go." The thumping of the tire-timpani stopped leaving only the high-pitched noise to settle into a rhythmic groan.

He reached over and turned the transponder off.

Outside, wind and engine noises resolved to a quieter cadence. He relaxed as he looked straight ahead. To the west, the purple mountain range carried faint-blue shadows which slowly melted as they drew closer, then vanished.

"Isn't this a great view."

Once through the pass of the Appalachians, the midwestern terrain opens up before it settles into a gentle rolling landscape. From the air the ground looks like a green and brown quilted carpet with roadways angling like so many pieces of uncut thread. Even from above, Sal and his two passengers knew they had reached America's industrial heartland.

An early-rising sun promised the small group of air travelers a steamy July throughout the Great Lakes, and ensured a clear approach for the small twin-engine. After landing at Hopkins International Airport, Sal, Gabe and Tom departed their aircraft and joined the milieu of air-terminal congestion.

To everyday travelers preoccupied with destination thoughts and flagging the next available cab, this small entourage represented little more than ordinary faces on routine business. The stern-looking trio with rugged Apennine features easily harmonized with the attaché-carrying crowd.

To educated eyes, however, their cameo appearances represented special concern. Instructed to observe and track their movements, the arrogant man would be expected to file a report on anyone coming in contact with the three men, no matter how casual. He was cognizant of a dubious and ill-kept mission that would be furtively tagged valuable information.

Any calculated defensive scheme executed today or tomorrow, would not sack this seasoned quarterback. Clapping his hands, Sal ordered, "It's time to split up. I'll meet you back at the aircraft. We'll leave in exactly twenty minutes."

Attempting to track the scattering squad was impossible, yet mindlessly following a decoy would be an unpardonable sin. Special Agent Martin P. McCoy[1] briefly glanced at his wristwatch before darting toward an

---

[1] FBI Agent McCoy's real name has been altered.

obstacle course of checkpoints. Flashing FBI credentials, he swiftly brushed past security personnel. With the elevator occupied, he chased the stairs leading to the glass-encased tower and the air controller on duty.

At the same time, Sal walked past the locker section, only to pivot himself and return in a still moment. He casually produced a key, inserted it into locker 12A, withdrew a white envelope and tucked it into his pocket. For an encore, Sal walked to a newsstand, purchased the morning paper, then left the terminal in a savvy stroll.

As they regrouped, McCoy pointed, "You see those three men boarding that small twin-engine over there? I need to know their destination."

"I think they're flying VFR" the controller revealed.

"Is there any way you can track them on radar?"

"Only while they're in our Terminal Control Area. Beyond that, we'll have to track the aircraft through Oberlin. ... Shall I ask the pilot his destination when I clear him for departure?"

"Can you do that without appearing obvious?"

"Sure. He hasn't filed a flight plan, so as soon as Ground Control hands him off, I'll inform the pilot that I have to vector him around other aircraft. It will take a moment."

After the aircraft was cleared for take-off, the controller motioned to McCoy. "The pilot says he is heading for Detroit Metro. That's about a half-hour's flying time from here."

"Hmm? Is there any way you can verify their destination?"

"That might be difficult," the controller responded.

"Why's that?"

"If the pilot wants to avoid detection, he might shut off his transponder while en route, or fly low. He might also fly tandem with another aircraft. Also, there are several small airfields in the Detroit vicinity, so we can't be exactly sure of their final destination."

McCoy jotted down notes, as he spoke, "I have what we need to know." He looked up and watched the aircraft turn toward the lake, then disappear.

While Detroit Metropolitan Airport was crawling with FBI agents, Sal was turning on the carburetor heat and lowering the flaps. He scoured the small airfield below, looking for a red windsock before identifying which runway to use, then guided the aircraft to an undisturbed landing.

While taxiing, Sal's brother fumbled with two sets of keys. "I'll see to the cars," Gabe suggested.

"While you're at it, check under the passenger's seat for the package," Sal instructed.

Gabe got the package from under a car seat. Everything had been planned down to its smallest detail, leaving no loose ends. A meeting was scheduled to take place at the Red Fox Restaurant located in the fashionable Detroit suburb of Bloomfield Hills. The subject would be anticipating to meet with Lenny Schultz, Detroit Mafia Boss Tony Gacalone, and Newark Mafia Boss Tony Provenzano, better known in organized crime as Tony Pro.

"I say we do it before he gets out of his car. We'll be out of there in less than a minute," Gabe murmured.

Sal smiled, and spoke without raising his voice, "Is there something wrong with your memory? Did mother raise you to be stupid? We've been over this a hundred times. We stick with Provenzano's plan. Period."

"I was merely making a suggestion."

"Your job doesn't involve suggestions," Sal reminded him.

"What if someone is with him? What if someone is following ..."

"That's your job." Sal poked Gabe's chest, "You're to make sure he isn't being followed, then pick him up. So he wants to see Tony Pro, Schultz and Gacalone." Grabbing the package from Gabe, he shoved it at Tom, "After he's out of the car, I'll walk him into the house. When his back is turned, put him to sleep."

Gabe located an inconspicuous spot to watch the restaurant. As expected, the subject's car quietly rolled into the nearly deserted lot. From a distance, Gabe watched every move. The subject began to pace. A half-hour passed. The subject walked over to a pay phone, and placed a brief call to his wife. Gabe glanced at his watch. It was 2:30 p.m. The subject's pacing resumed, then he returned to the pay phone. Gabe surveyed the flow of traffic. He spotted O'Brien down the street. "Okay. It's showtime."

Gabe informed the victim that he and O'Brien were to drive him to his scheduled meeting of July 30th. The vehicle disappeared down the road, and Jimmy Hoffa was never heard from again.

♦

On the evening of July 30, 1975, at 8:45, 100 miles away, located on the first floor of a downtown building, an unlisted telephone rang. In the presence of his armed protection, the heavy-set man reached to pick up the receiver.

"Yeah."

"I have some news," the caller announced. "The news is from Detroit. As of today, some merchandise was picked up. It was packaged and shipped. We'll be in touch. In the meantime, as we say in La Costa, have a nice day." — Click.

A sober expression came over his face as he quietly replaced the receiver. He glanced at the day-calendar page. Reaching across the desk, he placed his palm down over the sheet, then slowly crumpled the page. He opened the desk drawer and deposited it inside. In the corner he spotted a pair of cufflinks, a gift given to him on the evening of June 20, 1972, when he visited Richard Nixon at the White House.

The fat man had no reason to be nervous, but he was, for he was confronting the biggest change in his life.

*Chapter 2*

## Associations

Upon his election to the Presidency of the United States, John F. Kennedy appointed his younger bother Bobby to be J. Edgar Hoover's boss. As U.S. Attorney General, Bobby's first order of business was to disconnect J. Edgar's red telephone that had directly linked him to former sitting Presidents.

Symbolic or otherwise, J. Edgar perceived this as an unconscionable act to undermine his authority, challenge his power and castrate his influence. Washington insiders quickly concluded that J. Edgar's demise was in the making and his tyranny over the judicial system might be coming to an end.

Hoover recognized that distinct possibility. Having invested a lifetime in building the largest covert operation in the western world, he was not disposed to capitulating his authority to someone that he perceived to be little more than a spoiled brat. Nonetheless, Hoover would neither forgive nor forget, and he felt that the impetuous young Kennedy would have to be punished for his indiscretion.

The new Attorney General's second order of business was to launch a massive investigation into organized crime within the labor movement. Although the inquiry that followed appeared to be broad in scope, the investigation was limited to only one man and one labor organization. The motivation for the investigation stemmed from a political endorsement by the International Brotherhood of Teamsters.

The U.S. Treasury Department noted the conflict. Given the FBI's historic track record, the Treasury believed that the Bureau's manpower and resources were mischievously misdirected. The U.S. Treasury decided to launch a completely independent investigation. Since the days of Elliot Ness and Prohibition, the Treasury Department had been carefully tracking and monitoring underworld activities.

While the FBI focused its attention on non-quantifiable ventures such as exclusively targeting Jimmy Hoffa and Communists supposedly manipulating the American labor movement, Treasury agents applied a more pragmatic approach. The Treasury's efforts focused on a secret crime organization called *La Cosa Nostra*. The term, translated from Italian means '*this thing of ours,*' often substituted with the word *Mafia*.

With the 1961 arrest of Joe Valachi, a prolific hitman for New York's Genovese crime family, the Treasury agents were able to pursue organized crime from a different vantage and identify those who were really in charge. The Mafia, however, was only a microcosm of the total organized crime picture.

Under the direction of J. Edgar Hoover, the FBI's approach was to structure its massive investigation around rumors, spotty field reports and the belief that Jimmy Hoffa orchestrated underworld activity through the International Brotherhood of Teamsters. Throughout his career, J. Edgar had controlled the vital information U.S. Attorney Generals relied upon. His agency knew how to subjugate and manipulate information to ensure special interests.

By August of 1975, the separate investigations by the U.S. Treasury and the FBI eventually lead both government agencies to one man.

◆

"What the hell is this?" Jackie Presser wailed as his trusted bodyguard tossed the morning paper on his desk. *Hoffa Reported Missing.* "Is this suppose to be news?" He removed the newspaper and dropped it into the wastebasket, "For a moment I thought you were bringing me something important."

Tony Hughes folded his arms across his barrel-sized chest, "Okay, here's a news item. Guess who just came into town? ... Chuckie O'Brien."

"So? I've got no business with him either," Jackie responded. "I never in my life knew a guy who stood for nothing."

"Just thought I'd mention it. ... You think Chuckie had anything to do with Hoffa's disappearance?"

"Hmm. That's a very interesting angle, Tony." Scratching his chin, "I wonder what the hell he's doing here."

"He seems to have left Detroit in a real big hurry. ... Say, have you talked to Special Agent McCoy?" Tony asked.

"Why? I've got nothing to say to him."

"I just thought the feebees might want to ask you about Hoffa's disappearance," Tony noted.

"What for? We weren't close or anything. Far as I'm concerned Hoffa's always been a royal pain in the ass. If McCoy wants to get in touch with me, and it's really important, we'll set up a meeting. My ol' man is going to be getting out of the joint soon, and I want everything in order." While Jackie commenced shuffling papers, Tony lit up a cigarette and quietly took a seat across the room. As the silence mounted, Jackie had to get one more thing off his chest. "... You know, there's always the possibility the feds snatched Hoffa themselves."

"*Aaah*, I can't believe that," Tony responded in his graveled voice. "You just made that up to see my reaction." Tony was convinced that Jackie was merely putting him on, "Why would they want to do a thing like that?"

"I hear they do it to guys all the time."

"Don't be saying stuff like that, Jackie. Who did they do it to?"

"Oh? What about Kennedy?"

Growling, "*Aw*, come on Jackie. The feds didn't have nothing to do with that," Tony argued.

"Okay. Then tell me who authorized Kennedy's hit?"

"How the hell should I know," Tony complained.

"But you hear stuff. ... We hear stuff all the time, right? You heard Chuckie was in town ... correct?"

"Yeah, but that's different." Tony wasn't sure what Jackie was leading up to, but it was obvious that Jackie had something weighing on his mind.

"You met with Chuckie, personally?" Jackie abstractly inquired.

Smiling, "No, I got no business with him either."

"But you believe he's here, just the same ... right?"

"Sure," Tony responded confidently. "I know Chuckie's in town. What's your point?"

"Point being, you didn't see him ... you didn't even talk with him, but you believe he's in town."

"So?"

"I heard the Chicago Mafia had something to do with the Kennedy assassination, and that Sam Giancana might have given the *okay*, then ordered Jack Ruby to whack Oswald. Now I didn't see Giancana, I didn't talk to Giancana, but I heard something. Besides, he never got questioned about it."

"But that don't mean the government was involved," Tony pleaded.

"So who authorized the hit on Giancana?"

"How in the hell should I know. Why are we talking about this?"

"Just answer my question," Jackie demanded.

"I don't know. You're mixing all this stuff together. You suggesting that there might be a connection between Giancana's hit and Hoffa's disappearance?"

"Do we know who did either of them jobs?" Jackie snorted.

"I sure in hell don't. We don't know if he's actually been snatched. Maybe Hoffa has gone into hiding or something like that," Tony speculated.

"*Ooh* ... you know, you're probably right. I never thought of that possibility," Jackie reflected.

"Good. Now maybe we can change the subject. I was beginning to feel like I was preparing for a dress rehearsal or something. ... How's you're old man doing?"

"He thinks he'll be getting out soon," Jackie retorted as he continued browsing over papers without looking up.

"It was good of Big Bill to give you his seat on the Central States Pension. Now you can claim you have practical experience if he wants to retire."

"Yeah, I got that going for me," Jackie agreed non-plus.

"It's a good thing Bobby Kennedy never went after Big Bill like he went after Hoffa."

"Hoffa wasn't connected like my ol' man, either." Jackie made direct eye contact, "Hoover was scared of my ol' man's connections. That may have been why Hoover kept pushing Kennedy in all the wrong directions."

"Jackie ... you think Hoover protected guys like your old man?"

"Did you ever see anyone in any of the crime organizations on Hoover's Ten Most Wanted?"

"Now that you mention it, I never seen anyone important. Not even mass murders like Danny Greene or major drug operators like John Nardi."

"You answered your own question." Jackie looked up to reflect, "Until Treasury guys arrested Joe Valachi back in '61, Hoover was planning on Hoffa taking the blame for everything. Hoover knew you always have to

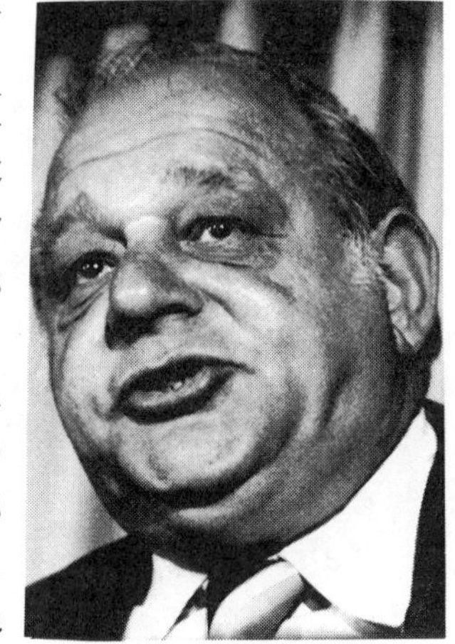

*Jackie Presser*

have a patsy to take the fall. Hoover tagged Hoffa with those honors. He was suppose to rollover, but Kennedy and Hoover underestimated just how tough that little bastard ... is."

Tony wasn't sure why Jackie had shifted the topic. "So you think Hoover was using Hoffa to get to Bobby Kennedy?"

"Of course. Look who runs the show ... the Mafia families out of New York and Chicago. One way or the other, everything has to go through them. Detroit and Kansas City answer to Chicago, just like Cleveland, Buffalo and Newark answer to the Genovese family in New York. There's a whole chain of command. Where did Hoffa fit in? He was an outsider. He didn't even belong to the Detroit Mafia. Kennedy wanted to nail him so bad that nothing else mattered."

"The heat Kennedy was applying on Hoffa ... do you think that's what made Big Bill and Hoffa part company?" Tony asked.

"Probably. Let's see ... yeah, they started falling out back in the early '60s after Kennedy ordered Hoover to lean on Hoffa. So what did the FBI do? They started opening his mail and following anyone who knew Hoffa. ... I heard that the FBI had all his Washington rooms and offices bugged. When none of that shit worked, the FBI sicced the IRS on him. Even that didn't work."

Smiling derisively, "I guess that's why they called Hoffa's trial down in Tennessee the Chattanooga Choo-Choo," Tony said.

"You know what's really funny ... they couldn't come up with one damn piece of evidence. Even the IRS couldn't find anything ... can you believe that? On top of that, they kept that crap up for years and not one piece of evidence ever turned up. And to top it all off, we have to pay through our damn noses in taxes for that horse crap."

"But Jackie, Hoffa still went to federal prison anyway."

"It's just like I said, the feebees always want to have a patsy handy to take a fall. How come with all that FBI surveillance and all those agents, they couldn't come up with anything? Huh? How come? Just answer me that."

"I don't know Jackie. You think they made the star witness an offer that he couldn't refuse?"

"You know damn well they did. Well they're never pulling any kind of crap like that on me or my people, 'cause we're too smart for 'em. I'm nobody's patsy. That's why I got an attorney like Climaco on my payroll to handle my problems."

"Speaking of problems, I always wanted to ask you, whatever happened to your Coliseum over in Eastgate?" Tony inquired.

The huge Eastgate Coliseum entertainment and recreational complex was the largest of its kind outside of Las Vegas.

"It went bankrupt about the same time Hoffa was standing trial. My ol' man hit the roof because he was the one who authorized the loan. Good thing the ol' man was able to lay-off a major portion of my debt, or he'd still be throwing that in my face."

"What did he do?" Tony asked next.

"He got Sammy Klein to take over the loan, but the ol' man had to throw Sammy some of his vending operations to get him to go along with the deal. It wasn't all my fault. If Uncle Al hadn't gotten so greedy, and the

FBI hadn't been constantly crawling all over the place and chasing away business, I could have scored with that joint. The feds were on my case every-which-way I turned. Since then, my life's been on the line. Take them assholes in our Locals. They'd love to take me out, not to mention a few others who want me whacked. ... Well it's going to be a whole new ball game from now on."

"How did you get the Coliseum off the ground, anyway?" Tony asked.

"Now those were some of the good ol' days. My ol' man finally came through for me on that deal. He set up a loan for $850 grand from the Teamsters' Central States Pension so that me and Uncle Allen could get the project going."

"Did Hoffa have to approve your loan?" Tony inquired.

"Hell no. He didn't know anything about it until it was a done deal. My ol' man and the guys on the Executive Board made all those decisions, then told Hoffa about it later."

"You think Hoffa knew your old man was running the Syndicate at the time?"

"Hoffa knew that he wasn't totally in charge, I know that much. But to say Hoffa knew the full extent of my ol' man's underworld connections, I kind of doubt it. The ol' man plays his cards damn close to his chest. I'll never forget the Coliseum's opening night. It was January 25th, '61. My ol' man ordered Sammy Davis, Jr and his Vegas act to open the place."

"The Coliseum should have been a gold mine, Jackie. What happened?"

"I made the mistake of letting Shonder Birns set up booking and gambling operations. I guess things got out of hand, but that wasn't my fault. Christ, in less than a month after we opened, the FBI was all over that place. I learned later that it was all Bobby Kennedy's idea. The moment Kennedy found out that Teamster funds were involved, he ordered Hoover to sic his guys on that joint."

"Over a little two-bit gambling?" Tony asked diffidently.

"Naw, that wasn't the reason. Kennedy was looking for a Hoffa connection. He ordered Hoover to send in a whole swarm of agents. But that didn't stop us. I have to hand it to Uncle Allen. He made a game of it. We were both skimming the hell out of that place, but they didn't catch us. Uncle Allen would actually wait until some FBI agent was looking right over his shoulder, and then he'd empty the registers and stick the cash in his pocket. Every night Uncle Allen would say the same thing. 'These clowns have gotta be dumber than dog shit.' It kinda makes you wonder what kind of operation the FBI is running."

"So neither of you got busted for any of that?" Tony responded.

"Like I said Tony, the Bureau was too busy looking for Hoffa. I mean, what did they think we were doing, hiding him in the toilet? That's why I think Hoover was doing a number on Bobby Kennedy. After they raided the place a few times, Hoover knew that Hoffa had nothing to do with my operation. I think Hoover must have been trying to set up Kennedy to make him look like a fool or get him sidetracked so that he would waste his time."

"You think Hoover was that clever?" Tony questioned.

"Oh-yeah, he was. Just look at how he treated the various Mafia families, not to mention my ol' man's huge crime Syndicate."

"Yeah, I guess you're right," Tony concluded. "I heard Big Bill had something pretty good on Hoover, and that's why the FBI left him alone."

"Hoover liked pretty little white boys. I've heard it from a reliable source that ol' J. Edgar was into kinky, big time."

Tony smirked and raised his eyebrows, "When did you first meet Hoffa?"

"It was when 'Babe' Triscaro invited him into town to see if the Teamsters wanted to sign up the stevedores with the Longshoremen's Association. Triscaro was running that day-labor service at the docks. My ol' man asked me if I wanted to meet Hoffa, so we met him at some restaurant downtown." Jackie reflected, "Lets see, there was me, the ol' man, Babe, Hoffa, and oh-yeah, that crazy bastard Danny Greene of all people."

"Who in hell invited Greene?" Tony asked in puzzlement.

"Triscaro, that's who. And, I'll tell you something else. Hoffa had Greene's number right off the bat. The moment Greene left the table ... probably to stick some junk up his nose, Hoffa leaned over to Triscaro and said, 'You oughta stay away from that guy. Greene's a nut case. I gotta gut feeling that something ain't right about him.' You should have seen the expression on Triscaro's face."

Tony added, "It just goes to show you, Hoffa's no dummy."

Jackie leaned slightly forward and with a grin whispered, "We have to do something about that crazy bastard. It's only going to be a matter of time before Greene tries to whack me or my ol' man."

"I know, but I don't think anyone can get close to him. He don't stay in one place too long," Tony remarked.

"I just don't understand it. He's killing people left and right. Sometimes he pops two guys at once. And it's not like he tries to keep it a secret. He then starts bragging about it all over town. Next time I see McCoy, I'll have to ask him about Greene. Somethin' not kosher."

"I don't understand why you're so worried all of a sudden. Nothing's gonna happen to you. ... Or is there something you haven't told me?" Tony questioned.

"Just the same, I have to change with the times." *Yeah, I need someone to watch my backside. I've known Uncle Al the longest, but I trust him the least.* Jackie spoke out loud, "Okay, so maybe I owed him once."

"What? Who? Who do you owe? You probably owe a lot of guys Jackie."

"I was just thinking about my Uncle Allen. I remember when we were kids. We always wanted to be gangsters, me and him. That's about the only thing we ever had in common. ... Did I ever tell you how I got involved in the rackets?"

Tony invited him to continue, "Tell me about it."

"After the war, I bummed around for awhile, working shit jobs. Then ma told my ol' man to put me on the payroll. So what does my ol' man do? He puts me to work with my two uncles, Allen and Harry, humping vending machines and jukeboxes. We worked small towns along the Ohio River and into West Virginia. I never hated anything so much in all my life. That kind of work is for niggers and hillbillies."

"You married one of them hillbillies," Tony noted.

"Yeah, my first wife's name was Pauline Walls. Ma hit the roof when she found out I had gotten a *goya* pregnant."

"So that was after you married Gypsy." Tony only recalled Elaine Gotlieb's nickname.

"I married Gypsy before divorcing Pauline."

"You're a bigamist!"

"Hey Tony, don't be mentioning that bigamist stuff in front of anyone. Nobody knows about that."

"Your secret is safe with me. So, did that happen before you got busted?"

"Keep a lid on that too. My ol' man got the court to destroy the records. As far as everyone else knows, I'm clean. ... Let me see, I got busted the summer of '49. I'm telling you Tony, the FBI thought they hit pay dirt when me and Uncle Allen were caught stealing cars. You'd have thought we committed the crime of the century."

"Was it that big a deal?" Tony asked.

"Naw. We must of snatched thirteen, maybe fourteen cars, tops. Strictly small time. Where we messed up was taking some of the cars across the state line."

"But you didn't have to do no prison time, so what's your beef?"

"Maybe so, but Uncle Allen didn't get off so lucky. The ol' man ordered him to rollover and do my time.

And don't think for one moment that Uncle Allen has ever let me forget it either. He keeps throwing that up in my face every damn chance he gets."

"Oh?"

"Yeah ... and he's sneaky about it too. He don't just come out and say it, he tells me shit like, 'When I was pulling time, the bigger guys made the weaker guys become their sex object.' Ugh! It gives me the willies just to think about what might have happened."

"Okay, I get the picture Jackie. You've told me all this before."

"Well I'm telling you again, I'm not pulling any time. Not now—not ever! I ain't going to give love to some muscle just to keep him from doing a pumpernickel on me."

"So you were telling me how you got into the rackets?"

"Where was I, yeah ... I married Patricia back in '52, before Bari Lynn was born. I didn't have two nickels in my pocket. We eloped to Indiana on July 30th of that year."

"Getting married got you into the rackets?" Tony asked with narrow eyes.

"I'm getting to it. Anyway, we got back to town. I couldn't afford a decent place to live and Patricia couldn't handle it. She packed her bags and split to live with some aunt in Arizona. The next thing I know, my ol' man is hitting the roof. He was tired of me getting married one week, and divorced the next. So he suggested we take a real honeymoon in Vegas. He made a couple calls to our people out there to set things up. I went to Arizona, picked her up, and took her on the honeymoon of her life."

"What about gambling money?" Tony asked encouragingly.

"Yeah, that too. Do you remember the godfather, 'Lucky' Luciano?"

Grinning, "Not personally."

"Now that story goes back to sometime after the war when Luciano got deported, but he snuck back in by way of Havana, Cuba. And that's where he and Meyer Lansky were making the slots for Vegas casinos." Snaping his fingers, "Remember that crazy Mormon, Howard Hughes?"

"Yeah," Tony acknowledged.

"Howard smuggled Luciano back into the country. Luciano along with Moe Dalitz and an half-dozen other Mafia members were in Vegas to greet us. I think that was when I was introduced to Jimmy Fratianno."

"Yeah, I heard the name mentioned a few times. Didn't he grow up with 'Babe' Triscaro back in the late 40s," Tony added.

"The point is, that's when I fully realized the ol' man was tied in to the whole universe of organized crime. I also found out that my ol' man was the one who financed the building of Vegas through the Central States Pension."

"Didn't Patricia get suspicious?"

"By the time we got back in town she was pregnant. She had Bari Lynn on Armistice Day in '53."

"I've always wanted to ask you about your daughter's name. Is Bari, Jewish?" Tony inquired.

"Naw, it's Italian. I chose it because that's where Luciano was born ... Bari, Italy. Anyway, between my ol' man and Luciano putting out the word, gifts started arriving. Some of those gifts came in white envelopes."

"So the two of you went from rags to riches overnight."

"I suppose so," Jackie laughed contemptuously.

Tony stood up and emptied his ashtray into the wastebasket. He glanced down at the newspaper, "So—What do you think really happened to Hoffa?"

"How the hell should I know!" Jackie shouted, "I was in town with you the whole damn day!"

"Hey, what did I do? I just asked a simple question. You don't have to get mad at me for asking a question. Okay, fine." Tony sat back down, "You were telling me about Bari Lynn. I suppose Big Bill started helping you out after she was born?"

"Not really. The ol' man was against me right from the beginning. Let's change the subject."

"Come on Jackie, what's the problem?"

"People ... you know what I mean. People are always making wisecracks behind my back. Some of these idiots think that because I don't write anything down that I don't remember so good."

"Well, maybe some people think you only remember what you want to remember."

"My problem is ... I've got too good of a memory."

Smiling to himself, "How can that be a problem? Sounds like you're in need of a woman." Tony's provocative suggestion failed to register.

"Yeah, well I remember plenty, and one of these days, everybody will be dancing to my tunes."

The private line lit up and Jackie grabbed the receiver, "This is Jackie." After a moment's pause, he scribbled down the coded message.

"Big Brother?" Tony surmised.

"Yeah. McCoy has set something up for tomorrow." Jackie walked to the window and gazed outside, drawing the images of the past into focus. ...

**1966**

"Jackie, you have to stop thinking about trying to get involved in *this thing of ours*. I'm telling you, it's a real death trap. It's not something like the Coliseum where you can walk away from it the moment things don't go your way." Big Bill had recited this several times.

*Big Bill Presser*

"Yeah-yeah-yeah. Well I'm a big boy now, pop. Don't lecture me about what to do with my life. If you were all that damn concerned, you'd be helping me more, rather than just standing in the way all the time."

"Don't you use that tone of voice when you speak to me."

"Christ pop, I'm your oldest, and you treat me as if I was a bag of shit. So do us both a favor, don't lecture me about anything."

"I just can't have anymore Coliseum fiascoes." It was not the subject Big Bill wanted to discuss, but it was something that had been eating on him ever since he had bailed Jackie out of the project.

"That was just as much Uncle Al's fault as it was mine. Besides, what was I suppose to do with all the fee-bees crawling all over the place? Huh? What made them think Hoffa was involved? By rights, that's what queered the deal. So don't be laying all that on me."

"Well I think our Master Hoover and Mister Kennedy are going to take care of our problem for us," Big Bill reflected.

"Huh?"

"I said, J. Edgar Hoover and Bobby Kennedy are going to take care of our problem. Hoffa has been taken into custody. He should be on his way to Lewisburg Federal Prison for the next eighteen years. By the time he gets out, he'll either be too old or too tired to mess things up for us."

"Uncle Allen says that's the worst hell-hole there is."

"Our problem is making sure he stays there. Frank Fitzsimmons is now in charge of the Teamsters. He's backed and supported by both the Chicago and Kansas City crime families, based upon my recommendations. I realize New York's Genovese family isn't too happy about it, but they are willing to let him serve until the next general election. They are taking my word that we will be able to control Fitzsimmons far better than Hoffa."

"Does Hoffa know about any of this?" Jackie inquired.

"If he doesn't, he soon will. I'm sure someone will get word to him. Let's just hope Hoffa never gets out of prison."

"Yeah, there's no telling what he might do if that happens," Jackie added.

"I think we can count on Hoover doing the right thing. I'm sure Hoover has enough on President Johnson to keep him from doing anything too stupid."

"You think Johnson's going to run for reelection?" Jackie asked.

"Personally, I don't think so, especially if he doesn't win this war in southeast Asia sometime within the next twelve months. That's why we're starting early. We start now, pick a winner, and come election time, it will be our call."

"Any ideas, pop?" Jackie was pleased that Big Bill was in a rare mood to share some ideas with him. The moment would be fleeting, however.

"I'd like to see our people financially support someone like Dick Nixon."

"Nixon! He's a loser," Jackie interjected.

"He didn't lose by all that much. And part of the reason for that was because our people were divided in our efforts. Besides, if Johnson doesn't run, and he probably won't, who do the Democrats have? Hubert Humphrey? The country needs someone who can rule with a strong hand. I think if we show Nixon enough money, he can be convinced to run. He'd have a good shot at it."

"Yeah, and then we'll own him, right?" It was a rhetorical question, and not one that Jackie expected his father to answer. "So, Hoffa's out and Fitz is in. Where does this leave the Syndicate?"

"In pretty good shape. You know this idea your Uncle Allen had about forming a new local?"

With indifference, “Yeah.”

“I’ve decided to call it the 507. With Hoffa out of the way, Fitzsimmons has assured me that I’ll have no problem getting his approval.”

“So where do I come in?” Jackie echoed.

“I’ll install you permanently as president of the local.”

“I thought so. That means Uncle Allen will be the Secretary-Treasurer.”

“No, I’ll appoint him to serve as a business agent. Harold Friedman’s going to be the Secretary-Treasurer.”

“You’re putting him in charge! He isn’t even family for crying-out-loud,” Jackie complained.

“I have my reasons. I’m not going to get into it, other than to say, he’s more responsible. He’s got a good head on his shoulders, and I must have someone in control who can take care of business. Besides, there will be nothing for you to worry about. I’ve covered all your day-to-day expenses. I’ve seen to it that you’ll be provided with bodyguards, a couple cars, daily expense money, an excellent pension, plus a decent salary. I’ll even see to it that you have an office and a secretary if you want one.”

“Hey, this sounds real good pop.”

“Don’t be a smart ass. I’m doing this for your own good.”

“I’ve got only one small question. Where in the hell will the money come from to cover all these benefits and expenses?”

“There you go again, flying off half cocked. This is why we can’t ever seem to communicate with each other. This is the reason why you don’t have any business getting involved in *this thing of ours*. I don't know why I bother myself with you."

"I'm sorry. You're right. I'm sure you know what you're doing. Harold's a good choice. So, just tell me what you want me to do besides collect a paycheck and keep my trap shut. That's all I'm good for, isn't it?"

"I'm not in the mood for this."

"Well I've got plans, pop ... big plans." Jackie's eyes flashed, "When you die, who's gonna take your place? Brother Marvin? Huh? ... No! ... What about Uncle Allen? You think the Mafia or the guys in the Syndicate will let one of them take your place? In a pig's ass they will. And everybody else you know has got a criminal record a mile long. You either cut me in, or ..."

"Don't you dare think of threating me. Hoffa tried that stunt, and look where it got him. He'll be damn lucky if they don't take him out of Lewisburg feet first."

"I'm sorry, pop. I don't know what came over me. I'm really sorry for blowing up at you like that. It's just that I've got a lot on my mind. Me and Patricia haven't been getting along, and I guess I had to take it out on somebody."

"If any of my men talked to me that way, they'd never make it to their car. You're damn lucky you are my oldest, or I swear to God I'd have my men kick you senseless."

"Yes sir," Jackie acquiesced.

"I completely forgot what I wanted to tell you."

"You were telling me how the new local is going be operated," Jackie reminded him.

"Right. Harold will run the day-to-day operations, is that understood?"

"Yes sir."

"Now, to get dues-paying members, I'll use my position on Teamsters' Joint Council 41 to seize any local that gets into trouble. Once it's been placed into receivership, I'm authorized to assign which local will be responsible for the members, dues and pension fund moneys. Naturally, I'm going to put them into Local 507. I've already found a local with 15,000 members to get you started. Then it will be Harold's responsibility to keep it on a financially sound footing. Within the first six months, the 507 should have at least a million dollars in financial reserves. Is all this registering? ..."

♦

"Yes pop. Now I understand."

"Hey Jackie. You all right?" Tony asked.

"What?" Jackie turned away from the window.

"You called me 'pop,' and something about, 'Now I understand.' You ain't never called me that before."

"I must have been thinking out loud. I was just thinking about the time we formed Local 507. Remember when we hired the PR firm to dress up the difficult struggle I had when I was appointed president of the local. What was it those two wrote ... 'Jackie has had to fight tooth-n-nail to force his father to make his appointment. It was a tough battle, and the members were an unruly lot of ingrates.' That was the damnest bullshit anyone ever wrote about me."

"Jackie, they were always writing stuff like that. Someday, someone will try and write your life's story, and they won't be able to figure out the facts from the bullshit ... at least not from the paper trail you'll leave behind."

"Listen, I want you to promise me that if anything ever happens to me, you or Gail, or both of you will burn all the records, okay?"

"Sure Jackie, but I don't have any of your records. Your attorney has most of that stuff. Maybe you should be asking him to do that."

"I'm thinking about getting rid of Climaco."

"No, you can't be doing that Jackie, not just now when everything is going so good."

"That's not the way I see it. Attorneys just use the system to get what they want," Jackie retorted.

"A whole lot of innocent people keep getting hurt by the legal system, and it's not suppose to work that way."

"Innocent my ass," Jackie stated. "Ain't nobody legit where I come from. The big fish eat the little fish. That's the way it's always been."

"I'm not going to argue with you Jackie, because I can see it's not going to do any good."

"What's there to argue about? I'm telling you like it is. Take my ol' man's case, for example. He's doing a little time for bribing five federal judges. It was only because he couldn't get to the prosecutor."

"That may be. So what's your point?" Tony inquired.

"The goddamn point is this ... none of those attorney judges who accepted bribes had to do any time. They didn't even have to answer up for their part. Not a damn one of them! And look at Senator Howard Cannon. He's been on the Mafia's payroll since Vegas opened."

"Okay Jackie, okay. You made you're point. I understand these things. ... Hey, how about we get laid tonight? What do you say?"

"I'm not in the mood. Besides, I've got other things on my mind."

"Are you worried about seeing McCoy tomorrow?"

"I think McCoy's an asshole. On second thought, maybe I'm the asshole for putting up with him. How many years have I been on their payroll?"

"I don't know, maybe five years, maybe a little longer. Why? What's got you started on McCoy?"

"He's an attorney, too. They're all alike. I just don't trust him. I think he's playing me for a sap. Christ, I shouldn't have fallen for McCoy's line. He'd never have got his hooks into me if it hadn't been for Danny Greene. We have to do something about him. Somebody has to whack that nut case before he gets all us Jews."

*Chapter 3*

## Cabal

PRESIDENT LYNDON JOHNSON was unable to deliver a knockout punch abroad and domestically. On the home front, the Great Society program faltered. Foreshadowed by the assassination of John F. Kennedy, Johnson's urban America exploded in violence, protests and psychological depression. The culmination of racial riots erupting in major cities, war protests springing up on college campuses, and an expanding drug culture mushrooming out of control, prompted Bobby Kennedy to challenge President Johnson as America's only hopeful Democratic candidate.

Johnson quit the race.

That same year, Dr. Martin Luther King was assassinated. Bobby Kennedy became a victim of the times when an assassin's bullets ended his campaign for the presidency.

J. Edgar Hoover was not disturbed with these events.

The climax of this turbulent era opened the door for former Vice President Richard Milhous Nixon to captured the White House with barely 500,000 votes in a three-way race. For the first time in eight years, Hoover felt that someone with the suitable agenda and ethnic background had ascended to the presidential throne. Hoover felt that Nixon understood his Victorian values of law and order. And even though he was beyond the age of mandatory retirement, Hoover felt secure in his position as the boss of domestic clandestine operations. Perhaps now, a new social order could be effectively imposed, and he would have an opportunity to resurrect his life-long ambition to fight the Communists in the labor movement.

To his chagrin, Hoover promptly discovered that men like H.R. Bob Haldeman, John Mitchell and other top Nixon advisors had their own agenda. One priority included installing their own man at the helm of domestic spy operations. The White House wanted someone who was both blindly loyal to the President, as well as someone it could completely control.

J. Edgar Hoover did not fit that profile.

After 46 years of handling covert operations for eight previous administrations, Hoover was proficient in reading warning signs and danger signals. By 1970, he had discovered the administration's hidden agenda to implement *The Huston Plan,* which would combine the CIA and the FBI into a national Gestapo agency. The new secret agency would require a new director.

He picked up the telephone and issued a top secret directive to all special field agents. Their emergency mission: Track down everyone who financially supported President Nixon and find out any improper underworld associations.

◆

"Let's see if we have our facts straight," Special Agent Martin P. McCoy remarked in a regal context. "IRS and the Justice Department both have solid cases against you. And what I'm hearing is that you want to keep Hoffa company in Lewisburg ... is that correct?"

"You guys got nothin'. If you've got a case, it's all bullshit, because I ain't done nothin'."[2]

"Yeah, right. And we didn't have *nothin'* on Hoffa either, but *nothin'* didn't save his ass now, did it?" McCoy paused. "Listen, I'm authorized to cut you a deal, here and now for information. You're not going to have a lot of time to think it over, because there are only two options. You either play ball with us, or I get to watch your life go down the tubes."

The rented downtown motel room sported out-of-date furniture, but the drab decor was not McCoy's concern. He merely needed a forum in which to perform. He stood center stage with his suit coat removed. Like a well-trained salesman, he had been working his potential prospect over before popping the question.

Jackie folded his arms, "Okay, I'm listening."

"We know that you, your Uncle Allen and your old man are dirty. The way we see it, between you and your uncle, the two of you have ripped off the Eastgate Coliseum for the better part of a quarter million."

"That's a bunch of crap," Jackie interrupted.

"It really doesn't matter how much the two of you hit the place for. What matters is that you did it. Even if you only skimmed half that amount, IRS would be real interested in collecting it's percentage."

"You're just fishing," Jackie grumbled.

"By the time IRS is finished, you'll be up to your ass with Treasury and narc agents, not to mention the Labor Department who would really like to nail your ass. ... Is any of this getting through?"

---

[2] An additional third party was present during this meeting, but wishes to remain anonymous.

"Whoever told you guys I was dealing is full of it. If you're looking for drugs, go see Danny Greene or John Nardi." Jackie ground his teeth.

"We're not communicating. Apparently I'm not making myself clear. ... Whether you're dealing or skimming tax-free money isn't the point."

"Okay-okay. What do you want from Jackie Presser?"

"We want you to join us as a paid informant. That way, we can protect you."

"Right." Jackie flashed a phony grin, "Well that certainly sounds wonderful to me. But I have one question? How the hell are you going to do that, Mister FBI, sir?"

"Listen and listen real good, fat boy. We have an old saying and it goes like this: He who has the biggest gang always wins. Who do you think has the biggest gang in town?"

"Yeah-yeah-yeah. Spare me your sentiments. All I hear coming out of your mouth are a lot of words, but you ain't saying nothin'. I still don't know dit-squat about how you guys are going to protect me. Wait ... don't tell me ... you want to protect me from myself."

"That's real funny, Jackie. I suspect that if the truth ever gets out, that's exactly what we'll probably have to do ... protect you from yourself."

"Like I said, I hear you talking and I see your lips moving, but you ain't saying much. How you guys going to protect me? Huh?"

"Actually, that's probably the easy part. We set you up with a secret code name. That way, your real identity is protected. If any charges get brought against you, we step in, take charge of the investigation, and in the process we foil or compromise the case. You read about this happening all the time."

"Yeah, right," Jackie retorted.

"It's been done before. Sometimes we leak information to the press, and sometimes the evidence becomes compromised. Bingo, the case gets dropped."

"If I get myself arrested ... you guys step in ... take charge and I'm off the hook. That sounds real good. Now, I only got one small problem with that. ... Let's suppose the Treasury boys or Labor Department don't let you do that?"

"Get serious. We're the FBI ... We can do any damn thing we want. Obviously, you've forgotten what we did to Hoffa. You know, everyone keeps telling me about your terrific memory, but it must be a real short one. Hoffa got in everyone's way, and now he's cooling his heels in the worst federal hell-hole we have. ... Oh, did I mention that he's been singled out for special treatment? ... I guess it really doesn't matter. We have your answer on the subject, so I guess I'll be running along."

Jackie flinched. "Okay, let's suppose for a moment that I do what you suggest. Won't some of my people start getting suspicious?"

Moving closer, "Not if we help you maintain the proper cover."

"What are we talking here? Are you suggesting that I set up a few deals, and take a cut of the action?"

"Possibly," McCoy encouraged.

"Something like putting a few ghost employees on the payroll and shit like that?" Jackie speculated.

"Something like that. Is that what you had in mind? Ghost employees?" McCoy invited.

"Oh-no you don't! I was just using that as a figure of speech. First, I have to know how this protection thing works?"

"We prefer to call it special privileges. First, we have to come up with a suitable code name, of course. How about something like ... 'The Tailor' A presser could also be a tailor, right?"

"I suppose," Jackie concurred.

"We place any information you furnish us under The Tailor code name. If and when an indictment comes down, we go to the judge or prosecutor, explain that the indictment interferes with one of our open investigations, and they drop the charges. It's that easy."

"Ain't nothing that easy," Jackie retorted contemptuously. "I got to have time to think about this."

"Sure, there's no rush. Take five minutes to think it over."

"I need more time than that," Jackie protested.

Grabbing the armrests to Jackie's chair, McCoy leaned into his face, "No! What you need to do, fat boy, is make a decision. You have to decide whose side you're on. Do you think the Treasury boys are going to cut you a deal like the one we just offered? If that's your game plan, well I have a nasty surprise in store for you." Standing up, he glanced at his wristwatch, then walked over and picked up his suit coat. Swinging it over his shoulder, he headed toward the door, "... Well, your time's up. I got other things I need to do today, like kick some asses." With his back turned, he opened the door, "It's time to shit or get off the pot."

"... Tailor."

A wisp of a smile across McCoy's face, "Are you sure?" He held the door open to leave Jackie with the impression he might change his mind, or worse, up the ante, "... I said, 'Are you sure?'"

"Yeah ... we got a deal. You can call me The Tailor." Jackie looked down at his fingernails and began biting down on one.

Returning to center stage, McCoy asked, "All right. Who are you involved with?"

"I'm not sleeping with Hoover if that's what you mean."

"Cute. ... Who can you get close to?"

"Let's see. There's a guy by the name of Alex Shonder Birns. He's into fencing stolen goods, prostitution, numbers and loansharking. I can approach Shonder without anyone getting too suspicious."

"What I had in mind was someone a little higher up in the underworld ... someone with real political power and influence. What about the local Mafia don?" McCoy asked.

"John Scalish?" Jackie shook his head, "That's not a good suggestion."

"Okay, what about Tony Milano, the underboss?"

"He don't see nobody these days. I've got no way of even getting in contact with him."

"All right, what about Angelo Lonardo?" McCoy suggested.

"Man, you sure know how to pick 'em. I can't get close to Big Ange Lonardo. He'd get suspicious the moment I opened my mouth."

"Look, we know you or your old man are connected to some of these guys. Surely there's someone you can get close to without raising too much suspicion?" McCoy probed.

"You don't know how it works. The Jewish Syndicate and the Italian Mafia have a chain of command. If I start asking any of them guys questions, I'll get myself whacked for sure. ... Hey, I got an idea. What about John Nardi? He's Milano's nephew. Besides, he's already in the Teamsters, and I have a contact that might lead to some of these other guys."

"Fine. We'll start with Nardi. Now, keep me posted on everything he does. Who he talks to, where he goes and even if Nardi changes his routine. I want to know everything. If I find out you're holding back, I'll deep-six our arrangement. Is that understood?"

"Yeah, I hear ya." Jackie felt emotionally drained.

While in the process of exiting for a second time, McCoy abruptly turned and took a more direct approach, "By the way, what's your political affiliation?"

"Say what?" Jackie puzzled.

"You heard me. ... Political affiliation?"

"It depends on who I'm dealing with. Right now me and my ol' man are politically supporting Dick Nixon."

"Why does that not surprise me?" McCoy rhetorically responded.

"Well, you know ... with Hoffa out of action, the Teamster Executive Board can pretty much back anyone who can do us the most favors."

"How does your membership feel about that?" McCoy asked.

"They ain't got nothing to say about it. ... Say, what difference is that suppose to make? Why all the interest in our political support?"

"Just thought I'd ask. ... Oh, one more thing. How well do you know President Nixon?"

"I don't, at least not personally. My ol' man received a 'thank-you-for-your-support' letter after the election and he was invited to attend his inauguration, but you know how that stuff goes. There were so many people there that he didn't have an opportunity to speak with him privately or nothing like that. Why the interest?"

"Nothing really. We just like to know who we're dealing with, that's all."

◆

Nationally and internationally, President Nixon's popularity was on the rise. Not since Franklin Delano Roosevelt had any President been able to garner such enthusiastic support in so little time.

But it was not enough. With the '72 national conventions little more than a year and a half away, the White House was in a state of turmoil and confusion. The fears of the last close election overshadowed common sense, and the battle cry coming from the President's top domestic advisers was that every last vote would have to be squeezed to ensure Nixon's reelection. A landslide would provide the necessary mandate to implement the new spy agency, and Congress would be impotent to impede it.

Absolutely nothing was to be left to chance. Jimmy Hoffa supporters would have to be either converted, neutralized or divided. The Vietnam War would have to be won, stopped or forfeited. The opposition party would have to be infiltrated, undermined and discredited. Even the top secret Huston Plan would have to be placed on hold until something could be done about Hoover.

Any other time, Hoover would have been delighted to have actively participated in these events, but he was being bypassed on every critical decision. His counsel, advice and feedback were neither solicited nor appreciated by the White House. Even covert operations were being assigned to someone else, and J. Edgar Hoover was not pleased about these new developments. He and the FBI had been reduced to little more than chasing down media leaks and following up on triviality.

"If there are no other questions, let's get out there and kick a few asses," the station chief commanded. "And Marty, I want to see you in my office immediately."

In less than a minute, Agent Martin McCoy was standing in the doorway.

"Come in and shut the door. ... Take a seat," the station chief invited.

"What's up Chief?"

"SOG has a special assignment for you, and it's being assigned right from the boss himself, so there better not be any screw ups."

"... Hoover?" McCoy asked.

"We don't have time for twenty questions. This is serious. I'm going to fill you in on some highly classified details. It's not to go any further than this room. Understood?"

"Sure. What's the assignment?"

"This is not going to be easy, because I don't have all the details. I'll bring you up to speed on what I have."

The station chief wasn't exactly sure where to begin, so he started with general background information. "Nixon may be in trouble."

"The opinion polls show that he'll win the election in a landslide."

"There's a lot the voters don't know about, and if it comes out, he'll be defeated in a landslide. Now listen, don't ask me any questions ... just take my word for it. There have been some serious leaks to the media coming out of the White House. Nixon's Chief of Staff, H.R. Haldeman wants the director to use the Bureau and find out where the leaks are and plug them up."

"May I ask what kind of media leaks?" McCoy inquired. "Does any of it have anything to do with these rumors about a new secret agency?"

"I'm not at liberty to discuss it. Besides, like I said, I don't have all the details, so let's not get sidetracked. What I do know is that our Chicago SAC office has found out that some secret White House plans are surfacing there. Some guy by the name of Harry Halfgod is going around claiming to have White House connections. He's using the name Harry Haler and Harry Hall."

"Let me write this down. Is Halfgod spelled like it sounds?" McCoy asked.

"I think so. ... Recently, this guy Halfgod started using the name Haler and left Chicago. He resurfaced in Las Vegas where our guys spotted him talking to Liberatore."

"As in Anthony D. Liberatore?" McCoy clarified.

"Precisely. Now here's where you come in. You're the one with the most contacts in the field. Who have you got locally that can get close to Liberatore?"

"Hmm? That's a tough one. Liberatore is crafty."

"What about Danny Greene? You think Greene could get close to Liberatore?" the station chief inquired.

"Not a chance. Those two are working at the opposite end of the spectrum. Liberatore wouldn't trust Greene even if he had a gun barrel sticking down his throat."

"Okay, is there anyone else out there who can? ... What about this new informant you lined up?"

"The Tailor? I doubt it. He's been practically worthless in terms of obtaining anything useful. I'm still developing him, but he's not really up to speed. He's got his own agenda. For now, I've got him assigned to watch John Nardi." McCoy knew he could have included more details, but why cloud the issue.

"Give it a shot anyway. I want to be able to report back to SOG that we're on top of the situation. See if you can come up with something. I don't need a bad efficiency report, and neither do you. If you can't get The Tailor on this, *pronto*, then get someone else who can perform the mission."

◆

Martin McCoy posed the question, "Jackie, what can you tell me about a guy named Harry Halfgod?"

"Halfgod? I don't know anyone by that name. I thought being an informant was going to be more exciting than this." Jackie put his feet on the motel's coffee table, "You think we should mess up the bedding so that it looks likes someone occupied the room?"

"If it makes you feel like James Bond, be my guest. ... Now let's get back to the subject. Do you know anything about a Harry Haler? Does that ring a bell?"

"Harry Haler? ... Nah, I don't know that guy either. I may have heard the name mentioned, but nothing comes to mind." Then Jackie asked, "You got a mug shot?"

"It's all the same guy. I can get a picture, but that takes time and at the moment, time is in short supply. But you're pretty sure you don't know him?"

"Yeah, I'm sure. I know at least a half dozen Harrys. Maybe I met the guy someplace ... if so, I forgot. So what's so special about this guy anyway?"

"I'm not at liberty to discuss it. What about a guy by the name of Anthony Liberatore?"

"Liberatore? Sure. Him I know. He's a wiseguy, a real wannabe. So what do you want to know about Liberatore?"

"Can you get close to him?" McCoy inquired.

"Man, this isn't part of our deal. Liberatore's dangerous. He killed an Irish cop back in the '30s. He'd have me whacked in a minute if he thought I was on some secret government mission."

"You don't have to get that close to him. Just see if he knows Harry Halfgod or Haler from Las Vegas."

"Yeah, sure. Who is this Harry guy anyway?"

"I can't get into that," McCoy said.

"I can tell you this much, he's got nothing to do with the rackets locally, 'cause if he did, I'd have heard about it. John Nardi's the one you guys should be worried about. His uncle, Tony Milano, is an underboss."

"We're not interested in ancient Mafia history," McCoy retorted.

"Fine. So what you want me to do? ... By the way, I put Nardi's son on my payroll like we talked about," Jackie announced. "My secretary, Gail, mails him a check for three-hundred each week. Nardi's real happy about that."

"Forget about Nardi. We want you to team up with Anthony Liberatore and this guy Harry Haler."

"You think I'm deaf or something? But I have to tell you, this may not be all that easy. If you really want to get close to Liberatore, you might want to do it through the mayor."

McCoy leaned forward. "Mayor Perk?"

"Yeah. The mayor and Liberatore are really tight. The mayor wants to stay on the good side of organized crime. Mayor Perk figures the best way to do that is by being extra nice to Liberatore."

McCoy briefly pondered the option before, "That's too risky. We can't take any chances by using an outsider."

"You're catching heat on this, aren't you?" Jackie surmised. "Okay, I might be able to set up a meeting. Let's see ... Liberatore might bite if I got my ol' man and Frank Fitzsimmons involved."

"Why do you have to involve others?" McCoy asked.

"Well me and Liberatore aren't exactly tight. But if Liberatore thinks that someone like the General President of the Teamsters is involved, he'll be real interested in setting up a meeting." Jackie reflected, "Now you said this guy Haler is in Vegas. So we'll meet in Vegas. ... But I'll do this only under one condition."

"What?"

Jackie pressed the issue, "I got to have a clue as to what I'm supposed to be looking for. What's the connection?"

"Look, I'll share this much. This Haler guy is a good friend of Liberatore's. Haler has been going around claiming he has White House connections, but I can assure you that he doesn't."

"Connections? As in presidential connections?" Jackie stood up.

"Something like that. ... Listen, it's all rumors as far as the Bureau's concerned. Just the same, we want to find out if there is any truth to it. You just have to get close to the guy and hear what he has to say."

◆

*Frank Fitzsimmons*

When the General President of the International Brotherhood of Teamsters learned from Big Bill that a man with presidential connections was holding a meeting, Frank Fitzsimmons canceled his appointments and flew to Las Vegas. Fitzsimmons saw this as a prime opportunity to get to Nixon and persuade him not to grant Hoffa a presidential pardon, regardless of how many letters and petitions the President had been receiving.

"Okay, let's all go over this one more time." Jackie pointed to Harry Haler, "Liberatore tells me you could get to the prez. Now I'm hearing something different."

"No. I don't think you completely understand how it works ..." Haler suggested.

"Oh? But we understand a con job," Jackie looked at his father before glancing at Fitzsimmons.

"What I'm trying to explain to you is that the PR firm I plan to create is just the vehicle, you know, a cover. Maybe funnel would be a better word. We take some of our excess funds paid to the PR firm, that's the funnel, which we control, and simply make an intelligent financial investment in our future."

"And by these 'excess funds,' you precisely mean our three-hundred thousand dollars?" Big Bill added.

"It takes money to prime the pump, for crying out loud," Haler complained.

"I don't like it," Fitzsimmons interjected.

"What's there not to like about a sweet deal like this? I kick back twenty-five gees each month, and invest the rest. You get a total tax write-off, and you're automatically going to be twenty-five grand richer. ... Let's see, that comes to three-hundred thousand a year."

"Yeah, right," Jackie responded. "We turn over three-hundred gees for you to hold, and trust that you'll kick back twenty-five gees each month."

"Well, when you put it that way, you make it sound like I'm trying to rip you off or something. I think we have to have a little mutual trust here." Haler's voice carried sincerity.

"Trust? ... You want me to trust you? Sure, I trust you. Whatever made you think I didn't? After all, people I don't trust have fallen off some very tall buildings. And god forbid, my ol' man here can't trust you."

"Why do I get the feeling you're leading up to something," Haler responded.

"You know why wiseguys like Liberatore are trusted?" Jackie baited.

"Because they take a secret oath?" Haler guessed.

"No. Because the Mafia's got something real good on each and everyone in the organization. ... Now I ask you, what do we have on you. Your word! Not good enough pal. As far as I'm concerned, if this cockamamie scheme of yours goes south, I'll just remind myself that I got your word. Oh yeah, I almost forgot ... this sheet of paper with the president's name on it. That doesn't means anything to us, pal."

"Okay Jackie, I see your point." Haler pondered the situation for several moments then, "Here's something nobody knows about. It could get me in serious trouble, but you all have to promise me not to mention it to a soul."

"Yeah, it better be pretty damn good, or we're out of here, and you can take this half-baked idea of yours to someone stupid enough to listen to it," Jackie said.

"First, promise you won't mention it to anyone."

"If you've got something else to say, say it quick," Jackie demanded.

"I used stolen bonds for collateral on a loan just before I left Chicago. There, are you satisfied? Now you have something on me."

"What's that? That's small potatoes. Who cares? You told Liberatore we could purchase direct access to the prez, and all I'm hearing is conversation. If all we wanted to do was launder a few gees, we can use our people. We don't need you laundering our bread." Turning to his father, "Right pop?"

Haler picked up and waved his letter, "If you want to get to this president, you will. Like I said, Jackie, I have a connection inside the White House."

"This so-called connection ... did you get that letter from your connection?" Jackie asked.

"Indirectly." Haler was not convincing.

"It figures. So you were hoping to set us up, skim some bread, and have a good laugh on us ... right?"

"No, honest. I'm telling it to you straight. This broad is right inside the White House. She told me that the best way to get to Nixon is through this Committee to Reelect the President. It being run by a guy very close to Nixon."

"In other words, if we want presidential favors, all we have do is make a sizable contribution to Nixon's reelection committee. Is that it?" Jackie surmised.

"Exactly, but the contribution must be in cash," Haler added.

"And we give this cash, our money, to the phony ad agency ..."

"Hoover-Gorvin," Haler interjected.

"Yeah, Hoover-Gorden, whatever, and they, meaning you, donate the cash to this reelection committee on our behalf," Jackie concluded.

"Yes! That's it, exactly. ... Now she tells me that the trick is to make large enough cash contributions so that you'll get noticed. But it all has to be done through a funneling operation, so there is a buffer. There can't be any paper trail. That's why we set up this dummy ad agency. We can't make it appear too obvious, because that could queer the whole thing."

"Why? What if I want to make donations myself? That way the prez will know he owes Jackie, Big Bill and Fitz favors."

"That's not going to work. No one individual's name can be directly linked to the cash." Haler leaned forward and whispered, "I hear the heat is on. Someone inside the White House has been leaking stuff to the media ... some newspaper guy by the name of Joseph Kraft. Without the buffer, this guy could catch wind of it, and Nixon's going to back off."

"So we make our donations in cash," Jackie refuted.

"No, I don't think you're getting the picture. The new campaign regulations make it against the law to secretly donate large amounts of cash. Some guy by the name of Sindona tried that, and Maurice Stans had to give him his million bucks back."

"Michele Sindona?" Big Bill queried.

Before Haler could respond Fitzsimmons asked, "Who's he?"

Leaning into Fitz's ear, "Sindona is tight with the Gambino crime family out of New York. He's sort of the unofficial consigliere between the Sicilian Mafia and the Vatican. He's very big in international banking." Returning to Haler, "So what do you think it will take to get noticed?" Big Bill asked.

"A hundred thousand. We wait a month, then pop in another amount that size. I guarantee, we'll get a call."

"It sounds like a high-stakes crap-shoot to me. What if it don't work?" Fitzsimmons remarked.

"Yeah, what if all we get for the money is a 'thank you for your support' letter like the last time. What then? We get to take you for a ride?" Jackie added.

"I assure you Jackie, so help me God, we'll get more than just a thank you letter."

"Yeah? How can you be so sure? You got an ace in the hole?"

"Maybe not an ace, but a high card." Haler paused for effect, "Listen, my gal tells me that Nixon has more shit going on at the White House than anyone can possibly imagine. She told me that they're planning something real big. Something called the Tom Huston Plan, but the White House wants it kept very hush-hush. I mean, just take a look at Nixon's staff. Even Vice President Agnew. My gal tells me even he's on the take."

"What's this Huston deal?" Jackie mentally noted the name.

"It's some secret project the White House don't want anyone to know about. I'm telling you, Nixon and Haldeman are really paranoid about plugging up leaks. My gal tells me Hoover himself has been over to the White House more than a dozen times in the last several months about some secret project. And let me tell you, she tells me Hoover hasn't been too happy."

Jackie looked at his father and Fitzsimmons before continuing, "So, what you're telling me is, these secret projects need special funds that can't be accounted for?"

"Exactly."

"I get the picture," Jackie said. "We put money where our mouth is, and don't ask too many questions."

"Does this mean we have a deal?" Haler stuck out his hand.

Jackie stroked his chin, and slowly noted, "We have a deal under one condition."

"What condition is that?"

"If this turns out to be a scam, I get to have you fitted for a pair of heavy boots. I'll watch, and just before you get dropped off the side of the boat, I'll remind myself that I took your word."

SIZABLE FUNDS from the phony public relations consortium began finding their way into the White House. President Nixon assigned Attorney General John N. Mitchell to find out what the Hoover-Gorvin Agency wanted.

"See, what did I tell you, Jackie? We did it! The U.S. Attorney General himself called to make the inquiry," Haler announced over the phone.

"No kidding. I'll be damned."

"John Mitchell himself, contacted me. Can you believe that. He wants to know if there was anything he could do for us? What shall I tell him?" Haler asked.

"No. You leave that to me and my ol' man. This guy Mitchell, did he leave you a number?"

U.S. Attorney General Mitchell received a telephone call from Big Bill Presser. The initial request was straightforward: *Keep Hoffa in prison until he dies*. Through Mitchell, Nixon relayed the message back that he would take their request under advisement, but that the request might not be possible.

In carefully weighing the options, the political fallout was risky. Hoffa's incarceration had made him more popular than ever, and every week new petitions and letters were arriving at the White House, requesting President Nixon grant Jimmy Hoffa a presidential pardon. To complicate matters, rumors persisted that the FBI had set Hoffa up, and the government's chief witness was now telling a different story in a sworn affidavit.

Mitchell returned the telephone call on behalf of the President, "Listen Bill, we're going to have to back off on your Hoffa request."

"How so?" Big Bill asked.

"We're catching all kinds of flack on this Hoffa thing. I'm not at liberty to go into all the sordid details over the phone, but suffice it to say, Hoover may have set Hoffa up just to pull Bobby Kennedy's chain. From there, things seem to have gotten out of hand."

"Oh?"

"Well, for one thing, that witness who claimed that Hoffa offered him a bribe has changed his story. It may not have been Hoffa tampering with the witness. You're going to have to come up with something else."

*John Mitchell*

"Yes, I see what you mean. I'll have to give this some thought. How soon can I get back to you on this?" Big Bill inquired.

"As soon as possible would be appreciated."

Frank Fitzsimmons and Big Bill were concerned about Hoffa having been setup by the FBI. If the Bureau could do it to Hoffa, could they be far behind? To distance himself from the transaction, Fitzsimmons suggested to Big Bill that his son serve as the buffer to deliver their decision back to Attorney General Mitchell.

"Here's what we came up with. If you feel you have no alternative, Fitz and my ol' man wanted me to inquire about Nixon granting Hoffa a conditional pardon?" Jackie conveyed.

"Hmm. Not bad," Mitchell responded. "I think we can live with that. We can give him a pardon on the condition that he not be allowed to participate in any union activities until the expiration of his sentence. Let's see, that would keep him out of action until March 1980."

"That's the good part. The bad news is that the ol' man doesn't think he'll accept it. My ol' man and Fitz know Hoffa pretty well."

"Oh. I didn't think of that, Jackie."

"So here's what they suggest. You might want to keep the terms of the pardon a secret until after he gets out."

"That's not likely to happen. There will be papers for him to sign, and my guess is, Hoffa or his attorney will read it over very carefully before he signs anything."

"Well my ol' man thought of that too. He suggests you wait until a day or two before Christmas. He said that Hoffa must be itching to get out of that hell-hole and, who could turn down being home with his family for Christmas."

"That's brilliant! I think I can sell that idea to the President. Listen, the moment I get the President's okay on this, I'll set something up with the warden over at Lewisburg."

"Well that all sounds real good, but just keep in mind, Hoffa is no dummy," Jackie advised.

"I see ... I've got an idea. I'll suggest to the warden that he walk Hoffa to the front gate with a car waiting to take him to the airport and then home, in time for the holidays. At that point, the warden then slips the paperwork under his nose to sign."

"Yeah, you got the idea," Jackie confirmed.

"If Hoffa doesn't sign his release, then it's all on his shoulders. I love it. This will get those damn Hoffa's supporters off our backs."

"Yeah, that might work. My ol' man has one more suggestion," Jackie added.

"Oh, what's that?"

"He said you should get Hoffa to sign his release first. You should wait until he's actually out of the joint before he's informed about the restrictions. He said that you should lock the prison doors first. Then he'll have to bang on the prison gates to get back in."

"God, I love it! Tell your old man for me, I think he's a genius ... simply brilliant."

◆

Two days before Christmas of '71, Jimmy Hoffa received surprise word from the warden at Lewisburg Federal Prison about a presidential pardon. Within two days, he would be free to walk through the gates and handed a package of paperwork to sign. Not included in the paperwork was a conditional restriction that would be handed to him once he passed beyond the point of no return.

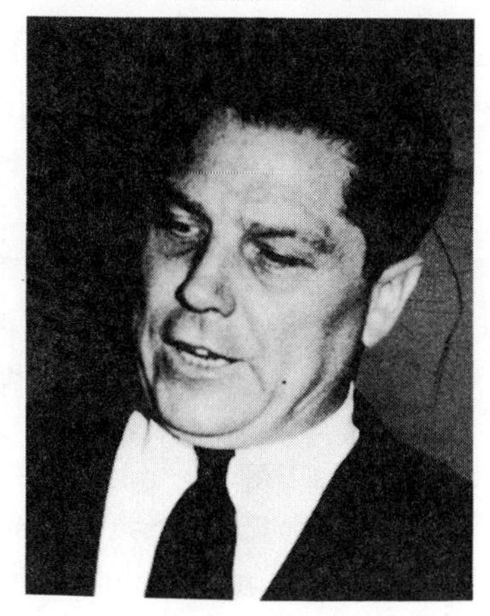

*Jimmy Hoffa*

When word of Hoffa's pending release reached Harold Gibbons, who was serving on the Teamsters' Executive Board, all hell broke loose. As a staunch Hoffa supporter, Gibbons was openly hostile to the idea of having the Teamsters directly or indirectly endorse President Nixon's reelection bid—pardon or no pardon.

Gibbons' support for Hoffa represented a major setback for the Teamsters who wanted to present a show of solidarity for the Nixon-Agnew ticket. The group was furious with Harold Gibbons—especially Syndicate boss Big Bill Presser.

"I don't know what Gibbons thinks he's going to accomplish by this?"

"Any ideas, pop?"

"I think I'll recommend to Fitzsimmons that he remove Gibbons from office. If he gives me any trouble, I'll suggest to him that he resign in lieu of me taking more drastic physical action. He'll get the message ... one way or the other."

Considering the source, Harold Gibbons knew the veiled threat was serious.

◆

As the new year rolled in, White House advisors were directly in touch with the Pressers. As an entity, Harry Haler became excess baggage, and the need to pipeline privileged communications through him no longer existed.

The White House was eager to show its appreciation. The Secret Service rather than the FBI was asked to conduct a discrete background check on Frank Fitzsimmons and the Pressers. It would only be a matter of time before new political appointments would be made, and the White House needed this discrete information.

The Secret Service quickly uncovered several problems. The agency learned that Frank Fitzsimmons was totally under the control of the Chicago and Kansas City organized crime families. Fitzsimmons was also beholden to Big Bill, who was heading up the largest crime Syndicate that maintained a close rapport with the Genovese crime family in New York.

The news went from bad to worse. Big Bill Presser dissolved his early-day business venture by fixing a bomb to his partner's car horn. Since then, he had ordered the deaths of at least a dozen men who got in his way. Then, there was Big Bill's involvement with an incident entangling a 15-year-old girl, who had mysteriously disappeared after becoming pregnant by Mickey McBride, the founder of The Yellow Cab Company.

When the Secret Service's investigation focused its attention on Jackie Presser, it found an equally hopeless situation. The White House was informed that appointing him to anything posed a serious predicament as Jackie did not project the type of public image the administration wanted to portray.

The Secret Service also pointed out that the Hoover-Gorvin public relations agency was merely a front operation for laundering campaign contributions and kickback money. That, however, was a salient point; the White House already knew where the money was coming from.

The White House Press Secretary's mission was to protect the President's media image, and to avoid situations that might prove to be publicly embarrassing before the election. Nixon's Press Secretary intuitively knew that the moment a new face began to regularly appear at White House functions, reporters would start asking questions: *Who is this guy? Where does he come from? What are his credentials? How long has he been close friends with the President?*

The litany of inquiries would be relentless and Nixon's administration would be hard-pressed to put a positive spin on the situation. The U.S. Treasury Department noted the investigation by the Secret Service and grew curious. Why wasn't the FBI called in to conduct these investigations? Perhaps the White House didn't want Hoover's boys digging into matters that could be traced back to the President's staff.

Meanwhile, the White House staff felt something should be done. The President's advisors suggested to Jackie that he could improve his public image by enlisting more experienced and professional talent. Within days of being contacted, he enlisted the services of Richard Bellamy and Peter Halbin. Their assignment: Rewrite Jackie's non-existent work history, and turn it into an exemplary track record of solid professional and civic accomplishments. In the event Bellany and Halbin were successful, the newly created individual would be formally invited to join White House personnel in an afternoon round of golf or perhaps dine at the White House with the 37th President of the United States.

*Chapter 4*

## Red-Letter Days

Since the early Roman Empire, death has served as the ultimate catalyst for change. Death expedites the process. Few men understood this concept better than J. Edgar Hoover. He had witnessed presidents and presidential candidates assassinated. His special agents had investigated and covered up a wide assortment of politically sensitive deaths so that the process of change could be continued without disrupting the public's perception of constitutional government.

Better than most, Hoover understood the complexities. He saw the big picture, and that picture included generating positive public relations, controlling information and surrounding himself with trusted confidantes who shared his values and beliefs.

President Nixon also knew the value in surrounding himself with people he could unquestionably trust, and he chose not to take Hoover into his confidence. When a special job arose, the White House picked a small group of talented professionals known as *The Plumbers Unit* to handle the assignment. One of their lessor assignments was to discretely enter the Watergate complex and install remote monitoring devices. Of all their special assignments, it was perhaps the easiest one they would be called upon to perform. For that reason, few precautions had to be taken, now that Hoover was no longer a problem.

◆

"The rumors about J. Edgar's death have not been greatly exaggerated."

Jackie was in no mood for light banter, "How did it happen?"

"Presumably, he died during the night. His housekeeper found his naked body sprawled over the floor when she arrived for work on May 2nd. So let's get down to bus ..."

"Natural causes?" Jackie inquired.

"What difference does it make? He's dead," Special Agent McCoy responded.

"Was he given a full medical exam?"

"Hmm? Strange you should mention that, Jackie. By Executive Order, President Nixon has decreed that his body is not to be autopsied."

"My people tell me that if something like cyanide gas was used, it would make it appear as if a person died of a heart attack."

"I don't think he had any immediate living relatives, so who cares?"

"I do, damn-it! This changes everything. You have any idea who's going to take his place?" Jackie inquired.

"The word floating around Washington is that William Webster will be tapped for the position, but it really doesn't matter. Can we get down to business," McCoy pressed.

"Who the hell is this Webster? Nixon should be appointing someone we can trust. Someone like John Mitchell."

"It's not my call. They forgot to consult me on the matter. ... What's the big deal, Jackie? I really don't understand why you're so concerned about who replaces Hoover."

"I'll tell ya what's got me concerned. We have an agreement. What's going to happen with that?"

"Is that what's bothering you? Listen Jackie, our agreement is going to be just as binding on the next director as it was with Hoover. Our mission hasn't changed. If we were going to close down organized crime, believe me, we'd have done it long ago." McCoy paused then added, "Look at it this way, ... we need you just as much as you need us."

Jackie mustered a short laugh, "Yeah. So, this Webster guy, who is he?"

"He's a Nixon insider. By that I mean he's loyal to the President. I can assure you, he's not going to do anything to upset the proverbial apple cart."

"I still don't like it," Jackie replied.

"Sorry, there's nothing I can do about it. Of course, there's always the possibility that we can wait a few days and see if the Bureau's Messiah will rise from his casket over at the Capitol."

"... What are you talking about?"

"Bad joke. ... Now, can we get on with more important matters?" McCoy could easily envision the entire day being wasted over trivialities.

"My attorney thinks I should get something in writing, ... you know, something that says I'm authorized to perform certain acts to maintain my cover."

"Tell your attorney to keep his nose out of Bureau business. Look, there is no point in making waves."

Jackie wasn't placated, "What if this friend of Nixon's isn't approved by Congress? What if some nut gets in there and starts messing things up for me and my people? What then? Huh?"

"If I were you, I'd be more worried about keeping a low profile. Who besides your attorney and your main bodyguard knows about our involvement?"

"Nobody. I tell everybody else I have to go to a Big Brother meeting when I split on short notice."

"Big Brother? ... I like that. It has such a nineteen-eighty-four*ish* sound to it." McCoy studied Jackie's face. "You're absolutely sure no one else knows?"

"Yeah, I'm sure," Jackie responded.

"What about Anthony Liberatore?" McCoy asked.

"Of course not."

"Angelo Lonardo?"

"No."

"Okay, what about this guy Harry Haler?" McCoy ventured.

"Are you kidding me? Why should I tell any of those guys anything, especially Haler?"

McCoy eased into the real topics of interest, "This Lonardo guy, how well do you know him?"

"He's been in the Mafia since '49, but he's been in the rackets all his life."

"Anything else?" McCoy pressed.

"Angelo's ol' man started up the first *La Cosa Nostra* crime family in America with a guy by the name of Charles 'Lucky' Luciano. His son, Big Ange, worked with the Jewish Syndicate on a few deals. And get this, he calls my ol' man's outfit the 'Jewish boys.' ... Why the interest? Is Angelo Lonardo up to something we Jewish boys should know about?"

"If I share something with you, can I have your word you'll keep your mouth shut?" McCoy challenged.

"You have my word, okay."

"We think Treasury agents are targeting Angelo Lonardo to become one of their informants. If that happens, they'll have a principal inside the Mafia, or *La Cosa Nostra* as you call it."

"I see," smiling, Jackie added, "you're afraid the Treasury is going to step in and start competing for your action, right? Well me and Angelo ain't exactly tight, so I don't think I'll be able to get close to him."

"Just the same, if you hear anything, I'd appreciate being made aware of it. ... By the way, a moment ago we were speaking about Harry Haler. Did you ever discover what he was up to?"

"He's a nobody. A zero." Jackie folded his arms.

"Did he, or perhaps Anthony Liberatore, tell you anything significant?"

"Oh, you mean about the leaks from the White House," Jackie clarified. "Nothing too important."

"I'll be the judge of that. What did he tell you?"

"Let's see. ... Haler told me he's got some gal in the White House he knows, but I got the impression he wasn't real tight with her."

"Oh? Why?"

"He didn't tell me what job she was doing, but it sounded like she might be a secretary or telephone operator, or something like that."

"Anything else?" McCoy pressed.

"I can't be too sure about this, 'cause I think the guy's a bullshitter, but he says that something big is going down, and that they were making some secret plans, but he didn't know any of the details."

"Now listen, ... can you remember exactly what Haler said?"

Jackie paused. "Nah, it's like I told, the guy's so full of bull, he can't tell fact from fiction. I wouldn't put too much stock in anything he says."

"Do me a favor. If anything he said to you about his contact inside the White House comes back to you, I want you to write it down, no matter how insignificant you think it might be. Then I want you to contact me a-s-a-p."

Jackie watched McCoy's disappointment. "Say, what about a contract? ... You know, something written down."

"Yeah, ... sure. ... That might take awhile. We'll have to wait until the next director of the Bureau is formally installed and briefed. You're absolutely sure Haler didn't tell you anything about any rumors floating around the White House?"

Jackie snapped his fingers, "Wait, I do remember something. He mentioned something about this broad telling him that Agnew, the vee-pee, was suppose to be on the take."

"Well, maybe today's a bad day for you. Just think on it. Like I said, if anything else comes to mind, the moment it does, just write it down."

Big Bill had imparted some valuable lessons with Jackie, and one of them was controlling critical information. Obviously, the things Jackie had selectively withheld from McCoy must have been of some value.

◆

On June 20th, Jackie received a telephone call from his father. It took him 45 minutes to dress and drive from his mistress' Van Aken apartment to his father's Glenville residence. Big Bill was waiting for him when he arrived.

"What's up, pop?"

"I received a telephone call from Attorney General John Mitchell. Come on into the den." Stepping into the room, Big Bill continued, "I have a delivery I want you to make. It's to be made personally and alone. I don't want you to pickup anyone along the way. And I don't want you to talk with anyone, coming or going. Is that understood?"

"Yeah, sure pop."

Big Bill walked about his desk, lifted a travel-size metal carrying case, placed it on top of the desk, and unsnapped the latches and lifted the lid to display the green. "I want you to deliver this case to Nixon, and personally hand it to him, or Mitchell if he's there. Is that understood?"

"Can I ask what's going on?"

"Like I said, I received a telephone call last night. It's taken me damn near the whole night and most of the morning to collect this cash. I'm half sick as it is, and too tired to make the trip myself."

"Sure." Jackie was pleased that his father had thought of him in his hour of need.

"Here's the situation as I understand it. It seems that a group of the President's men were on a special mission and went a little overboard. They need some cash to handle their defense. I've been asked to help out. I tried reaching your Uncle Allen, but he seems to be busy. So you're the only one available on such short notice."

"Gee, I'm almost speechless, pop."

"That's exactly how you're to handle it. Speechless. Don't talk to no one. Don't stop to help out any damsels in distress, and for god's sake, don't let this cash out of your sight."

"I've always wanted to see the White House. Maybe they'll give me a tour."

"Don't make a pest of yourself. You should be able to get in and out of there inside of fifteen minutes. Don't hang around. The longer you're there, the greater the risk someone will find out about it."

Jackie paused to make sure Big Bill was finished before asking, "Anything else I should know about?"

"The White House gate guard will be told to expect you at the last minute. So don't arrive too early. When you get there, all you have to say is, 'Pasquale has a delivery for the President,' and the guard will let you pass. You're to wait until after dark. Oh, and another thing, you're to go to the back entrance of the White House. The night doorman will let you in. Someone will escort you to wherever Nixon or Mitchell is."

"Is there any chance someone might ask me about what's in the suitcase?"

"Just tell them it's a special delivery for the President. Nothing else. As far as I know, everything has been taken care of, so you shouldn't have any problems. ... A round-trip plane ticket will be waiting for you at the airport. You should get to DC before five-thirty, so you'll have plenty of time to rent a car, grab something to eat and get there before Nixon retires."

"It looks like you thought of everything pop. ... I don't suppose you want me to get a receipt."

"Stop being a smart ass." Big Bill closed the lid, re-snapped the latches and handed Jackie the case, "Christ, I almost forgot. ... Keep your trap shut about Hoffa, unless one of them brings up the subject."

Heading toward the door, "Sure pop, I can handle it."

"We'll see. I'm not happy about your Uncle Allen being too busy."

◆

By August of '72, Jackie replaced Harry Haler with Duke Zeller.

Upon receiving this news, Haler was on the telephone, "Okay, so maybe in the beginning I was working on my own set of priorities, but damn-it, the thing worked! We got direct access to the President of the United States. Hell Jackie, you and your old man got what you wanted. What difference does it make how you got it?"

"What do I have to do, keep repeating myself? You're no longer in charge. That's not to mean you were ever really in charge, but if you ever thought you were in charge, you're not."

"You can't do this to me and get away with it."

"Pardon? Am I hearing a threat?" Jackie pushed himself back in his chair a little further.

"I'm telling you Jackie, you won't get away with it. I was the one who got you into the White House. It was all my idea, my game plan and ..."

"And my money! My money talks and your bullshit walks. Now, I hear anymore crap coming out of your mouth, and I'll see you get a boat ride." —Click

The following day, a public relations and advertising contract was signed for $10 million. Jackie, however, insisted upon his $25,000 monthly consulting fee. In the excitement of the paper-signing transaction, one minor glitch had been inadvertently overlooked.

The announcement of the new contract captured the business community's attention, including that of Anthony Liberatore. His participation in setting up the initial meeting with Harry Haler had been overlooked. Liberatore brought that issue to the Mafia don Scalish's attention. In turn, the don summoned Maishe Rockman and Angelo Lonardo to his Murray Hill residence. The don instructed them to remedy the situation. "This thing you're doing Jackie, isn't right," Maishe commented. He turned toward Angelo Lonardo.

"Jackie, you're going about this in the wrong manner. The Mafia as well as your father's Syndicate have traditions that must be upheld and honored," Angelo explained. He then turned to Maishe Rockman, "Perhaps we should have approached Big Bill about this."

*Big Ange Lonardo*

"But Liberatore, he didn't really do anything," Jackie argued.

Angelo interrupted, "That's not the way Liberatore sees it. He introduced you to Harry Haler, and set up your first meeting. I believe you met with him in Vegas."

"Now we find out that the meeting was successful," Maishe added. "As a result, you've just signed a multimillion dollar advertising contract with Hoover-Gorvin."

Angelo interjected, "The way we see it, none of this would have been possible if Liberatore hadn't made that initial introduction."

"But Haler was trying to scam us," Jackie continued.

Neither Maishe Rockman with the Syndicate or Angelo Lonardo with the Mafia wanted to hear side-bar arguments. Maishe held up his hand, "Now-now, according to tradition, Liberatore is entitled to something."

"He hasn't even been initiated. How come he's entitled?" Jackie protested.

Angelo felt compelled to address the question, "Well he's practically a made member. If it wasn't for the fact that the don refuses to take in any new members, he would have been initiated a long time ago."

"In fact, all the other members are in agreement on this," Maishe added.

Angelo nodded, "The moment anyone is made, Liberatore will be the first one inducted. So that's settled."

"Well I haven't been made into the Syndicate or the Mafia," Jackie argued. "Why should this tradition apply to me?"

Maishe paused, "We treat you just like family, don't we?" Jackie acknowledged Maishe's question with a sheepish nod. "If you're ever inducted formally, you'll have to show our members that you're a stand-up guy."

"If guys like Liberatore start complaining, or convincing other members that you have not honored your obligations, what then?" Angelo supported.

Maishe closed with, "You have to start now by showing proper respect appreciation."

*Maishe Rockman*

"Okay Maishe, whatever you say. We'll work something out," Jackie pondered. "What about if I get an additional two gees tacked on each month for consulting fees. Would that be okay?"

"Yes Jackie. Do that." Maishe was pleased with the offer.

Angelo nodded his agreement, "I'll tell the don. I'm sure he will be very pleased to hear about your cooperation on this matter."

"That's the kind of stand-up thing that we'll pass along to the others, should you be invited to join one of our organizations," Maishe remind him.

♦

The ultimate con had worked to everyone's benefit except for the man who had conceived the blueprint. With limited options, the time and effort Harry Haler had invested in the Hoover-Gorvin Agency amounted to lost opportunity through no fault of his own. He deserved satisfaction, but also realized he would have to settle for something far less satisfying—revenge.

Haler returned to Chicago and found himself walking the windy streets. His vengeance began when he entered the Chicago offices of the Internal Revenue Service to inquire about receiving a finder's fee.

Five hours and four cassette tapes later, IRS Agents Gabrial Dennis and John Daily knew they were on to something far bigger than anything they had ever handled. Kickbacks, death threats, Teamster funds, and secretly funneled large sums of cash to the President of the United States were only part of Harry Haler's story, which was totally unbelievable.

After Haler's visit, Agent Daily made the critical decision: U.S. Attorney General John N. Mitchell would have to be contacted, personally.

In an apologetic manner for disturbing the Attorney General, the two agents relayed Haler's version of the painful facts to Mitchell in a three-way conversation.

"I really appreciate the time and effort you boys put into this," Mitchell replied in a sincere tone. "Now, you mentioned something about the Teamsters, and the possibility that Teamster funds might be involved."

"That's what we've been led to believe," one of the agents responded.

"The way I see it, wouldn't that be a case for the FBI?" Mitchell asked. "I suggest you consider turning what you have, or at least that portion of it over to them. What I'm saying is, it might be better if you let them handle anything involving the Teamsters. You want to avoid stepping on the wrong toes or putting yourselves on the spot, ... you know, just in case you have to work with the Bureau in the future."

The Attorney General's suggestion made sense, and IRS Agents Daily and Dennis jointly responded with, "Good point."

"Now," Mitchell continued, "what do we know about this guy Harry Haler? Have either of you conducted a thorough investigation into his background?"

"No, we haven't pursued that angle."

"I think before we embarrass ourselves or even think about dragging the President into this, don't you think that might be a good idea ... now I'm not telling you gentlemen how to do your jobs. I want that understood."

"Of course not."

"I'm only suggesting that you might want to check out this guy Haler first. I'd hate to see either of you come out of this thing with egg on your face. Again, I'm merely suggesting that you might like to see if this guy is Mister Clean, if you know what I mean."

"We understand what you mean, sir."

"Listen, I want to be the first to commend you on the splendid job you've done so far. I appreciate you contacting me concerning this and keeping me informed. I would also appreciate being updated on any new developments," Mitchell suggested.

Mitchell wasted no time placing a call to FBI Director William Webster. The essence of that conversation found its way back to Jackie in a hastily arranged meeting.

◆

"I got the strangest call yesterday from the Director," McCoy said as he ushered Jackie through the motel room's door.

"Strange? How so?" Jackie's entire life was at sixes and sevens, and strange merely constituted the norm.

"The Director called me without going through channels. Oh-well, ... do you remember when I asked you if Harry Haler knew anything about your arrangement?" McCoy inquired.

"Yeah, so? It's like I told you, he doesn't know a damn thing. Haler's out and someone else is in. If he's still making noise about it, he's wasting his time."

"Apparently, Haler contacted the IRS in Chicago, probably looking for a finder's fee."

"Oh, brother. I suppose he's mentioned something about my ol' man and Frank Fitzsimmons."

"Haler has been screaming to two IRS agents about you receiving kickbacks and funneling cash to the Nixon. It sounds to me like the guy has taken leave of his senses."

"You got that right. I don't know where he's coming up with this crap."

McCoy added, "Rumor has it, he might even file a law suit against either you or your father."

"Is there a story here, or am I supposed to play twenty questions?"

"For some reason, Attorney General Mitchell wants Haler taken out of action, and my assignment is to find out if you have any recommendations? ... I can't believe I'm actually saying this."

"Haler's an ass. Nobody's going to take him seriously. Like I told you, the guy's a bull-shit artist. But I suppose if the Attorney General wants him whacked, I can make a few calls," Jackie posed.

"Oh god no. Maybe I didn't state it correctly. Headquarters wants to use some other type of ammunition to bring him down."

"Ah, I see. So you want to send Haler to someplace like Lewisburg. Well, you have your ways, and we have ours," Jackie reflected.

"Do you know anything in this guy's background that the Bureau might be able to use against him?"

Scratching his jaw, "Not a bad idea. Let's see. ... I remember the time we first met in Vegas. I didn't think anything of it at the time, but I told Haler I didn't trust him. So I pushed him a little."

"Pushed him?" McCoy asked.

"You know, I leaned on him a little. I told him I didn't have anything on him."

"And?"

"So, he told me about some stolen bonds he was using as collateral for some bank loan he made in Chicago. I don't know if it was true or not, so I probably didn't mention it."

McCoy snapped his fingers, "Perfect!"

♦

Agent McCoy dutifully telexed Jackie's information back to Washington headquarters. In turn, the FBI Director notified the U.S. Attorney General Mitchell about Haler's illegal possession of stolen bonds. The following day, Harry Halfgod, alias Harry Haler, was arrested in Chicago.

The government was not interested in Harry Haler's complaint or Jackie's extracurricular criminal activities. The Pressers were not going to be the target of a massive criminal investigation, he was. As Haler pondered the reality of serving serious prison time, he came to one inescapable conclusion: ... Somebody had to be talking.

Haler had been wasting his time and efforts with the wrong audience. He would send a message to someone who would listen. Someone with serious connections. ... Someone like Anthony Liberatore.

*Chapter 5*

## Karma

BIG BILL PRESSER's role in the Syndicate shielded his children and relatives from public limelight. Because of his influence over local and state politicians, local and state judges, and a wide assortment of business interests, his children and their families escaped the normal scrutiny that an opulent lifestyle normally attracts.

Even when a multi-million dollar construction project arose, the public was unaware that the Pressers were directly involved. Big Bill had maintained a close friendship with the principals who had created and developed the project, and he saw this as an excellent opportunity for his oldest son to earn a few extra dollars. Jackie was quietly invited to acquire one-third interest in the project for a token amount of less than $40,000. The project would be named The Front Row Theatre, a state-of-the-art entertainment complex that specialized in booking Las Vegas acts and other nationally known talent.

"We understand you might be interested in getting into the entertainment business," McCoy threw out as an opening salvo.

"It's a possibility," Jackie responded. "It isn't a done deal."

"If it's not too personal, what do you see as your possible involvement in The Front Row project?" McCoy inquired.

"Now listen, you have to stay away from The Front Row. I can't have you going around behind my back, beating my action and scaring business away like you did with my Coliseum project."

"The Coliseum was different. I understand that Teamster money was involved," McCoy reminded.

"Teamster money my ass! You guys were looking for Jimmy Hoffa."

"Now that you mention it, we never did figure out how he was involved," McCoy reflected.

"Other than to see that the money got paid back, he wasn't," Jackie replied.

"Oh? How could you get your hands on that amount of Teamster money without Hoffa being involved?"

"Because he wasn't the one authorizing the loan." Jackie stopped short of mentioning his father's involvement. "Well I can assure you, Teamster funds aren't involved in this transaction and neither is Hoffa. Hoffa hasn't had anything to do with the Teamsters since he got out of prison."

"Let's hope it stays that way. ... So, off the record, what's going on? We hear the Theatre is having some labor problems."

"One of the original partners withdrew from the project and transferred his interest to me. It's no big deal," Jackie said.

"And you were invited into the project to make sure they don't have any union problems?"

"Okay, so maybe they have some labor problems. I was approached and asked to use my influence to intervene."

"As in 'intervene' with the Teamsters?"

"Damn-it, I'm calling in a marker on this one. ... I have a chance to make some serious bread off this deal," Jackie said turning away.

"Okay Jackie, we'll leave The Front Row alone. By the way, speaking of influence, have you spoken with anyone at the White House lately?"

"Not lately, I've been too busy. Why?"

"Oh nothing in particular. I just thought you might have heard something, that's all."

"Those conversations are private," Jackie said.

"Nonetheless, it might be a good idea for you to avoid any further contact with the Nixon White House."

"Why? What's going on? Is there anything I should know about?" Jackie probed.

"Let me put it this way. There are certain matters we can take care of for you, and there are some we can't. You have to meet us half way and do your part."

♦

President Nixon's landslide victory immediately began falling apart. His vice president, Spiro T. Agnew, was forced to resign, followed by one resignation after another. Each new resignation raised new questions, and the President's extraordinary escapades and illegal covert operations were becoming national interest. The President's 18-minute encounter with Big Bill's son Jackie was on the verge of exploding, because it provided the one direct link between Nixon and organized crime.

The solution: Have the meeting obliterated from the White House visitor's log and direct Rosemary Woods to erase their conversation. Then Henry Kissinger could claim he was discussing matters of state with the

President. The only oversight would be a brief reference to the $1 million cash needed to defend five members of The Plumber's Unit.

Word was passed along to John Mitchell, who in turn informed the Pressers to keep their mouths shut. Jackie concluded from this that meant the FBI.

♦

Among those being kept in the dark and psychologically controlled, included Jackie's daughter. Bari Lynn discovered she was comfortably naive about the circumstances contributing to her affluent surroundings. She knew her father and grandfather held an assortment of business interests, but the nature of those activities were carefully guarded as though great national secrets were involved.

Based upon the volume of telephone calls arriving from the White House and the U.S. Attorney General's office each week, she surmised that both Jackie and Big Bill were deeply involved with matters of national interest. Somehow, the culmination of their private businesses and the direct access to world leaders magically transformed itself into *la dolca far niente*—the best of everything.

She knew that it would be impolite to inquire about certain matters, or ask where the large sums of cash came from, or why so many bodyguards were needed. The new public relations team had performed wonders to improve Jackie's wardrobe. They had even persuaded him to limit the amount of four-letter words coming out of his mouth. And since teaming up with the Nixon White House, her father had also developed the luxury of arrogance. Jackie now divided everyone into one of two social classes: We who have power and influence, and everyone else whom he referred to as 'the little people.'

Those little people amounted to nothing more than passing strangers, and she could hear them using foreign-sounding words, spoken in disquieting whispers and lowered tones. They would say such things as *Syndicato*, *La Cosa Nostra* and *Mafioso*, then turn their heads away.

Perhaps some of these little people knew far more about her family and their businesses than she did. Outwardly, she dismissed their off-the-cuff remarks, but internally, she felt quiet anxiety.

One thing was for certain: Jackie knew many people who were very rich and very powerful, and the list was growing every day. Rumors persisted that Nixon might appoint Jackie to a Cabinet post. The prospects of having direct access to the President of the United States prompted many to seek his advice, even on matters he knew nothing about.

In a quiet moment, she thought that to be particularly strange: Jackie wasn't an authority on anything. He refused to read books and he could barely write. His interests were limited to playing cards and golf, watching dirty movies and chasing an assortment of women.

The after effects of her father's lifestyle motivated Bari Lynn into Sacred Heart Church. For the first time since converting from Judaism to Catholicism, she felt shaken in her faith as she headed toward the confessional booth. She sat quietly, not sure how much or what she wanted to confess. The moment passed all too quickly, and she heard the priest close the outer door and slide back the panel covering the screen.

The priest recited a familiar incantation, "Yes my child. Why are you here? Speak from your heart, for all thoughts spoken shall be held in my word and in God."

"Forgive me Father, for I have sinned."

"What is troubling your soul?"

"It is my conscience, Father." It was a safe response, for one could always claim a guilty conscience without damaging one's immortal soul.

"Speak from your heart."

"I am perplexed, for I am in conflict with my father on earth and the teachings of the church." Bari Lynn felt trapped in her own words.

"You must detach yourself from all earthly things, and abandon yourself to God's Will."

"My father is fornicating with other women while married to my mother. He lives openly without the spiritual blessings of God." She had spoken her mind, and the magic of the confessional had lifted one of her burdens.

"It is not for you to comply with such acts. God shall guide you in accordance with acts that are pure."

"Father, I know that without peace of conscience, I shall forfeit the felicity of Heaven. I do not want eternal punishment for the sins of my father and grandfather."

The priest consoled her with, "Have patience. In time, God's Truth shall set you free. Go with peace in your heart."

With the priest's words still echoing in her mind, Bari Lynn left the confessional to confront her fear. She had decided to meet one of her father's mistresses.

Jackie was waiting for her outside to make the half-hour drive to South Russell, a fashionable community known for its bucolic scenery.

"I'm ready, I suppose," Bari Lynn announced.

"You damn well better be, and you better not pull anymore stunts."

"Why father, I haven't the slightest idea what you are talking about."

"You know damn well what I'm talking about. This converting to Catholicism nonsense. You're just doing it to spite me."

"Well father, if it is so important to you, why didn't you say something before now."

"You're going to stop the smart-ass attitude starting right now. You're going to behave yourself in front of Carmen, is that understood?" Jackie demanded.

"I take it you're still going through with this marriage idea.".

"Climaco should have my divorce thing finalized any day now."

"Really now. Don't you think that having a wedding on April Fool's Day to a ..."

"Watch your mouth," Jackie warned.

"I wonder who the two of you think you're going to invite to this thing?"

"Hmm, that reminds me." Jackie spoke to himself, "Maybe I should set up a Big Brother meeting so we can take a honeymoon in peace."

As Jackie and Bari Lynn approached the community of South Russell, the homes became more secluded and the neighbors more affluent. Occasionally, an electronic security fence could be spotted to protect property, signaling first-time visitors they had entered a community where the poor were not invited.

The driveway to the new accommodations dipped slightly before crossing over a small bridge, and continued onward over a lengthy paved, tree-line pathway leading to the ranch. To the right, Bari Lynn saw a private lake next to an in-ground swimming pool. The car stopped in front of the attached garage.

Noticing a small fleet of unfamiliar vehicles, Bari Lynn felt relieved. "It looks like you have company. Yes father, I know, remain cordial and polite at all times."

"Why don't you stay here, while I go in to see who's here. Smoke a cigarette and take in the grounds if you like." Jackie proceeded inside.

Despite all the accusations she had heard, Bari Lynn would give Carmen the benefit of the doubt, "Let's see, her assets are supposed to include being voluptuous, brazen, sensuous and the epitome of desirable pleasures."

She surveyed the grounds by foot, as her mind wandered back to her lonely childhood. We have so much, yet we have nothing. The family is broken, and all the money in the world can't make it better. Focusing her eyes at the vast acreage, I wonder if this place goes all the way back to that line of trees. "I'll bet he has spent a million bucks for this place."

She passed the pool and noticed that it was empty except for a few dead leaves lying on the bottom. Jackie knocked on the window from inside the house, signaling her to come in. A woman with dark-almond eyes greeted her at the front door.

"I'm so pleased to meet you. Do you prefer to be called Carmen or Carmella?"

"Please, call me Carmen."

"Well Carmen, I've heard so many interesting things about you. I'm sure they're all true."

She was much darker and much shorter than Bari Lynn had envisioned. Her petite stature helped Bari Lynn to feel less threatened as she entered what was to be her new residence. The pungent smell of Carmen's gardenia perfume filled her head. Her attire was plain, and Carmen wore no jewelry, not even a ring on her finger. Her hands were un-manicured, which struck Bari Lynn as odd, as she had been told that Carmen was employed as a pedicurist catering to business executives. *Well I'll bet she enjoys a lively afternoon trade,* Bari Lynn mentally noted.

Carmen conducted a tour of the spacious rooms. As they strolled through the house, which would eventually end when they reached the back patio, Carmen recited her extravagant redesign plans for the property. As Carmen checked-off her proposed itineraries, Bari Lynn tried to imagine living here. She knew she had come a long way from her happier days on Meadowbrook Road.

The pending marriage was not being well received by family members. Jackie was especially anxious to have at least one family member provide moral support for this fourth wife. Bari Lynn thus became Jackie's logical choice, and perhaps other family members would follow. For the rest of the Presser-Friedman clan, however, Carmen's features were a little too dark, her views a little too opinionated, and her disposition a little too hot tempered. In Carmen's absence, family members used less flattering terminology to express their prejudices about the attractive woman from Puerto Rico.

♦

As promised, the FBI stayed away from the operation, and on July 5th, 1974, The Front Row Theatre opened on schedule with entertainer Sammy Davis, Jr. Bari Lynn was vaguely aware that Jackie was preoccupied with new business ventures, as well as a new circle of friends associated with The Front Row. Access to Jackie was becoming increasingly difficult. Between his secretary Gail, and his new wife, Carmen, Jackie's schedule was tightly controlled, and obtaining direct contact had turned into a game of wits. If she needed to see him during the day, he told her to clear such an audience in advance with Gail. If it was after business hours, she would have to check with Carmen for her approval.

The litany of responses appeared to be endless. "Sorry dear," Gail would say. "Your father has important business to attend to. He'll be in Washington all this week to see Fitzsimmons." If he wasn't in Washington to see Fitzsimmons, then it was to see someone on the White House staff. Upon learning that he might return soon, she was informed that her father had to rush off to La Costa for a round of golf with Richard Nixon, or to Las Vegas to meet with Moe Dalitz and Allen Glick. And if he wasn't in the process of going somewhere, then it was a matter of him not having returned.

In town, the excuses followed a similar venue. "Sorry dear. Your father will be tied up all day with his attorney," or "I think he went to a Big Brother meeting." One thing was certain: Jackie was rarely home and rarely accessible, in or out of town.

*One of these days, I'm going to follow him,* Bari Lynn promised herself. *I'll bet these Big Brother meet-*

*ings are nothing more than getting together with a group of his new friends and going to some hotel or whorehouse to get laid.*

The following Sunday her suspicions were confirmed. She heard Jackie rise early and quietly leave the house. She waited for him to exit the drive before she started her car to follow. Jackie headed directly toward downtown and a motel. She watched from a distance, and it appeared as though he had not taken the time to check in, but proceeded directly to one of the rooms.

Inside the motel room, a small group of high-ranking officials had assembled and were patiently waiting.

"Hey, what gives? Who are these guys?" Jackie addressed his question to McCoy as his eyes surveyed the room.

"Never mind who they are," McCoy announced. "We'll skip the formalities of making any formal introductions, other than to say, Gentlemen, ... this is The Tailor.

Each individual nodded politely, but said nothing. McCoy took hold of Jackie's upper arm and pulled him to the side, "They've come here on a special assignment from Washington. This Watergate thing has gotten out of hand, and they want to ask you a few questions."

"What does that have to do with me?" Jackie asked.

"Just answer their questions, damn it. No notes will be taken or written reports filed on this. That's why they've come here to see you personally," McCoy clarified.

"Am I suppose to have a problem with that? What the hell do I care what you guys put in your FBI reports, so long as you keep my name out of it."

"That's the problem," a no-named individual remarked. "Your name *has* come up. Your name appears all over the White House telephone log and visitor's sheet for June 20th, 1972."

"Damn. I thought Mitchell was going to take care of that shit," Jackie responded.

"It's a little more complicated than that. The Secret Service has possession of the logs, not us. And whether you were aware of it or not, Nixon taped your conversation with him on June 20th while you were in the Oval Office."

"No shit!"

"Look. Let's cut the crap. We have to know what you talked about. Did you mention anything to Nixon about working for us or being a registered FBI informant?"

"Hell no!"

"Do you remember approximately what you might have said or how long you were there?" another individual inquired.

"I don't recall exactly. It wasn't too long, I mean it wasn't like I was there for dinner."

"What was your business with the President?" another agent inquired.

"It was personal. I'm not at liberty to discuss it. Hey, why don't you guys ask Nixon or Mitchell?"

Mitchell's name brought the room to silence, and it was obvious that McCoy was not in charge. "We understand that Nixon received a million dollars on-or-about the time you were there. Did you deliver that money?"

"I don't know what you're talking about." Jackie turned to glance in McCoy's direction.

"Who gave you the money? Was it your father?" another agent asked.

"I got nothing to say," Jackie responded.

"Your Uncle Allen, ... Friedman I believe, ... didn't he also meet with John Mitchell? What was that about? Did that involve a second delivery of cash?"

Jackie's silence brought forth another question. "We have a complete list of the telephone calls you've received. I suggest you avoid playing games with us."

"If you want to know why my Uncle Allen met with Mitchell, you should ask him."

"Did you discuss your trip to the White House with anyone?"

"No." Jackie's response was not convincing.

"What about your main bodyguard, Tony? Did you say anything to him."

"I went alone."

"What about your current wife or your attorney?"

When Jackie failed to respond, McCoy spoke up, "He generally tells anyone that he has to go to a Big Brother meeting."

The individual who had first spoken, motioned for McCoy's attention. In a hushed tone, "It's obvious this meeting is not going to be productive." He turned back to Jackie, "Ah, Mister Taylor, just tell us one thing. What do you know about an organization called The Plumber's Unit?"

"I take it, this doesn't have anything to do with the plumber's union. Is this some special hit squad or something? If that's the case, you're wasting your time. ... I want to speak to McCoy in private."

"Sure."

McCoy followed Jackie into the bathroom, leaving the door slightly ajar. "Look, I don't know what these guys want. My business with Nixon is nothing I can talk about in front of strangers. Know what I mean? What I want to know is, what you're going to do to keep my name out of this? I'm in the process of closing a major deal, and I don't need any shit cropping up at this time."

"I wish I could give you some answers, but I can't. It's not my call. That's about all I can tell you. But I'll share your concerns. Better you leave now. I'll be in touch in a day or so."

♦

On the evening of August 8th, 1974, Richard Milhous Nixon, the 37th President of the United States, appeared on national television. In a brief message to the American public, he announced his resignation of the presidency that would take effect the following day at 12 noon. Following his resignation, Gerald R. Ford was sworn in as the next President. He appointed Nelson A. Rockefeller as Vice President.

The rapid turn of events compelled Jackie to transfer his ownership in the Forge Restaurant to Carmen, telling her it was a wedding present. Within three short years, Carmen had progressed from Jackie's mistress, to his wife, and now a full-fledged partner in one of his business interests. Unlike his third wife, Patricia, Carmen desired to play a more active role in her husband's day-to-day affairs. She wanted to be able to keep up with other socialites, should she be invited to accompany Jackie to White House engagements.

In all, Jackie had plunked down $39,420.11 for his one-third interest in The Front Row project. It would prove to be an excellent investment. Within the next ten years the entertainment facility would be bought back and sold on paper time and again. Percentage of ownership would fluctuate, but Jackie's prudent investment would pay-off in million-dollar jackpots.

Throughout the summer of '74, Jackie had been consulting with Moe Dalitz while working with Allen Glick from Las Vegas and Delbert Coleman, a businessman from Chicago. Coleman was a personal friend with another principal involved in The Front Row. Collectively, the alliance approached Jackie to structure a $62-million loan from the Central States Pension Fund. The money would be used to purchase Coleman's Recrion Corporation, which owned and operated The Stardust and Fremont Hotels in Las Vegas.

Coinciding with the transfer of the Forge Restaurant to Carmen, Jackie and his attorney, John Climaco, formed the Wilson Mills Entertainment Company. In turn, a general partnership would be formed with the Dalitz-Glick-Coleman alliance. Two weeks before Christmas '74, the Wilson Mills Company secured a loan for $2.5 million, allowing Jackie a direct access into Las Vegas operations.

The combination of purchasing a million-dollar estate, national entertainment enterprises, multi-million-dollar loans, and ownership in Las Vegas hotels and casinos went unnoticed by the public. It caught the attention of the major underworld crime families stretching from New York to Chicago. Maishe Rockman was summoned and asked to look into the matter.

"Now Jackie, you have to understand one thing. If one day, you were to be permanently installed to sit on the

Central States Pension Fund Board, you have to demonstrate to the New York Commission and Chicago that you know and understand the rules by which *this thing of ours* operates. If you don't do the right thing, then someone else within our ranks will take Big Bill's seat and serve in that capacity," Maishe advised.

"I can assure you Maishe, I know the score. But whatever you say, that's the way I'll go. I'm sure you know what's best for all of us." Jackie had heard this lecture from his father. Now his personal liaison with the various crime families was conveying the message.

Maishe responded with, "We're having a problem."

"Oh? What's that?"

"We've set up Vegas operations a little differently than the way you are handling things. The commissions you've been earning must be shared with our other associates."

"What do you want me to do?"

"From now on Jackie, I'll collect the skims and distribute your share. This way, no one will be left out of any future transactions."

"Yes sir."

"That's the spirit."

◆

Pondering his first big score, "Christ Tony, this is how my ol' man did it right under Hoffa's nose."

"Yeah, but you have to be careful, Jackie. You can't mess this up."

"I have to think things through and get it right the first time. Life isn't some dress rehearsal. I'll have to get some help on this."

"Maybe Climaco can help you?" Tony suggested.

"His attorney fees are eating me alive. I have a better idea. Suppose he helps me launder my bread? In return, I can set him up with some big name clients."

"Yeah, you know a lot of them people. Besides, anyone you don't know, you could get Big Bill to make an introduction."

"You're right. I can set him up with Sammy Davis, Dean Martin, Jerry Lewis, and maybe some other movie stars like Frank Sinatra."

*John Climaco*

To alleviate potential tax problems, Jackie's attorney began structuring an elaborate maze of funneling operations with multiple holding companies. To avoid detection of large-dollar transactions and circumvent the Bank Secrecy Act, Seaway Acceptance Corporation was selected. This would allow Jackie to shift large amounts of cash from one account to another without alerting the Treasury and IRS.

The rapid sequence of transactions would be so convoluted, not even the IRS would be able to track who owed what to whom, or how much money actually fell through the cracks. Stock A would be exchanged for B, split or sold to C, while ownership would be subdivided and sold off to subsidiary D, and ownership would then be transferred back to company A. The financial gymnastics would one day baffle whole teams of special strike force agents, accountants and lawyers.

One transaction involved Coleman's King Music Company. Once the deal was finalized, King Music was purchased and drawn into the already complex transaction. King Music transferred its stock to Seeburg Industries. Then, with a simple corporate name change to Xcor, which in turn would buy or sell The Front Row Theatre, depending upon whether a financial gain or a tax loss was needed. Another transaction involved Golden Nevada Resources, a paper company created to camouflage the Las Vegas transactions. Although merely a holding company on paper showing zero value, the same was not true about the major Las Vegas casinos in which it held a financial interest. The revenues generated allowed for new investments in tax-free bonds, overseas investments, as well as a substantial purchase in large fast-food and drug store chains. In the final analysis, A became B and was transferred to C which was sold on paper to D and transferred back to A. The money laundering process would be washed and re-washed until Jackie's assets were clean and respectable.

Jackie understood the process of doubling, then redoubling his money. One million rebounded into two million and two returned four. From his original token investment of $39,420.11 in The Front Row, the man who 13 years earlier had been penniless, now found himself pole-vaulted into tax-free wealth He decided the effort was well worth Climaco's million-dollar retainer fee.

*Chapter 6*

**The Turning Point**

THE PRESSER'S FINANCIAL assistance was not deemed to be a critical factor in the upcoming presidential election. Other than soliciting a positive endorsement from the International Brotherhood of Teamsters, there was little interest for a nice guy like Gerald Ford to become actively involved with anyone directly engaged in underworld activities. Other than a few missing POWs, the Vietnam war had ceased to be a major campaign issue, and the Republicans were only confronting an unknown candidate from the state of Georgia.

Each passing day, Big Bill spoke more openly about retiring. The prospects of having to deal with Jimmy Hoffa getting back into the Teamsters, a new administration in Washington, his federal conviction for bribing five federal judges, and Danny Greene taking a more active interest in controlling the rackets were beginning to take its toll. His deteriorating health condition exacerbated the situation.

Owing to the $1.6 billion in the Central States Pension Fund controlled by Big Bill, the various organized crime families were only concerned with that exclusive issue. The five New York crime families comprising the Commission directed Maishe Rockman to setup a meeting to discuss Big Bill's intentions.

"This is serious, Bill."

"I agree Maishe, but you also know that I've been thinking seriously about retiring. I'm getting tired, what with my health and all the other problems we'll have to confront, I'm just not up it. Faye wants us to move to Florida after I get out of prison."

"I know, and so does the Commission, but it's out of the question until we have a suitable replacement," Maishe added.

"I'll only be in the joint for a year at the most. With any kind of luck, I should be back on the outside in six or seven months. Maybe by that time we'll have someone to take my place. We should pick someone from within our immediate ranks," Big Bill replied.

"Bill, we've already discussed that, and it's totally out of the question. Everyone either has a criminal record or is being so closely watched by the Treasury boys that it's impossible."

"What in the hell are they on our case for this time?"

"For one thing, they know we have the Teamsters' national election coming up," Maishe pointed out.

"I see."

"Even if it was possible, who among us could we trust with such large sums? Who would impartially distribute funds without showing favoritism?"

"So what you're telling me is that we're back to square one?" Big Bill concluded.

"One idea is to appoint someone as a stand-in trustee. The Genovese family wants us to resolve the matter as soon as possible. Fat Tony personally wants to know who you control. In other words, who could be trusted to give back the position after you get released?"

"Under those conditions I can only think of two. Harold Friedman and my son Jackie," Big Bill offered.

"Do you think Harold would be willing to sell us his soul?" Maishe inquired.

"Not a chance. Scratch Harold. I mentioned him only because of his position with Local 507. I certified the Local, and by-God I can dissolve it if he got out of line. But as far as him selling his soul to *this thing of ours*, I don't think he'd do it. He certainly wouldn't do it for the long haul."

"That leaves Jackie," Maishe winced. "I realize he's your flesh and blood, but I have to tell you, none the families on the Commission would be too keen on that idea. His Coliseum venture didn't go very well, and with all the heat that came down, ... I just don't know, ..."

"That wasn't all Jackie's fault. I know my boy isn't perfect, but most of the difficulty with the Coliseum was because the FBI was climbing all over the place looking for Hoffa."

"I didn't mean for that to sound like it did. Personally, I like Jackie, and if it were solely up to me, I wouldn't fight you on this."

"You know Maishe, Jackie has come a long way in the last couple years since running his skimming operation. He's become more sophisticated in how he handles his affairs. Look at this Front Row Theatre operation. Jackie has practically handled that on his own. He's working closely with his attorney, and for once in his life, he's taking sound legal advice."

"Okay, because it's you Bill, I'll present Jackie as a possible candidate for your position on the Central States Pension, but it's going to be a difficult sales job. By the way, speaking of the Teamsters' Pension Fund, I understand Jimmy Hoffa is coming to town next month. Any idea what that might be about?" Maishe asked.

"I think he wants to set up a sit-down. I think Hoffa is serious about getting back into the Teamsters and running against Fitzsimmons for the International's presidency."

"I hope you're not serious about having a sit-down," Maishe clamored. "The Genovese family won't allow him to get back in. We just can't control him like we do Fitzsimmons."

"I'm not going to be here, remember? I'll be taking a little sabbatical," Big Bill perfunctorily reminded him.

"Oh. ... Well, who do you think Hoffa's coming to see?"

"Eddy Lee with Local 407. He'll probably try to line up support with the larger locals. He might even want to see my number-two man, 'Babe' Triscaro."

"Have you talked to Fitzsimmons lately?" Maishe queried.

"Not in the last couple days. I was planning to before doing my stretch. Why? Is there something I should know about?"

"Are you aware that Fitzsimmons approached some attorney by the name of Russell Bufalino to approach Fat Tony to authorized a hit."

"And?" Big Bill prodded.

"Fat Tony approved it. All the details haven't been worked out, but it's definitely in the works."

"Who did Fat Tony give the contract to?" Big Bill asked.

"He gave Tony Pro the contract. He'll use three of his wiseguys from the east coast to carry it out."

"I'll tell Triscaro not to waste his time seeing Hoffa. I don't want to know any more details, Maishe. Just see that they do it clean. We don't need a mess."

"Tony Pro has picked professionals. They'll clean up after themselves," Maishe assured. "Some day he'll just disappear without a trace, and our problems will be over."

♦

"What's this about, Maishe?" Jackie asked.

"Well Jackie, I just returned from New York. Before I left, I spoke with your father. He would like to appoint you to his position on the Central States Pension board while he's in prison."

"Yeah. Is there some problem with that?" Jackie politely questioned.

"To be quite frank about it, yes there is. But, before you get yourself worked up over this, perhaps something can be done to resolve the appointment."

"Good. I'd like to cooperate with the Commission anyway possible. What do you suggest I do?" Jackie invited.

"The Commission is having a problem with your selection."

"Damn. What the ..."

"Now before you say anything Jackie, I want you to understand that there is nothing personal in this. It's just that we've never been faced with a situation like this before. Your father has always been our eyes and ears on the Central State Pension board ever since it was first established."

"I understand that. So what's the problem with me filling in for him?"

"Now let me finish. The fact is, you've never gone through either a Mafia or Syndicate initiation. Let me put it this way, as far as I'm concerned, you'd probably do fine. If it were up to me alone, I'd say, no problem."

"I know, it's nothing personal, 'cause you're speaking for the five families of the Commission."

"Exactly," Maishe confirmed.

"I suppose you want me to whack someone, is that it? How about Danny Greene?"

"Oh my God, no. We don't require that anymore. That went out with Joe Valachi in the sixties. Nonetheless, you have to be able to demonstrate that you're a stand-up guy. Now-a-days, we call them goodfellows."

"I think I see what you're driving at. You want me to prove myself—is that it?"

"I can't begin to tell you Jackie how relieved you've made me feel about this whole matter." Maishe sat back in his chair.

"What do I have to do to prove myself? You know how I feel about Greene. We have to do something about him before he gets us."

"Well that was sort of what we had in mind. ... Perhaps you could put up some funds to cover some, shall we say, ... expenses?" Maishe proposed.

"Say no more. When are you planning to have the guy whacked?" Jackie inquired automatically.

"I wouldn't be too concerned about the specific details. In fact, the less you know, the better off you'll be. That way, you can always claim you weren't directly involved."

"So what you're telling me is that to demonstrate to the Commission that I'm a stand-up guy, all I have to do is put up the expense money? How much?"

"We were thinking somewhere in the neighborhood of twenty-five grand, preferably in cash," Maishe suggested.

"That's no problem. When do you want it?"

"There's no rush. In a month or so," Maishe revealed.

"You think we should wait that long? He might get one of us first."

"The point is this, now I can go back to New York and tell the Commission you've been a stand-up guy about this. You have to think about your future. This could lead to a permanent position, if your father retires."

Jackie blinked. "... That's it?"

"Yes Jackie, that's it." Maishe stuck out his hand, "I want to be the first to officially welcome you into our Syndicate. Now remember, your word is now your bond with the organization. No matter what you say, do or tell others, you must never break our trust."

*'Babe' Triscaro*

Within days of Jackie's casual acceptance into the world of organized crime, Babe Triscaro was calling on an old business associate from his past to whisper a few pieces of interesting news Triscaro learned second-hand from Big Bill. Jackie had been formally accepted into the Syndicate. He also mentioned that a contract had been approved by the

New York crime families, and the hit was currently in the works.

'Babe' Triscaro knew there were a few individuals he could trust with this information. Great care would have to be exercised in not disclosing too many details. Only those with a vested interest or heavily involved in their own criminal activities could be relied upon to keep such a secret. Triscaro believed Danny Greene fell into that group. As Triscaro saw it, it was a good idea to have someone as dangerous as Greene on your side.

It was good news for Special Agent Martin McCoy when he received word from Greene about the scheduled hit. Although it was only third-hand information, which qualified it as an interesting rumor, the Bureau justified its covert operations by recording provocative gossip.

Whether the rumor was true or not, the Bureau immediately authorized a team of special agents to place Frank Fitzsimmons under 24-hour government surveillance. Fitzsimmons' dilemma quickly spread throughout the underworld and the overworld.

Jackie needed little persuasion to keep a low profile and distance himself from Fitzsimmons. After all, it was his father who was close to him. If controversy toppled Fitzsimmons, the International's presidency was within grasp. Unlike others, Jackie had not confronted a knock-down-drag-out struggle to make his way through the ranks. And unlike his father, he had no ties, or even a moral obligation to the Teamsters' upper management. Considering Jackie's new appointments, Fitzsimmons represented an obstacle to his ambitions.

"That kind of power will go right to Jackie's head, and knowing him the way I do, he'll start flaunting it, and attracting too much attention," Big Bill surmised. "Besides, it's a real death trap, and I don't think he can handle the Commission the way I do. You can't make idle promises to them, not even in jest. You break your word to one of them, and you're dead. And if they don't get him first, he'll end up getting himself indicted on some federal wrap. I just know he will."

Bari Lynn understood her grandfather's words. She knew this was a serious moment. Big Bill was not prone to idle chatter nor sounding off unless he had something to say. He was a man who chose his words carefully.

Though he may not have expressed it in words, Big Bill was concerned about Jackie's inability to understand the concept of sharing. *Taking* was Jackie's forté, and taking the offer to finance an assassination was simply too easy for him to refuse.

Then there was the issue of making loans from the Central States Pension Fund. If loan deals could be properly structured, and an extra five or six million were to be kicked back, the loan carried with it an implied obligation for him to share those excess funds with the various Mafia families and crime Syndicates throughout the country. There was no telling what Jackie would do once he had direct access to an endless supply of cash.

While Big Bill was coming to terms with the reality of serving time, one of Jackie's previous business associates was coming to terms with his situation. Harry Haler had been formally indicted in Chicago for using stolen bonds as collateral in a loan transaction. Only one name came to mind as he retraced his footsteps.

Haler felt he had nothing more to loose. The jig was up and Haler was down to his last chip. He had only one alternative: Tip-off Anthony Liberatore that Jackie Presser was a potential government snitch. It was a desperate act performed by a desperate man, and fortunately for Jackie, that was exactly how it was perceived.

"We've got a small problem Jackie."

"Oh, something wrong?"

"Liberatore received a telephone call from a guy by the name of Harry Haler," Maishe announced.

"Oh for crying out loud. You can't believe anything Haler has to say."

"Well, just the same, the don asked me to look into the matter. Haler told Liberatore that he suspected you were a government informant," Maishe stated.

"Yeah-right. What a crock. I got a couple of ghost employees on the payroll, a few money laundering projects, not to mention a few insurance scams going on. You yourself just supported my induction into the Syndicate. So now what do you want me to do to prove myself? Like I said, who in his right mind would believe a liar like Harry Haler?"

"Do you have any idea why Haler's doing this?"

"I'll tell you why, it's because I kicked him out of the Hoover-Gorvin deal. You should tell Liberatore that if he doesn't stop listening to that liar, he can forget about the two bills I've been sending him each month."

"Those are excellent points. I'll bring these issues to the attention of the don. There's just no way the FBI or any other government agency would allow an individual to be actively involved in such activities simply to maintain an informant's cover," Maishe surmised.

"Good. And another thing, if this guy Haler keeps it up, I might ask for a contract on him myself."

"No doubt it's like you've said. He's probably just blowing smoke over the Hoover-Gorvin contract. So I guess I can report to the don that it's all a matter of sour grapes. It's obvious that Haler concocted this whole informant story in retaliation."

◆

Danny Greene's most trusted stick man, Enos Crnic, turned onto the apron of Christie's Lounge and drove to the back parking lot. Enos selected a a spot at the far end of the quiet lot and parked his car. He noticed the dark Continental Mark IV parked in its regularly reserved spot.

Enos waited a moment, then got out of his car, walked to the back and unlocked the trunk. He reached down and removed a package, then quietly re-closed the truck lid. Enos knew the evening atmosphere without going inside Christie's. Alex 'Shonder' Birns would be seated at his reserved table in the back. A line of customers would be patiently waiting to see him, either to complain about a numbers payoff that hadn't been made, or to pay interest on an installment loan that was coming due, or perhaps to discuss liquidating some personal property that had been acquired, and Shonder knew better than to ask his clientele questions.

Since the closing of Jackie's Coliseum, Shonder had relocated his business operations to Christie's Lounge. He enjoyed a mentor's reputation in the community of underworld activity, and was well liked by both the Syndicate and local Mafia crime family. To maintain the peace, especially in the black community, he selected a young African-American by the name of Don King to serve as his enforcer. King would one day parley his education to become a world-famous boxing promoter.

After being voted out of office from the Longshoremen's Association, Shonder picked up the freelance services of Danny Greene, who was eager to demonstrate his alent presence of Greene proved to be an invaluable asset in reducing outstanding receivables and avoiding unnecessary business competition.

Recently, however, Greene had expressed an interest in branching out. Greene felt he could earn far more money in prostitution, narcotics and contract killing than playing second-fiddle bill collector for Alex 'Shonder' Birns. To launch one of his new ventures, he needed $75,000 up-front money, and suggested to Shonder that it might be in his best interest to float him the loan.

In turn, Shonder approached Angelo Lonardo to have the local Mafia put up the money. The transaction was finalized, and if all went well, Shonder would realize a return on the investments within a month.

Immediately, the deal went 'bad.' The $75,000 Greene had obtained was invested in narcotics turned out to be worthless. Greene was left holding merchandise he couldn't move. To Greene's way of thinking, under the circumstances, he should be excused from repaying Shonder any of the money.

Shonder saw it differently. He pointed out that the money wasn't his. Because of Greene's erratic and unpredictable disposition, it was decided to forgo interest, but the local Mafia insisted on having the principal repaid.

Those terms were not acceptable to Danny Greene. He countered the offer by suggesting that he kill any three people of their choosing in full repayment of the loan. Greene's generosity was refused. Things were going too well to throw the community into a state of panic, or create any unnecessary law enforcement problems.

Outside Christie's, night lights offered Enos just enough light to crawl beneath the Mark IV to attach the package under the driver's side floor panel. Believing such a well-built vehicle might require a little larger charge, Greene had decided to triple the recipe. Enos backed out from under the vehicle and headed back to his car when Shonder emerged from Christie's back door.

"Hi Alex," Enos called out.

"Hi, my foot. And don't call me Alex. Where's Greene?" Shonder demanded.

"I thought he was inside." Enos continued casually walking toward his car, as another patron walked out the backdoor.

"Hey, there's Tommy, the guy who prints up his numbers. Maybe you should ask him."

*Danny Greene*

"Have you seen Greene?"

"Not today," Tommy confessed. Shonder's tone signaled Tommy to keep walking and avoid a confrontation.

Shonder reached his Mark IV. "When you see Greene, you tell him that I have to have the money, or I'll have to make it good out of my own pocket."

"I'll deliver your sentiments Alex." Enos closed his car door and sat there looking straight ahead. He waited until he heard Shonder slam his car door before slowly leaning over on his right side.

The evening tranquillity abruptly ended with an explosion. The force of the blast could be heard within a ten-mile radius. Enos took a deep breath and smiled. He sat up, started his car and drove away.

Shonder's death signaled the beginning of the gang wars. Unprecedented was the fact that Danny Greene immediately began bragging about the murder, and the community was thrown into a state of panic. Jackie Presser and Harold Friedman grew more concerned for their safety. They responded by running down to police headquarters and registering their handguns, as well as their complaints. They wanted to know why neither Enos or Greene was arrested for Shonder's death.

Jackie and Harold soon discovered that Danny Greene's criminal activities were off-limits. Police officials quietly whispered to Jackie that he was not the only one in town with connections. Without fanfare, a special undercover unit with the Cleveland Police Department had been set up to investigate not only Shonder's bombing death, but several other killings that were connected directly or indirectly to Danny Greene.

"I don't need this type of aggravation," Jackie complained. "How in hell is he getting away with this crap?"

Agent McCoy smiled, “I don’t know what you’re talking about.”

“Greene! He’s going all over town telling everyone how he built the bomb that Enos Crnic used to kill Shonder Birns? Can’t you guys do something about slowing him down?”

“There could be more behind this than meets the eye.”

“Yeah, like what?”

“If I were you Jackie, I wouldn’t be too concerned about anything Greene’s bragging about.”

“Am I missing something? Greene’s telling everyone how he had Shonder killed, and he don’t even get himself arrested or questioned.”

“I think he just wants to make himself look tougher than he really is.” Before dismissing the topic, McCoy added, “In fact, we’ve heard the police already have six people who have claimed responsibility for Shonder’s death, so which crackpot should they arrest?”

“Yeah. Well tell me, do any of those other suspects know how to make a bomb?” Jackie echoed.

“Look, it’s a local police matter, okay. If a federal crime was involved, don’t you think we’d be on top of it?”

“Yeah, well I’ll bet if it was one of your guys you’d be doing something about it,” Jackie bitched.

“Speaking of assassination ... we did pickup a rumor that your father’s old pal, Jimmy Hoffa, was scheduled to be hit. Did you hear anything about that?”

“Hoffa? ... Whacked? You’ve got to be kidding,” Jackie mused. “You know, come to think of it, I did hear a rumor, but that’s all it was—just a rumor.”

"That's the name of the game. We're in the business of investigating rumors."

"I overheard someone mention something about a group in Detroit that might be planning something," Jackie revealed.

"Anyone specifically?"

"I just told you, it's just rumor shit. There weren't any names attached to any of this."

"The Bureau has picked up on some of those rumors. We've heard that Chuckie O'Brien is part of a conspiracy and plot to have Hoffa killed. Did his name come up in any of the rumors you've heard?" McCoy asked next.

"Yeah, as a matter of fact it did. It makes a lot of sense when you stop and think about it. I mean, Chuckie being Jimmy's adopted son and all. He could get close to him, find out his schedule, set him up, and stuff like that."

"That makes sense." Casually, McCoy continued. "... What about Frank Fitzsimmons?"

"What about him? I haven't spoken with Fitz in months."

"Word has it that he's the one calling for the hit."

"Hmm, that's very interesting," Jackie pondered with a grin. "Who's your source on that shit?"

"Come-on, you know I can't divulge that information. What about an attorney by the name of Russell Bufalino? Has his name come up?"

"I don't know him," Jackie immediately responded.

"Now listen Jackie, if you've heard anything, I'd like to know about it with as many details as possible."

"Honest, I'm leveling with you. Like I said, it's just talk that's been going around. If you guys want a source, see what Chuckie's up to. I understand he's the one spreading the rumors about Hoffa being an FBI informant."

"Oh—that's choice. It really is," McCoy mussed. "I'll have to share that one with our guys downtown."

Jackie realized this scenario was not being taken seriously. "Hey, look at it this way. What better and easier way could someone use to set him up and get him taken out?"

"I suppose so," McCoy said as he jotted down a note.

"Sorry I couldn't be of more help, but if I hear anything, you'll be the first to know."

"Well I guess that about wraps it up. If anything new develops at our end, I'll be in touch." Agent McCoy closed his notepad.

"Sure. But you do like I said. Keep a close eye on that little fat-fart, Chuckie." As McCoy headed toward the door, Jackie appealed, "Say, what about some protection?"

Turning around, "What are you talking about? You've got four or five bodyguards now."

"Yeah, sure. I even got a rack full of guns too, but that's no good against someone like Danny Greene sticking a bomb under my car. Or suppose John Nardi takes a notion to have me whacked?" Jackie speculated.

"I'll see what I can do to obtain authorization for some special equipment. Say, what about a wire so you can record some of these rumors you've been hearing?"

"Nah, a wire's no good. If I got caught wearing, I'd be dead on the spot," Jackie protested.

"Okay, what about a nifty, miniature-size tape recorder? Something disguised as a key-ring holder? You could carry it right with your keys or leave it setting on the table. If you had to drop it someplace, you could get rid of it easily. It's real James Bond stuff."

Jackie acquiesced, "All right, I'll carry that, but what about protecting me from Greene blowing me to pieces in one of my cars?"

"That requires special authorization, and it would have to come right from the top. ... I'll see what I can do, but it might take a few weeks. In the meantime, I suggest you maintain your bodyguard protection."

"Yeah, well it would be a whole lot easier if someone went after Greene and took him out of action," Jackie suggested scornfully.

"Speaking of 'action,' that reminds me. You're holding your father's position on the Central States Pension, is that correct?"

"So? What does that have to do with anything?" Jackie challenged.

"Has Allen Dorfman from Chicago been in touch with you?" McCoy came back.

"No. I got no business dealings with him. Why?"

"Our Chicago office thought there was a good chance Dorfman would be contacting you directly about securing loans through the fund, that's all." McCoy proceeded to leave when he suddenly stopped and turned back into the room. "Say Jackie, I almost forgot. ... Do you ever come in contact with the Provenzano brothers from the east coast?"

"Are you kidding? All I know about the Provenzanos is that they are nobody to be messing with. Those guys specialize in turning big packages into little cubes. I keep as much distance between me and them as possible. And don't be asking me to see if I can get close to them or start making inquiries, 'cause I can't. And even if I could, I won't do it."

◆

Jackie had many balls in the air. He bounced his expanding itinerary off Tony, "You know what this public relations firm wants me to do?"

"No Jackie, I haven't the slightest idea."

"They want me to be fitted for a new wardrobe and begin taking public speaking lessons as if I didn't have anything better to do with my time."

"Well you're getting up in the world. That might not be such a bad idea."

"Yeah, well speaking lessons will have to wait. I've scheduled a meeting in Las Vegas with Allen Glick on some major pieces of property."

"You want me to go along with you? Were you planning on driving or taking the plane?" Tony asked.

"On second thought, maybe Gail can call Glick and get that put back a few weeks."

"It sounds like you got a lot on your mind, Jackie."

"I don't want to get into it right now, but you're right."

"Didn't you say something the other day about reviewing your investment portfolio with Climaco?" Tony recalled.

"Yeah and that's another thing. I can't understand half that shit. What I want to know is where's all my money? And we're not just talkin' about a few million either."

"You have to stay on top of all that stuff, but you should be thinking about what to do with Harry Haler."

Jackie turned red, "If he keeps it up, I'll get a couple of guys to take him out of the picture."

"Hey, did I tell you that I heard a rumor that someone might have let out a contract to have Jimmy Hoffa hit?" Tony inquired.

"Listen, we hear rumors all the time. I don't have time to think about stuff like that. I have to worry about Greene and my own skin. Christ, I almost forgot, we have to start thinking about our national elections."

"You think Fitz is going to stay in the race?"

"I'll tell you what I think. I think Fitz's days are numbered. I hear he's catching all kinds of federal heat, and if he's not careful, he may wind up in federal prison."

"Speaking of taking people out, I hear Danny Greene killed another couple of guys down near the lake. You think the police know he did it?" Tony asked.

"I don't think they even care. We may have to take matters into our own hands. Something has to be done about that Irish bastard, and none too soon. I wouldn't be too surprised if someone takes out a contract on Greene."

Jackie's concern was addressed on the evening of May 12th. Mo Kiraly, better known as *Mo The Mechanic,* had been discretely tracking Greene's elusive movements. Mo followed Greene to a girlfriend's second-floor apartment. He waited to see if Greene was planning to stay the night, but the lights failed to come on in the dark apartment. He decided to wait.

Quietly, Dottie walked up the backstairs and unlocked her rear apartment door. As she reached for the light switch, a hand grabbed her wrist, "Jesus Christ! ... You scared the hell out of me."

"I know, Dottie. I have that affect on people," the voice in the dark responded.

"I didn't see your car," Dottie observed.

"You weren't suppose to."

"What if I had someone with me?" she asked.

"Then I'd get to watch."

Dottie ran her hand over Danny Greene's bare chest, "You'd like that, wouldn't you? You'd like to see my young naked body with some big stud."

"You know what I'd really like?"

"You want you and your friends to have your way with me. Tell me what you really want me to do."

Pulling her hand away, "I'd really like to make sure you weren't followed. Why don't you go over to the window and make sure," Danny ordered.

Dottie walked to the windows overlook the street and glanced in both directions, "It looks pretty quiet outside. What am I suppose to be looking for? A cop?"

"The police are never my problem. You should know that by now. I want you to get undressed in front of the window while I watch." Danny turned on a small lamp that cast a shadow of Dottie standing in front of the windows. He took up a position to peek outside and survey anything or anyone who might be interested in watching the apartment.

Dottie slowly removed her clothes. "How long to you want me to stay in front of the window? I feel that there are a thousand eyes watching me."

Danny did not respond but kept watching until he spotted a lonely vehicle and driver parked in the shadows across the street, “You’re absolutely sure you weren’t followed?”

“I’m pretty sure, but I wasn’t really paying any attention. Why?”

“You’re a very pretty girl, Dottie. I’d hate to see anything happen to you that you didn’t deserve. You now have my permission to move away from the window.”

Dottie past a small table as she headed toward the bed in the one-room efficiency, “What’s in this box?”

“Death.”

“Can I look inside?”

Danny moved away from behind the curtain and the corner of the windows, but avoided casting a shadow that might otherwise reveal he’s presence to the driver parked across the street. “You asked far too many questions, Dottie. A pretty girl such as yourself should only be asking questions that will keep me happy.”

“If you don’t want me to know, I won’t look inside. I was just curious, that’s all.”

“You’ll just have to trust me. You do trust me, don’t you?” Danny politely asked.

“Yes, of course I trust you.”

Danny pushed her onto the bed. As he began removing his pants, “The real question is, can I trust you.”

“You scare me when you talk like that. I don’t have to know what’s in the box, honest. If you don’t want me to know, just tell me it’s none of my business.”

“Oh, it’s business all right. Dangerous business.”

Smiling, “Fine. ... I’ll believe it’s anything you want me to believe, you know that.”

"Lately, you've been asking too many of the wrong types of questions. A pretty girl could get herself badly hurt asking too many of the wrong questions."

"Please. Don't hurt me too badly. Don't mark my face or chest, please. I promise I won't ask any more questions. Just tell me what you want me to do."

Danny picked up a rag and rolled it into a ball before turning out the light, "I want you to open your mouth and take your punishment like a good little girl. Don't scream."

Once the apartment lights dimmed, Mo carried five gallons of gasoline up the building's back stairs and placed it against the door. He set the timer and returned to his car to retrieve a second device consisting of several sticks of dynamite, which he placed under the windows. The timer was set to detonate a few seconds before the gasoline would be ignited, thus engulfing the entire upper floors in flames. If both systems went off as planned, no one would walk out of the apartment.

At the precise moment, the dynamite Mo had installed under the window exploded, hurling Greene across the room and into the refrigerator. Mo waited for the second explosion that would engulf the unit in flames. The moment never arrived. As the sounds of wailing sirens from police, fire and ambulance vehicles converging on the scene, Mo drove off into the darkness.

Mo's failed attempt to end Danny Greene's life only served to heighten the myth that he was the luckiest Irishman alive. His reputation for being invincible prompted John Nardi to contact him two days later to propose they join forces for the purpose of taking over the rackets. Aside from any formal affiliation with Danny

Greene, Nardi had his own agenda. The local don, Johnny Scalish, had refused to formally induct him into the Mafia, irrespective of the fact that his aging uncle, Tony Milano, had served as the organization's underboss since the '40s. Leo 'Lips' Moceri's appointment to replace John Nardi's uncle, Tony Milano, as the underboss of the crime family angered Nardi. Lips had earned his Mafia membership during Prohibition, while serving as a prolific hitman for Detroit's Purple Gang. Lips' appointment represented one thing: The don had no intention of installing Nardi as a Mafia member. Therefore, the don had left him with no alternative but to take matters into his own hands and force the issue. Nothing sent a clearer or stronger message to the don than the recruitment of Danny Greene into Nardi's camp. Their combined forces would be able to successfully challenge both the Syndicate and the aging Mafia family.

*Chapter 7*

## The Cover Story

BIG BILL'S PRISON SABBATICAL left Jackie in charge to handle more than one assignment. Besides holding his father's position on the Central States Pension Fund, a ceremony to honor Big Bill was scheduled for June 22. The Israeli government wanted to demonstrate its appreciation by bestowing the country's highest honor and decoration on Big Bill for his enthusiastic and financial support in promoting the sale of Israeli Bonds.

Making such a public presentation to someone who was serving time for bribing five federal judges, however, posed a potential source of international embarrassment. The U.S. State Department was not pleased that one of its staunchest allies had chosen the boss of the largest crime syndicate for this prestigious honor.

To remedy this awkward situation, Jackie was selected to serve as a substitute recipient in place of his father, but there was some question as to his religious convictions. Jackie was merely Jewish by an act of birth. His interest in Judaism was little more than a religion of convenience. He knew no Hebrew and spoke no Yiddish. Jackie refused to practice any of the customs or observe any of the High Holy days, thus presenting him with such a high honor appeared to many as an exercise in hypocrisy.

The Deputy Prime Minister had been originally scheduled to make the presentation, but owing to the change in plans, a substitute official was sent to present the honors, plaque and medallion. As the dinner ceremony drew to a close, a high-ranking general with the Israeli Army approached Jackie to exchange a few social pleasantries.

"We're very appreciative of your family's support."

"I really appreciate you thinking of me like this," Jackie rejoiced.

"Yes, of course. If there is anything we can do, let us know." It was one of those polite gestures that officials sometimes throw out in the spirit of the occasion, not something to be taken literally.

"Well General, maybe there is something," Jackie invited.

The General returned a polite, "Oh?"

"My ol' man tells me you people are going to start getting into some secret building projects."

"I'm not sure I know what you mean. What have you heard specifically?" the General inquired.

"You know, resettlement projects if your army has to invade southern Lebanon."

"That's mostly speculation at this point in time. Naturally, something is always in the planning stage. I'm not in a position to discuss any details or promise anything. Why?" the General pondered.

"Is this resettlement program in the works?" Jackie pressed.

"I can neither confirm or deny that, but I don't see how that would be anything we would be able to assist you with."

"Well General, I understand you people are going to build a couple million houses, and I was wondering if there might be anyway I could get in on some of them building projects? You know, maybe supply materials such as windows, you know, something like that?" Jackie speculated.

"First, you must understand that I'm not at liberty to award such contracts, but there is something I can do. I'll mention your interest to the proper authorities, and have them get in touch with you directly."

♦

As July rolled around, Maishe Rockman arrived to finalize their agreement. "You remember that little matter we discussed earlier?"

"Yeah, I was beginning to wonder whether you had forgotten all about it," Jackie responded hesitantly.

"It's that time. Do you have everything ready? If you need a few extra hours, I can come back."

"No problem, Maishe. I've got it in the safe. Do you want to count it?"

"That won't be necessary. I'm sure it's all there. I would appreciate it if you could put it in an envelope for me."

"Sure Maishe." Jackie withdrew a fresh white envelope from the desk, "I guess you heard that Mo missed when he tried to hit Greene. Talk about being lucky, ..."

"Yes, we'll definitely have to do something about Mister Greene, but that's a local matter."

"Well like you suggested, I shouldn't be too interested in the details."

"Exactly. Oh, I might make one small suggestion. It might be a good idea to keep yourself very busy the last couple days of this month. You know, keep a full appointment schedule."

"Thanks for the suggestion, Maishe. I'll keep that in mind."

The following evening at 8:45, Jackie's unlisted office line rang. In the presence of his armed protection, the heavy-set man reached to pick up the receiver.

"Yeah."

"I have some news," the caller announced.

"Oh?"

"The news is from Detroit. As of today, some merchandise was picked up. It was packaged and shipped. We'll be in touch. In the meantime, as we say in La Costa, have a nice day." —Click.

Jackie glanced at the day-calendar page for July 30th, 1975. Reaching across the desk and slowly crumpled the page before opening the desk and dropping it inside. He spotted a pair of gift cufflinks from Richard Nixon. Jackie looked up and let his deep brown eyes survey his office.

"Anything the matter, Jackie?" Tony tendered.

"Naw, I was just thinking about Nixon. Did you know he had the Oval Office bugged?"

"That doesn't surprise me. Nixon was always up to something," Tony responded scornfully.

"I was just thinking, maybe I should get that ex-chief of police, John Joyce, to put in one of those taping systems in this office. ... You know, just in case."

"I don't know Jackie. You really think that's such a good idea?"

"I can't be too careful these days. ... Where could we hide the bug?"

"How the hell should I know Jackie."

"What about the shelf or behind one of the pictures?" Jackie ventured.

"I don't think so. What if someone found it while they were cleaning?" Tony observed.

"You're right. That eliminates the desk, too. Maybe we could hide it in the ductwork?"

"You really think that's a good idea? You'd be better off just hanging it over your desk or something like that," Tony offered.

"Good idea. It would be out of the way, and yet pick up everything."

The red light on his second private line began flashing. "Yeah? ... What do you want?" ... No, don't count on me being there. I've got more important things to attend to. I can't be bothered right now. We'll talk about it tomorrow or the day after. Better yet, from now on, when you call, I want you to talk to Gail first to make sure I'm not busy." He punctuated his orders by slamming down the receiver.

"Anything wrong?" Tony submitted.

"Bari Lynn. I need another family get-together like I need an extra fifty pounds."

At 348 pounds, Jackie was a bundle of struggling obsessions, and moving his ponderous frame across the room was the result of wasted emotions and inactivity. Coupled with his paranoid preoccupation with Danny Greene, there was little time available to accomplish anything productive.

Pressing in the sequence of security codes seemed to cause him bother. Lines of tension began showing on his face. A trickle of sweat rolled along the side of his face and began traveling down toward his collar. He caught it with his finger, then flicked it to the side as he stepped outside the security of his Maginot-fortress. He plodded down the corridor. The echo of his heavy walk announced his arrival before reaching Harold Friedman's office door. He cracked the door, poked his head inside and waved a parting gesture.

Other than briefly nodding, Harold offered no social discourse to this titular role-playing dilettante. Jackie could fool politicians and the unwashed public all he wanted, as long as he stayed out if his way. At the moment, Harold was far too busy running the two Locals to exchange pleasantries with his junior partner.

Jackie continued toward the solid-steel backdoor exit. He felt his father's diamond-studded ruby ring on his small finger. He was now in charge, so why did he feel left out of all the union activities? Jackie knew that once his father departed the union stage with his private army of soldiers, he would be left defenseless, and perhaps cast into playing the part of the union's court jester, the only role which most people felt he was profoundly suited. His problem would be to accomplish some mission that would allow him to leave his own footsteps, if only in the sand. But how could he achieve that mission before his father died or retired, or better yet, before Big Bill's release from prison.

Jackie withdrew a small black radio-controlled transmitter Agent McCoy had provided him for added protection. Before unlocking the door leading to the parking lot, one bodyguard peeked through a small portal and spot-checked the immediate area. He emerged first and Tony followed, each gripping the handles of their 45-

caliber pistols. The two bodyguards focused their attention in opposite directions of the now-quiet street before nodding their heads to signal the heavy-set man that it appeared safe to step out.

Since the bombing of Shonder Birns the evening before Easter, this security precaution had developed into a nightly routine. Jackie knew that his list of enemies in both the union and the underworld was growing at an alarming rate.

From the top step, Jackie extended the directional antenna and pressed the button as he aimed it at each vehicle in sight. The two bodyguards continued to inspect moving traffic at an equally safe distance. Nothing happened. He re-set the switches to repeat the process on another frequency. Still nothing happened. He could now breathe a little easier. Nothing had exploded.

"I'll meet you guys at The Forge Restaurant," Jackie called out, as he hurried with a quickened pace under the protection of shadows toward his bullet-proof Lincoln Continental. Tonight, as was his preference, he would chauffeur himself, but the two well-chosen escorts would never venture more than a car's length away.

Once the locks snapped shut, he was alone, and for the moment he could review his life and the situation. "I wonder who the hell I can really trust? ... Okay, let me see, there's Climaco and Gail, but who else? Harold's no good. He doesn't trust me, so how can I trust him? I'll have to think of someone else. Uncle Allen is totally out of the question, that bastard would blackmail me for the rest of my life. Just who in the hell can I trust?" He stopped at the red light quietly waiting.

... *No one came to mind.*

♦

Special Agent Martin P. McCoy replaced the telephone receiver in time to join his fellow cadre of black-tie loyalists who were marching their way down the gray carpeted hall to the FBI briefing room. Maybe he would share his information with his fellow brethren, then again, maybe not. Much would depend on the tone and atmosphere of the briefing.

A younger special agent, Robert S. Friedrick noticed McCoy's uncontrollable smirking expression as he joined the small procession. "You look as if you just received word that Howard Hughes died and left you his fortune. You got something interesting?" the younger agent inquired.

"Yep," McCoy responded rudely.

"Does it have anything to do with Hoffa being snatched?" Friedrick probed.

"Yep."

"You going to share it with us?"

"Maybe."

As the group assembled and took their regular chairs, the Station Chief entered the room, which brought the rustle of noise to a measure of silence. Like all the rooms, it was decorated with government-issued furniture and supplies. Included in the decoration scheme were framed portraits of the President and their now-deceased leader, J. Edgar Hoover.

Unlike past presidents, whose portraits were quickly snatched from the walls with the end of their administrations, J. Edgar's portrait, supporting a tough bull-dog image, still hung in homage to his almost 49-year reign as the undisputed commissar of American justice. Until recently, the rooms and hallways had been decorated with a full Rogue's Gallery of their former leader's dubious conquests, that stretched as far back to the day "Machine Gun" Kelly surrendered outside Memphis, Tennessee.

Leaning to his right, and wanting to appear as inconspicuous as possible, Friedrick spoke in a controlled whisper, "How in hell did you know Hoffa was going to be snatched in the first place?"

"Good informants," McCoy whispered back.

"... Good morning gentlemen. May I have your attention," the Station Chief announced as he looked in McCoy's direction. "... As most of you know by now, our favorite public enemy, James R. Hoffa, was reported missing late yesterday afternoon." Polite applause immediately followed the announcement. "Our informed sources tell us, he was picked up at approximately 3:30 yesterday afternoon, and driven to a remote house, approximately 20 minutes from the Red Fox Restaurant in Bloomfield Hills. We believe that he may have been shot a couple times in the back of his head, and his body placed into a car's trunk, then disposed of."

The briefing room erupted into mild cheers, amplified with slightly louder applause. "Try to contain your excitement. We're working on a number of different theories at the moment and should be releasing a cover story for the media. In the meantime, let's keep a lid on what we know so far." The Station Chief paused long enough to survey the room and see if his comment had registered. It would simply be a matter of leaking one lie to cover-up another. "Today's assignment is to find out if anyone locally may have been involved. I mention this only because the rumors about his pending assassination originated locally, so there is a strong possibility of a Murray Hill connection. So let's get out there, twist a few arms and kick a few butts. Now, before I leave, are there any questions?"

Agent Friedrick raised his hand.

"Yes," the Station Chief acknowledged.

"Do we know who did it?"

"I'll leave the response to that question to Agent McCoy. He can fill you in on any of the minor details. Are there any other questions?" Seeing no hands, the Station Chief walked over to Martin McCoy. Laying a heavy hand on McCoy's right shoulder, "Try not to keep this going too long. I want everyone in the field sometime before lunch." Nodding to the others, he excused himself.

The moment the Station Chief left, Friedrick announced, "Okay, let's have it. What's the rest of the story?"

"Not so fast. Besides, not everyone present may be interested, in which case, you may be excused." McCoy wanted to hold court, not necessarily share everything on his plate.

"Listen guys, Marty just got off the telephone with one of his snitches before the meeting. He knows something," Friedrick insisted.

"I come from the old school, remember. Back during J. Edgar's day, if you didn't have a solid network of reliable snitches, your ass was grass," McCoy reminiscently reminded his audience.

"Please Marty, no war stories," Friedrick pleaded.

"Yeah, I have to be home for dinner in another eight hours. Tell us about that call you received," another agent interrupted.

"Okay, guess who just arrived from Detroit? ... On second thought, you'll never guess. Chuckie O'Brien."

"Hoffa's adopted son? What the hell is he doing here?"

McCoy smiled rudely, "One of my snitches tell me he's looking for someone who can provide him with some answers. I'll bet my money on the possibility he's also looking for an alibi."

"You think he was involved?"

"As J. Edgar might say, 'Who cares.' The point is, he's running scared, which means he's ripe as a plum. If he isn't involved directly, my second guess is that he knows who is, or he's here trying to cover his ass."

"Like the Chief just said, the rumors started here, so why wouldn't he want to see if he's being set up?" a younger agent snorted.

"Speaking of Hoover, did you ever meet him personally?" Friedrick inquired.

"Christ, why did you have to ask him that? I just told you, I have to be home for dinner!" another agent sarcastically remarked.

Ignoring the side-bar comment, McCoy continued, "When I joined the Bureau, everyone had to get J. Edgar's personal approval. I met him, ... let's see, it had to be well before the FBI television series started."

"I guess things have changed a lot since he died," Friedrick speculated.

Picking up on that cue, another agent chimed in, "I'll say things have changed, and a little too fast to suit my taste." Dropping his voice to a serious whisper, "I hear they're thinking about letting women and niggers become special agents if the Democrats get in."

"You can damn well bet your ass that none of this would have happened if Hoover hadn't been taken out," McCoy grunted.

The room's atmosphere fell silent. Darting glances passed from one agent to another. Special Agent Patrick Foran broke the silence with a cough. The moment he made eye contact, it was a clear signal to McCoy to change the subject.

"Marty, are you suggesting that Hoover may have died of something other than natural causes?" another agent challenged.

Foran stood up. At six-foot-four, his height drew everyone's attention. "Well gentlemen, I think it's high-time we changed this subject and proceeded with something more productive."

Throwing up his hands, McCoy acquiesced, "No problem. I was in the process of sharing with our younger brothers the value of having good snitches."

"Yeah, was that Probex who was on the phone?" Friedrick asked.

"No," McCoy bluntly replied.

"How did you come up with a code name like that?" Friedrick inquired.

"It wasn't too difficult. Probex was a professional boxer in his younger days. I just shortened his old occupation to *Pro*-Boxer, ... Probex," McCoy acknowledged. He was pleased with his ability to simplify the mysterious.

"That's neat. What about that other guy you're working with?"

"You mean The Tailor?" McCoy clarified.

"Yeah. What does that code name stand for?"

"That one is so easy, I'm almost too embarrassed to tell you," McCoy smirked contemptuously.

"Does it have anything to do with his occupation?"

McCoy offered, "What other name fits a tailor or someone working in a dry cleaners?"

"Let me think, ... a dry cleaning operator, ... ah, press operator or someone who presses cloths. ... That's it! A presser. Jackie Presser is The Tailor!"

"Like I said, it's simple." McCoy paused to take a sip of coffee, "The real trick is not coming up with the code name, but finding an informant's Achilles' heel. Take the Tailor, for example. He's scared to death about going to prison. Once you use this technique, all you have to do is give it a little tweak now and then to pinch his active nerve. He'll fall apart like an overripe plum."

"You make it sound easy," Friedrick replied.

"Listen, you guys spend your days and nights running your asses off, it's okay by me. I can wrap up a week's worth of work in one meeting, milk it for enough information to keep me busy for a month."

"I heard it was Probex that led you to The Tailor?" Friedrick inquired.

McCoy held up his cup, "Say, I just realized this stuff is cold. We'll pick up this conversation later when I have time to do it justice."

As McCoy made his way down the hall, Friedrick cornered him. "Marty, are you suggesting that Hoover was assassinated?"

"Assassinated? I don't recall using *that* word. What gave you that idea?"

"Well it was sort of obvious," Friedrick retorted.

"If you had been paying closer attention, what I said was, if Hoover hadn't been taken out of the picture, and by that I meant, his untimely death ... that Watergate thing would never have happened."

"Oh. Well, he was getting old anyway. I heard he died of heart failure."

"Yeah, something like that, ..." McCoy responded in a retiring manner.

"It was a heart attack wasn't it?"

"Let me bring you up to speed on something. There wasn't anything wrong with Hoover's heart. Sure, he had a few minor medical problems at his age, but none of it was life-threatening."

"I see ..."

"No you don't. Hoover and Nixon were on the outs. In fact, Hoover was fed up with the whole damn lot of them, especially Mitchell and Haldeman."

"Why, over what? The Watergate break-in?"

"No, it was over some guy who worked in the basement of the White House by the name of Tom Huston. In fact, I think they called it The Huston Plan."

"What was the plan?"

"It had something to do with combining our domestic operations with those of the CIA. They even had plans to setup concentration camps throughout the entire courtry."

"Something like a new Gestapo agency?"

"Whatever. The point is, when Hoover found out he wasn't going to be put in charge of this new operation, he deep-sixed the idea. ... Later, after Hoover's death, Watergate became a matter of Deep Throat taking his revenge. The threat of exposing Hoffa's pardon in exchange for secret campaign money became the issue."

"Come on ..."

"Hoover didn't give a damn about The Plumber's Unit, protecting the Nixon crowd or laundered campaign money from the Syndicate."

"How did Hoffa fit in?"

"After Hoffa got pardoned by Nixon in late '71, Hoffa moved to have his restrictions overturned," McCoy quipped.

"Back up. I missed something. Are you saying we set Hoffa up for political reasons? Why?"

"Nixon was coming up for reelection in '72 and needed money and votes. Whoever gave Nixon or Mitchell the money on June 20th was probably the same individual behind Hoffa's secret pardon restrictions."

"So where did we come into the picture?" Friedrick queried.

"Before Hoffa got set up and sent to prison in '66, we were literally bugging the hell out of him, and had been for almost five years. We probably could have pinned the Kennedy's assassination on him if that little son-of-bitch hadn't been standing trial down in Chattanooga when it happened."

"I heard a rumor that Hoffa might have been involved in that."

"Yeah, right under our noses, I suppose. Hoffa couldn't have farted without us knowing about it. We even had the jury room and the jury's hotel suites bugged."

"What for?" Friedrick submitted.

"There was this young prosecutor trying the case. He was four or five years out of law school, and wanted to make a name for himself. So Hoover made sure that the prosecutor began receiving profile information on which jurors to select."

"So you think Hoffa was set up?"

"Once Hoover successfully sold Bobby Kennedy the idea that Hoffa was running organized crime, Bobby was convinced he could make the charges stick."

"But I thought we were following him because he was a suspected Communist?" Friedrick surmised.

"Organized crime, Communists, what's the difference. When that didn't work, we simply shifted the music to a new theme."

"I heard he was totally under the control of the Mafia anyway, so I guess he got what he deserved," Friedrick responded.

"Mafia my foot. When we couldn't get the organized crime charges to stick, we found a witness who was willing to say that Hoffa bribed him."

"What are you saying? Couldn't we come up with anything solid to convict Hoffa?"

"It's like I said, Watergate had to be covered up to conceal far more serious crimes. The fireworks started after Hoover's sudden death."

"And that's when Deep Throat started blowing the whistle."

"Precisely. As far as Hoffa was concerned, he was dead set against supporting Nixon's reelection efforts. When Big Bill and the Teamster's Executive Board threw its support to Nixon, Hoffa and Hoover were standing in their way."

"So that's why Hoffa's file is classified top secret," Friedrick stated.

"Hell yes. We can't have our bugging operations exposed."

"And I suppose none of this was authorized," Friedrick concluded.

"You got that right," McCoy retorted. "When the Watergate break-in occurred, it provided us the perfect cover story to misdirect everyone's attention."

"So, do we know who blew the whistle?"

"Deep Throat?" McCoy reacted.

"Yeah. All I ever heard was that it was some guy who was a heavy smoker, and was supposed to be living in Arlington, just outside D.C."

"My educated guess is that it was Clyde Tolson."[3]

"Hoover's second in command? I find that hard to believe."

"After Hoover's unexpected death, Tolson got really pissed when Nixon didn't appoint him to replace Hoover. So, you tell me, who had a better motive? No one. Who besides Tolson had direct access to that information? Who else besides a heavy smoker like Tolson knew where to look for the skeletons? Unless you believe in pure coincidence, only one person fits that profile."

"That makes sense when you think about it." Friedrick paused. "So, do we know who hit Hoffa?"

---

[3] The primary source for this information did not come from the FBI, but rather one of the undercover agent who served in a liaison capacity with the Bureau.

"Wrong question, young man. Do we care who hit Hoffa?"

"Well, do we?"

"I've already told you too much for your own good. But I'll make one solid prediction," McCoy offered.

"What's that?"

"Now that Hoffa's been taken out, I'll bet we don't put more than one, maybe two agents on his assassination."

"Oh?"

"Headquarters will assign some young or inexperienced agent to go through the motions for show and media purposes. It'll go down just like the Kennedy assassination, just another unsolved mystery."

"What about this guy Chuckie O'Brien? You think he had anything to do with it?"

"Give me a break. You think he's smart enough to mastermind something like this? Besides, he's practically in love with Hoffa. Chuckie worships the ground Hoffa walked on. But it really doesn't matter. It will make an excellent cover story in case John Q. Public starts clamoring for its pound of flesh."

"So you think he might be an Oswald-type patsy?" Friedrick suggested.

"Maybe. Actually, the name that came to my mind was Bruno Richard Hauptmann, the guy we set up, framed and executed for the kidnapping of Charles Lindbergh's baby."

"Hmm ... now that you mention it, I do remember hearing something about that," Friedrick reflected. "Wasn't there some guy by the name of Fisch involved?"

"Hey, Isadore Fisch left the country. Somebody had to pay for the crime."

"If it's not too personal, Marty, I'd like to ask you one more question."

"Shoot."

"Did the Tailor or Probex tell you Hoffa was going to be hit?"

Disappointment drew on McCoy's face. "Neither of these guys are my main source, but one of them confirmed it for me. I've learned not to put all my eggs in one basket. I put my source in my report to SOG." McCoy used Hoover's acronym for headquarters, which stood for Seat Of Government.

"Hey, how are we ever going to learn this stuff if you older guys keep us in the dark? ... Come on, who told you?"

McCoy took a sip of coffee, "It was Greene."[4]

"Danny Greene! What's his code name? —Psycho or nut case!"

"Keep your voice down. He may be a nut case, but he's *our* nut case. Besides, I've got him properly motivated. My problem is keeping him alive, which is a full-time job in-and-of itself. If Greene can avoid getting himself killed, the drug traffic coming into town will be under our complete control."

"Christ, DEA and ATF will be mad as hell if they find this out."

Leaning into Friedrick's face, "So who says we have to tell them."

---

[4] Two confidential sources independently substantiated that Danny Greene was not only an FBI informant, but that Greene provided the FBI with the initial details on Hoffa's pending assassination.

"For crying out loud, we have to work with enough assholes as it is. Why do we have to maintain an alliance with a crazy like Greene?"

"Look, if anything goes south, we're the ones taking the heat. If you think SOG is going to cut you any slack, think again. Mark my words, you get yourself in trouble out there in the field, and you're on your own. Develop your own snitches. Remember, you don't have to share them with anyone. If you do, the next thing you know, SOG will be leaning on you for more information. Before long, you're faced with double the amount of paperwork. We slip some of these bastards millions, and what do we have to show for it? Nothing! If you younger guys want to work your tails off to earn a few extra brownie points, be my guest."

Friedrick stood there as McCoy walked away. He would have liked to have asked McCoy if he had ever shaken-down any of his informants for serious money or special favors, but some things were better left unasked.

◆

Within days of Hoffa's reported disappearance the FBI assigned Special Agent Robert J. Garrity from the Detroit office to conduct a routine investigation and follow-up on leads. His assignment was simple: If there was no hue and cry for justice, target a suspect in the event the media or the public give the matter thumbs down and demanded its pound of flesh.

Locally, McCoy had made several attempts before establishing contact with The Tailor. "I suppose by now you've heard that Hoffa is presumed to be dead."

"I wouldn't take that too seriously. My guess is it's all a hoax. Just one giant media stunt," Jackie grumbled.

"That's novel. We never thought of that angle."

"He'll turn up in a couple days, you mark my word. It's just a publicity gag to recapture the Teamsters' presidency."

"But what if it isn't?"

"I see. So you're looking for a lead. My other guess is that maybe it could be someone from Chicago or Kansas City."

"A special agent from our SAC Office in Detroit will be conducting the formal investigation. It's just routine, but he may want to interview you."

"Interview me! What for?"

"Why are you so alarmed. It's just routine, but just so there are no surprises, may I assume that you can account for your time on July 30th?"

"I'll have to check with my secretary. As a matter of fact, I was in town because I was sitting at my desk when someone called and told me they had heard something about Hoffa on the radio."

"Good. Besides, I think we already have a couple of solid leads, so you probably have nothing to worry about. Our agent from Detroit might not even want to see you."

◆

By mid-August '75, skyrocketing oil prices overshadowed the media's attention paid to Hoffa's disappearance. Occasionally, someone from the media or Hoffa's family would make an inquiry. In response to such inquiries, the FBI assured interested parties that every possible lead was being followed up. There was, however, only so much one special agent could do.

Because Sal, Gabe and Tom had passed through Hopkins International Airport while en route to Bloomfield Hills, Michigan, Special Agent Robert Garrity touched base with Special Agent Martin McCoy. They briefly reviewed the information McCoy had gathered, and in the process, the decision was made to conduct an interview with a high-level informant known to SAC offices throughout the country as *The Tailor*.

"Mister Tailor, Agent McCoy tells me that you are convinced the Hoffa disappearance is merely an elaborate hoax," Garrity inquired. "When do you think he'll be coming out of hiding?"

Jackie's gambit had run its course. "Yeah, but I also said that Chuckie O'Brien might have set the whole thing up. Tell him, Marty."

"Let's not waste time playing games, Mr.Tailor."

"I don't know what you're driving at," Jackie relayed.

"Frankly, the idea of a hoax, or your O'Brien story doesn't make sense." Garrity turned to McCoy, "Have you questioned this guy thoroughly?"

"He's the one with the contacts," McCoy tendered.

"Jackie?" Garrity called out.

"Yeah? Would you repeat the question?"

"You told Agent McCoy about the possibility of the Chicago Mafia being involved. How does that fit into this equation?" Garrity continued.

"Well you know, when Hoffa got out of prison in '72, he began demanding a piece of the action from Dorfman."[5]

"*The* Allen Dorfman of Chicago?" Garrity clarified.

"Yeah."

"I'm still not sure I see the connection."

"You see, Dorfman is in charge now that Sammy Giancana is out of the way."

"Oh? I find this totally fascinating." Garrity turned to McCoy, "I wonder if our Chicago office knows anything about this?" Back to Jackie, "Please continue. I'd like to know more about this. So what you're saying is that Dorfman took over the Chicago Mafia after Giancana was hit, is that it?"

"Well my guess is that Dorfman had him whacked. But it's only a guess, mind you. That's why he's running the show, so-to-speak."

"'Running-the-show-so-to-speak?' That's utterly fascinating. The only problem I'm having with your conjecture is that I'm not sure what you mean?" Glancing at McCoy, "What the hell is he talking about?"

McCoy shrugged and Jackie continued, "You see, it's like this. Dorfman refused to allow Hoffa any direct involvement in the Teamsters after he got pardoned by Nixon. Hoffa got mad at Dorfman and threatened to run for the Teamsters' presidency, if you know what I mean."

"No, not exactly," Garrity retorted. "Our info indicated that Hoffa was on pretty good terms with Dorfman. Other than insuring the Central States Pension Fund,

---

[5] The majority of this information was gleaned from FBI files not necessarily provided by the FBI. There is no evidence to support that Allen Dorfman was directly or indirectly involved in Hoffa's death.

what does Dorfman have to do with running the Teamsters? —Or the Chicago Mafia for that matter?"

"Well-yeah, but that was a long time ago. Look, if I was you guys, I'd be looking at the Kansas City Mafia."

"I see. Now it's Nick Civella with the Kansas City Mafia," Garrity mused. "That possibility just never occurred to us."

"Oh? Why is that?" Jackie asked rudely as his eyes narrowed.

"No, let's not change the subject. I want to know how Kansas City ties in?"

"You guys obviously don't realize that Civella's people are friends with Chuckie O'Brien in Detroit. Didn't Marty fill you in on all this stuff?"

"Give me a moment Mister Tailor. I want to speak to Agent McCoy privately." Garrity and McCoy moved to the far end of the motel room. "Marty, I thought you said this Tailor guy was a reliable informant."

"I didn't say he was the best informant. It just seemed to me that he appeared to know something. Why? What's the problem?"

"I should have worn my hip boots. Your Mister Tailor is so full of bullshit, I don't know where to step," Garrity rebutted.

"Without making it too complex, can you fill me in?" McCoy whispered back.

"The names of those wiseguys you gave us, Sal, Gabe and Tom are from the east coast. They all work for the Provenzano brothers out of New Jersey. Now, according to a note in Hoffa's calendar, he had an afternoon appointment to see Tony Provenzano the same day he turned up missing. As you know, Provenzano takes his orders from Fat Tony Salerno, who heads up the Genovese crime family with the New York Commission. We believe that Frank Fitzsimmons asked for the hit contract on Hoffa. We think he went through an attorney by the name of Russell Bufalino, who obtained Fat Tony Salerno's permission. So you see, none of the stuff this guy is trying to pawn-off on me, tracks. In fact, it doesn't even come close. I'm telling you, this guy's full of shit."

"Hmm. I don't understand what reason he would have for sending us on a wild-goose chase," McCoy reflected.

"Did it every occur to you that your Mister Tailor may have his own agenda. What kind of stuff is this guy into, anyway?"

"And did it ever occur to you that we might be the ones heading in the wrong direction? It's happened before. Now this guy is right on the inside of organized crime. His old man heads up the largest Jewish crime syndicate in the country, so I wouldn't be too quick to dismiss what he has to say." McCoy turned toward Jackie, "Perhaps you could tell Agent Garrity why you think Chuckie O'Brien is involved?"

"Sure. I can do that in one question and one answer. Who could have gotten close to Hoffa? It could have only been someone like Chuckie."

Garrity cut in, "We're exploring similar scenarios, but what I'd like to know is, do you have anything concrete?"

"Listen, I've told you what I know. If you want to listen to all the bull-shit rumors floating around, go ahead. I know what I'm talking about, but if you're just looking for a patsy to take a fall, then I got nothing else to say. That's it. *Fenito!*"

Jackie's information implicating the Chicago and Kansas City Mafia was immediately telexed to both FBI SAC offices. Two separate follow-up investigations would be conducted to evaluate The Tailor's story and theory.

♦

Jackie's forty-ninth birthday was observed with confrontation. Bari Lynn had arrived at his office without an appointment, but before any birthday pleasantries were exchanged, the topic of conversation shifted to Jimmy Hoffa's disappearance.

"How can you be so happy over this? Hoffa is probably dead, and you're, ... you're ... gloating!" Bari Lynn screamed.

"I don't want to discuss it anymore. Like I told you, Hoffa stepped out of line, so just keep that in mind. Now, that's all I have to say."

"Well, I think you're sick! It sounds to me like you knew this was going to happen. I think it just stinks!"

"I don't care what you think. Get the hell out of my office." Jackie turned toward the window and began humming.

Jackie's behavior over Hoffa's disappearance was unsettling. She turned to leave, then paused, and thought briefly about the wrapped gift she was holding. For as far back as she could remember, this was the first time she hadn't given him a gift on his birthday. Perhaps he had forgotten what day it was.

Upon returning to her apartment, she opened a ledger-size book and began her first journal entry. During the next several years, she would eventually fill six volumes about her relationship with Jackie and her grandfather, Big Bill. The entries included their power and wealth, as well as Jackie's wives and his affairs.

Her attempt to see her father on Labor Day was futile: Jackie's appointment calendar was full and he had no time to see her. He would be seeing a man from New York concerning the purchase of The Front Row Theatre. All she learned about the transaction was that if the price was right, Jackie might sell it again. That too, appeared strange, as he had already sold it once or twice.

Jackie's attorney structured a lucrative deal: James J. Hughes represented Seeburg Industries, which would serve as the holding company to purchase The Front Row Theatre for $2.9 million under a seven-year contract. Jackie received $100,000 as a cash bonus in appreciation for signing the paperwork.

The Dolin family would be retained as the on-site management company to run the day-to-day operations to protect their mutual investment. The transaction provided the ideal vehicle for laundering sizable kickbacks, and provided the perfect tax shelter. The Presser-Dolin group would be able to transfer the theater back and forth to each other without loosing control of the facility. The legal gymnastics were necessary to avoid violating the Taft-Hartley Act.

The success in setting up this financial cover boosted Jackie's mood, and in a luncheon at the Clubhouse racetrack, Carmen revealed their plans to Bari Lynn.

"You know, it might be a good idea for your father to be out of town for a few days. What do you think?"

"Is something wrong?" Bari Lynn queried.

"Oh-no. In fact, everything is now wonderful. I was just thinking that a trip to Vegas might do Jackie some good, and us too," Carmen suggested.

"How many will be going?" Bari Lynn inquired.

"I think it would be much better if just the three of us went, don't you?"

Sipping her drink, "Sounds wonderful. ... Which horse did you bet on in the fourth?" Bari Lynn wanted to keep the conversation light.

"I don't remember the horse. I use their numbers."

Bari Lynn took another sip, "Will Jackie be seeing anyone while we're out there?"

"No one you would know, but I think his name is Harry Haler. He's been causing your father some problems, but it isn't anything too serious."

"Is there anything else I should know about?"

"It's not good for us," Carmen revealed. She then turned serious, "We're just staying together for his public image, but I don't want to talk about it."

"Okay, we won't talk about it. ... What are your plans?"

The gatepost bell sounded and the horses bolted from their positions. Bari Lynn divided her attention between the race and Carmen's facial expressions.

"Jackie's been treating me like shit. But I don't want to talk about it."

"Of course not," Bari Lynn agreed.

"I'm going to spend a lot of his money when we get to Vegas, you wait and see."

"That will get his attention," Bari Lynn replied with a smile. She knew from first-hand experience just how much Jackie hated to part with a buck, unless he was merely taking it out of one pocket to stash it into hiding from IRS.

"Jackie's got more money than he knows what to do with. You should see how much he's got in his office safe. He has to have close to ten million in cash. Who knows how much he has hidden in his Washington safe? ... And I'll tell you something else. He has safety deposit boxes all over the country."

"Yes, I know, but you don't want to talk about it."

On November 18th, two weeks after they returned from Las Vegas, Bari Lynn noted in her journal that Carmen had been secretly contacting high-ranking Mafia members while in Las Vegas. Bari Lynn reflected on their luncheon at the Clubhouse, and suspected that Carmen may have said something negative about Jackie in an effort to get back at him.

For the first time in her life, Bari Lynn felt threatened. Invisible forces seemed to be closing in on her, and she began confining herself to her apartment. Days passed until Jackie's private secretary, Gail, called. "How have you been? No one has heard from you in several weeks."

"Oh, I've been staying close to my apartment."

"Listen dear, the real reason for my call is to inform you that you might be subpoenaed."

"Oh?" Bari Lynn echoed in mild surprise.

"Yes. Jackie may want you to testify for him," Gail informed her.

"What's this all about? What's wrong? What would I be testifying about?"

"We can't get into all the particulars over the phone. It has to do with the Central States Pension Fund."

"I can't testify about anything having to do with that. I don't know anything about it. What's going on?"

"I just told you, we can't discuss things like this over the telephone. Now, I have to have your answer. Jackie wants to know."

"I can't give you an answer, because I don't know what's involved."

"I'll see what Jackie has in mind." —Click.

Jackie stopped talking to John Joyce when Gail said, "I'm not sure you can count on her. She didn't seem to be overly receptive to the idea."

"I want to talk to you some more about this. We're about finished, so don't go away." Turning to Joyce, Jackie continued, "Okay, you're supposed to be good at this sort of thing. Here's your opportunity to prove it."

"Shoot."

"I want you to start setting up some phone taps. I also need you to keep tabs on a few individuals for me."

"No problem. Give me the order in which you want me to begin." Joyce took notes.

"First, I want you to start with Carmen. Find out if she's sleeping with anyone."

"Film ... or will photos do?"

"Film! You think you might be able to catch some action shots?"

"Whatever's your pleasure," Joyce responded in a matter-of-fact tone.

"Yeah, film would be a good idea. I don't care what it costs if you can get me something interesting."

"Film it is. Anyone other than your wife you want me to keep tabs on?"

"Yeah, Danny Greene."

"That might be a tough one, but I'll see what can be done. Anyone else?"

"Yeah, put a tap on my kid's line. I want to know what Bari Lynn is up to, who she's sleeping with and if she's on any junk."

"Right. Okay that's three. If it's all the same, I'd like to cut it off at this point. With Greene in the picture, I'm going to be kept pretty busy. By the way, do you want any interesting footage on who Greene's sleeping with?"

"Naw, not unless it's with someone I know. I think Carmen's seeing some car salesman. But I need something good in order to keep her off my damn back."

"No problem. As soon as I have something I'll get it to you."

Jackie held up his hand like stopping traffic, "I want to be the only one to know."

"Ten-four."

♦

Between Christmas and New Year's Eve, Seeburg officially purchased The Front Row Theatre. To insulate Jackie from the transaction, his attorney created a series of subsidiary companies. Seeburg Industries would turnover day-to-day operations to the original owners, thereby making the sale of the property merely a paper-shuffling transaction.

Within the next year and a half, Seeburg Industries would show a $27 million loss for tax purposes, officially change its name to Xcor, and Jackie would become the major stockholder in the new company. At the same time, The Front Row would restructure its stock ownership to remove Seeburg Entertainment and become Seeburg Theatrical Enterprises.

To compensate for legal services, John Climaco suggested to Jackie that he could use his authority to appoint him as the attorney-of-record for Ohio Teamsters, thus replacing Robert Rotatori.

♦

Gail rose from Jackie's lap when John Joyce entered the office. "You got something for me? I hope it's interesting."

"Yes, but I'm sure there is more that I'll be able to come up with," Joyce speculated.

"What have you got on Greene?" Jackie asked in a deliberate voice.

"That's the one category where I'm coming up short. Greene's difficult to track. The guy's never in one place long enough to establish a routine. He doesn't even make two calls from the same telephone booth."

"So, what did you bring me besides nothing," Jackie responded in a grumpy manner.

"Let's see." Joyce flipped open his notes, "Carmen is sleeping with a guy by the name of Fred Barr.[6] You were right, he's a car salesman. You want more on that?"

"Sure," Jackie chuckled.

"She sucks his ... toes. You know, kinky stuff." Holding up a package, "You want the footage?"

It was a provocative invitation and Jackie displayed mild interest, "Okay, leave it with Gail. Anything else?"

---

[6] This name has been altered.

"Your daughter is sleeping with John Nardi's youngest boy. That's an easy camera setup, so if you want some footage, I can have it for you by next week."

"Yeah, do that. What's next?"

"Now this is nothing I can say with any degree of certainty, but I think Carmen may also be seeing some guy by the name of Dominic ... besides the car salesman," Joyce reported.

"Am I supposed to be surprised?"

"If she is seeing Dominic, it's nothing regular, and I may have difficulty setting up a camera, because like Greene, they never meet at the same spot twice."

"Stay on Greene," Jackie ordered. "He's got to slip up somewhere, and I want to know the moment he does. And listen, I'll take good care of you for this information."

*Chapter 8*

## Time Bombs

COLLECTIVELY, the Treasury Department, the Labor Department's Investigative Unit and the FBI appeared ineffective with their efforts to solve Jimmy Hoffa's kidnapping and presumed demise. Some Washington insiders were beginning to suspect that the outgoing administration had orchestrated a massive cover-up.

Each investigative branch maintained the position that unless tangible evidence surfaced to indicate Hoffa's body had been transported across the Michigan state line, no federal crime had been committed. Therefore, the case was a local police matter and not something that required federal intervention.

Behind closed doors it was a different situation. The FBI had been assigned the initial responsibility of handling the investigation. That investigation, however, appeared to involve covering up leaks and disseminating an assortment of false cover stories for the media. The Hoffa family became livid and tried to use its influence with loyal Teamsters who shared Hoffa's values and beliefs.

Lack of progress combined with Fitzsimmons' known ties to organized crime and the former Nixon administration, prompted a group of indigent Teamsters to form an independent organization called the Professional Drivers Council, better known as PROD. With the anticipated change in the White House, the PROD organization believed it could build a coalition that would be able to democratically challenge Fitzsimmons' corrupt ties. If they failed to succeed in that effort, PROD felt it could force Fitzsimmons to be more responsive to the Teamster membership.

The formation of PROD alarmed Jackie's attorney and his public relations firm. They knew that Big Bill's close ties with Fitzsimmons would make Jackie highly suspect. Furthermore, Jackie's ties to Nixon raised doubt about his labor-management philosophies. If PROD was successful in ousting Fitzsimmons as Teamsters' President, the chances of replacing Fitzsimmons with another suitable, anti-labor candidate would be difficult.

Big Bill had advised Jackie that the time to stand-up and be counted was before the race started, not after it was won or lost. The issue became: What would be the winning strategy to use at the '76 National Teamsters' Convention to defeat PROD's efforts? Before presenting his advisors' recommendations, Jackie reviewed their strategy with Frank Fitzsimmons in a private meeting.

"My attorney and PR guys think we can turn this whole PROD thing to our advantage," Jackie submitted.

"I don't see how," Fitzsimmons responded. "Jimmy's death has turned him into something of a martyr. He's more of a problem now that he's dead than when he was alive. That's just what your father and I wanted to avoid. So, what do these guys suggest?"

"They want me to label them as Communists."

"Are you serious?"

"The PR guys say once PROD gets painted with that brush, we can claim that they're part of a Communist conspiracy, taking their orders from Moscow."

Fitzsimmons laughed, "That would be great, but no one's going to believe you, let alone take you seriously."

"No? That's how Hoover did it. Any time someone started making trouble or getting in his way, Hoover labeled him a Communist. My guys tell me if we label PROD as Communists and they're not prepared, ..."

"Yeah, it could take them by complete surprise," Fitzsimmons concluded.

"My attorney agrees with the PR guys that this strategy would change the whole focus of the convention, and away from our affiliations."

"That might put PROD on the defense."

Jackie knew he needed to demonstrate his loyalty to the various crime families who were maintaining Fitzsimmons in office. The Hoover-Gorvin PR firm's plan worked, and PROD's efforts were effectively shouted down during the convention. For the first time in his life, Jackie basked favorably in the national limelight. He was publicly lauded for taking a strong and decisive stand in exposing the true foreign-inspired enemy within the Teamster ranks. As for Fitzsimmons, his close ties to organized crime never became a topic of discussion.

♦

The various organized Mafia crime families across the country expressed their appreciation for Jackie's support through Maishe Rockman.

"Jackie, I've been asked to inform you that the families are very pleased with your performance at the national convention."

"Thanks Maishe. I appreciate that, and hearing it from you means a lot."

"Well, it goes much further than that. We want to show you how much we appreciated your support of Fitzsimmons. It was suggested that you should start thinking about higher office."

"Are you suggesting that I should be thinking about making a bid for the International?"

"I'm not in a position to promise anything, but who knows. You continue to demonstrate the kind of leadership we saw at the convention, I believe I can speak for the families in saying, a day will come when you may be able to throw your hat in the ring."

Maishe's words of encouragement both excited Jackie, as well as intimidated him. On one hand, he realized it would be impossible to bid for the General Presidency of the International without broad Mafia support, but he also knew he needed something in the substantive category in which case, he was grossly deficient.

As an important meeting of the Executive Board approached, Jackie's initial enthusiasm began to wane. Questions of Jackie's dubious performance worried his attorney and the public relations team. Writing a speech and telling Jackie what to say to which audience was one thing, but the time was rapidly approaching when someone, perhaps the media, would start asking serious questions, and he knew that his cameo image and phony work history could be easily exposed.

"Ah shit, Tony. I just realized something."

"What's wrong Jackie?"

"I can't walk into that board meeting with nothing. I have to have something for an encore. One anti-Communist speech may not cut it with the board. What if someone stands up and says something stupid like, 'Say

Jackie, how many new members have you personally been able to recruit into your local?' I can't blame that on the Communists!"

"Maybe Harold has some ideas," Tony suggested.

"What's your problem?" Harold Friedman demanded.

"I've got this Executive Board thing coming up. I was wondering if you had any suggestions on how we might boost our membership sometime between now and then?"

"This is a little short notice, don't you think?"

"Come-on Harold, you're good at this sort of thing. Think of something," Jackie pleaded.

"Okay, give me a moment."

Jackie fumbled with small talk, "I tried bouncing a few ideas off the PR guys, but they've got their heads up their asses on this one. Besides, they haven't got your brains for something like this."

"Right," Harold responded sarcastically. "Okay, I have an idea. I can't promise you it will work, but it's worth a try."

"Anything. Let's hear it," Jackie invited.

"Your Uncle Allen—"

"Ah-shit, not Uncle Allen," Jackie bitched.

"You want to hear this or not? Now, Uncle Allen is very sick with that heart problem of his."

"Yeah, I know. I hope that shithead kicks off real soon."

"You may get your wish. There's a good chance he won't pull through another operation," Harold continued.

Jackie quipped insultingly, "Awe, wouldn't that be a shame. He's dying, so what other good news can you tell me?"

"If you're simply looking for warm bodies, he's got Local 752. Why not have him sign those members over to us before he starts pushing up daises?"

Local 752 was a hodge podge of tobacco and vending machine workers that didn't fit nicely into other locals. The membership amounted to little more than a crate of lemons, but to Uncle Allen, they were his pride and joy.

"You've got to be crazy. Uncle Allen! Part with his members! There's no way in hell he's going to sign over his members to our Local 507. He'd go to his grave first, and if he could, he'd take his members with him."

"You know what one of your problems is, Jackie? You've got a bad attitude. Besides that, you don't think things through."

"Are you suggesting I pay him? 'Cause, if so, I ain't. He's going to be dead soon. Why should I pay him a fuckin' dime?"

"Do what you want. You're going to do what you want anyway, so why did you bring me this problem?"

"Because I'm running out of time, damn-it!"

"The way I see it, you either wait around until your Uncle Allen kicks off, or you make him a tender offer. Besides, even if he dies this afternoon, it's going to take a while before you can legally have his members transferred. But then you might encounter two more problems. First, it will appear to the Executive Board as if you simply inherited the members just like all the others."

"*Ooh,* that wouldn't look too good, would it? ... So what's the other problem?"

"What would happen if his members decide they want to line up with another local? You given that any thought?"

Jackie began to pace, "Damn, you're right. Besides, Uncle Al's already had one heart attack. What if he was to have a sudden relapse? What would happen to his poor, abandoned members? Hell, anything could happen. That local isn't in that good of financial shape as it is. Those poor bastards might get themselves taken over by someone else, and then, their membership dues would go somewhere else. We can't very well let that happen. Okay, what the hell ... let's try it."

Two days after making this startling revelation, Jackie invited Harold to accompany him to The Cleveland Clinic to see how serious Uncle Allen's condition had become. Bernie Charms, Allen's cardiologist, informed them that Jackie's uncle didn't have long to live. In his professional medical opinion, it was a hopeless situation.

"Listen Harold, we have to act fast on this. How do you think we should do it?"

"First, you have to make him an offer he can't refuse. How about offering him a thousand a week for the rest of his ... well, you get the idea."

"A grand a week! Are you out of your mind!"

"Do what you want. I merely threw out a figure that might get his attention. If you're not serious about this, you shouldn't have asked me for my suggestion."

"Okay, I'll have Climaco draw up the necessary legal junk. We've gotta get him to sign over his members before he makes a turn for the worse. You think he'll go for it? What if he asks for two gees a week?"

"Better hope that's not the case. A thousand a week, plus expenses, is all we can afford at the moment. It seems like our cash reserves are being drained, considering all the money we're supposedly pumping into public relations. And while we're on the subject, what's this deal with Anthony Liberatore? What kind of public relations consulting work is he supposed to be doing for two grand a month?"

"I knew you were going to say something like this! —I just knew it!" Jackie screamed. "You're tying my hands on this, I want you to know that. I'm going to hold you personally responsible if Uncle Allen doesn't sign a deal for those members."

With some reluctance, Jackie's uncle signed over his members to Local 507, and accepted the first installment. Allen Friedman was a man of great passions and addictions. His courage to take great risks right down to the wire had allowed him to develop a measure of intestinal fortitude when things got tough, and although he was close to death's outer door, the thousand-dollars-a-week offer plus expenses, was sufficient motivation for cheating the grim reaper. Or perhaps it was because he knew how much Jackie hated to part with the money, and just for spite he would hang on long enough to be fully compensated.

◆

While Uncle Allen's condition continued to improve, the same was not the case with Johnny Scalish, the silver-haired Mafia don of the Cleveland organized crime family. On the morning of May 26, 1976, he quietly passed away at his home in Murray Hill, while Maishe Rockman sat at his bedside.

Within hours of his death, except for the aging underboss, Tony Milano, the elite of the organization's remaining members assembled at the don's home. Maishe closed the door to the room before addressing Jack Licavoli, Frank Embrescia and Angelo Lonardo.

"Before the don passed away he told me that he wanted Jack Licavoli here, to succeed him as the don. Those were Scalish's last wishes," Maishe announced.

"What about Old Man Milano?" Angelo inquired. He knew that as the underboss for the family, Milano was automatically next in line of succession.

"My guess is that he figured the *Old Man* is now at the point where he is too old," Maishe pointed out.

"Well I'm not so sure I want the honor of being the don. I'm not all that young myself," Licavoli replied. "Christ, I'm nearly seventy. It's a lot of responsibility. Maybe we could select someone a little younger, you know, more aggressive."

"That's the problem," Lonardo pointed out. "We haven't initiated any new members since I was made back in the late 40s."

"Maybe it was a mistake not inducting Milano's nephew, John Nardi," Frank concluded.

Maishe bristled, "Absolutely out of the question. He's far too heavy into gambling and narcotics. Now I understand he's into running guns. It will only be a matter of time before the Treasury boys start watching him, assuming of course, they're not already doing so."

"Nobody's got any respect for the old ways anymore," Licavoli added.

"Yeah, I know what you mean," Lonardo agreed. "Speaking of the old ways, does anyone remember how *sub rosa*[7] is suppose to be performed?"

Lonardo's question brought a moment of silent embarrassment. Not one of them could remember the procedure or the ceremonial words.

"What about Lucky Luciano?" Frank suggested.

"No one knows where to find him," Maishe said. "He could be in New York, Chicago, Vegas or San Francisco. He might even be out of the country for all we know. Besides, he's been officially retired since '68. I doubt whether he'd do it, even if we could locate him."

"What about Jimmy the Weasel Fratianno?"

"Good idea," Maishe said. "In the meantime, someone will have to break this bad news to Old Man Milano. Anyone want to volunteer to convince him to gracefully step aside?"

Seeing no volunteers, Lonardo said, "I'll do it. I've probably known him longer than anyone else. If he had to receive bad news, he'd probably appreciate hearing it more from someone like myself."

Maishe accepted, "Good. Now, let's get down to the serious business. We've got to induct some new blood. We've received permission from the Genovese family to induct up to ten new members. I suggest we get started as soon as possible."

Each member knew they were facing an explosive situation, and that each passing day allowed Danny

---

[7] *Sub rosa* is an ancient Mafia custom that borrowed the tradition from Roman and Greek mythology, when Cupid offered a rose to Harpocrates, the god of silence, not to betray the amours of Venus, the goddess of love and beauty.

Greene to grow stronger. It would only be a matter of time before he took the notion to kill everyone of them.

Maishe added, "Each of us should make a list of proposed members. In the meantime, I'll contact *the Weasel* and find out when he's going to be in town. In fact, he should be here anyway for the don's funeral."

The announcement of Jack Licavoli's appointment to serve as the Mafia don brought a quick response from John Nardi. He demanded that he be put in charge of the crime family, or else.

Or else what?

Or else he would have to take matters into his own hands by force, if need be, and that was not an idle threat. Member or not, Nardi meant business. His 91-year-old uncle, Tony *Old Man* Milano, was the underboss, and therefore, technically he was next in line of succession. Nardi reasoned that if his uncle could not serve, then the position rightfully belonged to him, and he meant to have it—one way or the other.

In response to Nardi's threat, Angelo Lonardo was appointed to serve as the new underboss of the crime family. Nardi realized that with Lonardo's appointment, he was not going to be installed as the new Mafia don. To add insult to this personal affront, he wasn't even going to be proposed for membership.

News of John Nardi's retaliation plans against the Mafia and Syndicate were picked up by Leo *Lips* Moceri. Lips approached the new underboss with the news. Lonardo decided to set up a meeting with the don in his bachelor-pad apartment, and asked Lips to wait. It was not something Lips looked forward to, and he fumbled with his car keys as he impatiently reviewed how he should present his information to Licavoli—a man known for having a hot temper and generally bad disposition.

"Lips has some disturbing news," Lonardo whispered into the don's ear.

"Bad news, I suppose."

"I thought it best if you heard it directly from him in case you have any questions." Lonardo motioned for Lips to step forward.

"It's good of you to see me, boss," Lips said with a measure of respect, tempered with hesitation.

"What's so important?" Licavoli snapped.

"It's like I told the underboss, John Nardi has joined forces with Danny Greene. Together, they're going to set up a competing operation."

"Go on," Licavoli ordered.

"They're even going to change the old Irish Gang's name to The Greene Gang. Between the two of them, they have enough connections with the Hell's Angels to cause us some serious trouble."

"This is not good," Licavoli responded.

"I'm afraid he hasn't gotten to the bad news," Lonardo added. "Go on, finish the rest of it."

Lips continued, "Nardi's ultimate plan is to wipe out all the Jews on the Teamster Executive Board, and any Italians who refuse to side with him. He plans to seize control of the Central States Pension Fund. Nardi says it's time for the Bill-and-Jackie-Presser dynasty to retire, and turn over their power to the new outfit."

"And by that you mean Nardi and Greene?" Licavoli inquired.

"I'm afraid so, boss. The way they see it, Jackie is a weak contender to take over his father's responsibilities, not only in the Syndicate, but on the Teamster Executive Board."

Licavoli flicked his cane to dismiss Lips then turned to Lonardo, "I want you to get Maishe Rockman here as soon as possible. Have him inform the Pressers personally. Big Bill should be out of prison any day now."

The news, coupled with his deteriorating health, was more than Big Bill could handle given his advancing years. He decided it might be better to announce his retirement at the upcoming October Teamsters' Executive Board meeting. Big Bill's primary concern would be to place Jackie back in charge of the Central States Pension Fund before retiring. Upon his release from prison, the decision was make to go to La Costa to discuss details of his retirement.

Jackie's qualifications for a permanent position on the Central State Pension Fund fell measurably short of the mark, but the alternatives appeared worse. It was a precarious situation. As head of Local 410, John Nardi would be throwing his hat into the arena the moment the position became available, and if Jackie failed to get the nod, the Presser dynasty over the billion-dollar trust fund would be lost.

When the Pressers returned from La Costa, Danny Greene was informed by John Nardi that Jackie expected to be permanently installed to serve as his father's replacement. Enough time had been wasted and Greene took matters into his own hands. Greene set up temporary residence which offered him a strategic vantage point to watch Jackie's daughter across the street from her apartment complex. With any Irish luck, he would be able to watch Bari Lynn's coming and going, discretely follow her, determine her routine.

Consequently, Bari Lynn felt uneasy. She felt she was being watched, but she saw no one. It was one of those suspicions she couldn't put her finger on, yet she believed that at any moment, something was going to happen. This premonition was confirmed when a tenant's car identical to her own, exploded after parking near her regular spot. To fuel her anxiety, the following day one of her friends was found stripped with her throat slit and her gut cavity filleted.

Bari Lynn became too terrified to leave her apartment. By mid-July '76, she limited her outside activity to buying food. On the afternoon of July 26th, she remembered walking to the windows and draw back the drapes. The outside world appeared to be normal until she glanced directly across the street. Someone was standing in the front window opposite her apartment. The individual appeared to be looking at her with his hands on his hips. Her eyes began to focus more closely on the man who was still standing there. A chill of cold sweat began to run down her spine.

Danny Green reached down and picked up an object. He held it up for a moment, placed the butt-stock to his shoulder and aimed the rifle at her. Bari Lynn dove to the floor. The walls seems to shake in silence. She could not get any lower as she began crawling on her stomach and dragging herself toward the kitchen, realizing that at any moment the front window's glass would explode.

♦

Maishe Rockman traveled most of August informing the various crime families throughout the country of his new co-underboss position. While in Los Angeles, he met with Jimmy *The Weasel* Fratianno, inviting him to conduct the formal initiation of new Mafia members. En route, Maishe received word that Jackie wanted to see him.

"Maishe, this business with Nardi and Greene has really gotten to us. I never thought I'd see the day when anyone would be able to intimidate my ol' man, but Greene has succeeded," Jackie lamented.

"I understand Jackie. Not even Jimmy Hoffa or Bobby Kennedy could have got to your father like this," Maishe retorted.

"Yeah. Anyway, the reason I wanted to see you is because the ol' man is going to announce his retirement at the upcoming Executive Board meeting in San Francisco."

Maishe nodded, "I can't say this comes as a total surprise. The families were hoping he could stay on until after Fitzsimmons' reelection."

"That isn't all. He intends to have me replace him at that time."

"We've talked about that," Maishe responded.

"I want to reassure you where my loyalties are, and that the Mafia families can rely on me, just like they have with my ol' man."

"There are other issues involved. And while I personally think it's a good idea, you must understand that this is not my decision alone. In the meantime, I'll relay Big Bill's decision to the other families. I can't promise you anything, but I'll put in a good word."

"I appreciate that, Maishe. If there's anything I can do in the meantime, just tell me what you want done."

Maishe maintained eye contact, "The biggest favor you can do both of us is to stay alive until we can eliminate our mutual problems."

"I know what you mean. My kid tells me Greene is trying to kill her, but I can't take her too seriously. That kid's got a runaway imagination. She's just moved to another apartment. She claims that Greene has been following her around with a rifle."

"That may not be totally fabricated. Greene's been telling everyone that he's going to kill all the Jews. I'd be extra careful where you park your car," Maishe warned.

"I've assigned John Joyce, an ex-Police Captain, to follow him. Joyce tells me that he's damn near impossible to tail, and he told me that Greene won't even make two telephone calls from the same phone. Can you believe that?"

"It's true. Part of Greene's problem is that he's so hooked on junk, he's totally paranoid. We've even heard that Greene's numbers runner, Tommy ..."

"Yeah."

"Well, Tommy is so scared, he's left town, fearing Greene might take the notion to whack him."

"He'd do it, too, probably in broad daylight, just like he gave it to Frato. How in the hell is he getting away with this crap? Joyce tells me the U.S. Marshal's Service must have a half dozen arrest warrants for Greene just sitting on their desk. Why can't they do something?"

Maishe responded, "Just be damn careful. We've got several guys trying to keep tabs on him. Sooner or later, he'll make a mistake."

◆

It took Maishe the best part of the following month to make the rounds from Kansas City to Chicago, Pittsburgh to New Jersey, and finally to New York, before getting back to Jackie on the Commission's decision. With Maishe's endorsement, each crime family confirmed its willingness to let Jackie hold Big Bill's former position.

"Remember Jackie, you'll be expected to do the right thing. I told each of the families that I got your word on this."

"You got my word. I'll do the right thing," Jackie replied.

"Not to change the subject, but I suppose you've heard about Lips?"

"I heard he's missing. What's the story?" Jackie asked.

"Lips was expected in Murray Hill last night to see Lonardo. His girl friend reported him missing. The police found his Lincoln, and except for one small spot of blood in the trunk, he's nowhere to be found," Maishe stated.

"Any idea who might have made the hit?"

"We figure it was Danny Greene or one of his wiseguys. The point is, Lips' death must be avenged. We have to do something immediately, or this could turn into a national embarrassment. Licavoli has officially approved a hit on both Nardi and Greene. I'll keep you posted."

"Thanks. If there's anything I can do, just say the word," Jackie offered.

◆

Weekly meetings were set up with don Licavoli and one of Jackie's bodyguards. Now Jackie could be kept abreast of ongoing developments. After their initial meeting, the bodyguard returned with the news.

"Listen Jackie, the don wanted me to inform you that Nardi is planning on whacking your whole household," Tony announced.

"Oh," Jackie mused but without showing any outward alarm.

"The don said that Nardi and Greene plan to wipe out all the Jews involved with the Teamsters, and that includes Maishe and Harold," Tony elaborated.

"Christ, I knew those two crazy bastards were planning something. Any other good news?" Jackie inquired.

"Yeah. The don said that once the entire group has been wiped out, Nardi plans on taking control of the Pension Fund."

"I guess I should be grateful for being tipped off like this. Next time you see the don, tell him I owe him one."

"You got any plans?" Tony asked.

"Yeah. Tomorrow I'm going to get a permit for carrying a concealed weapon."

◆

In response to Maishe's invitation, Jimmy Fratianno arrived from the west coast the first week in September. He met with Tony 'Dope' Delsanter, a *consigliere* with the crime family, to work out arrangements, accommodations and set up a proper meeting place.

Nardi's hit was scheduled for the evening of September 10$^{th}$. The moment Nardi would be hit, it was expected that Greene would go on a killing rampage. New Mafia members would be needed to form a barricade of protection.

At precisely 11:30 on the evening of the 10$^{th}$, Nardi stepped outside the Italian-American Brotherhood Club. The club had been a part of the community of Murray Hill where the Mafia dons had resided since Prohibition. The area was understood to be off limits for anyone making trouble, and Nardi was aware of this tradition. This tradition did not protect him as he walked the street that night, because Nardi wasn't a Mafia member.

He slid into the front seat of his Olds parked on the street. A dark-colored van pull along side. Nardi wasn't sure why the vehicle had stopped, and turned his head toward the other driver. Without words being exchanged, the driver lifted a handgun and fired. Nardi's driver-side window exploded, showering him with glass. Nardi threw himself to the floor and a volley of rifle shots began hitting the car.

They missed their target. As the van pull away, he slowly picked himself up and drove home. While en route, Nardi realized he knew the van's driver, and quickly associated the possible firing-squad members. He knew exactly who he wanted Danny Greene to target in retaliation.

Greene assigned Enos Crnic the responsibility of installing the bombs as fast as they could be assembled. The failed hit squad went down quickly. Alfred was the first to go. Frank Percio was blown to pieces when Al Calabrese's car exploded.

Eugene Ciasullo escaped death only by a few seconds. The bomb intended for him was slid into a crawl space, strategically positioned below his bed. Once in bed, he abruptly decided to go to the bathroom. As he reached the bathroom, the bomb below his bed blew up.

Aside from Nardi's gun-running and wholesale drug-smuggling businesses, the sequence of bombings caught the attention of the U.S. Treasury's Division of Alcohol, Tobacco & Firearms. A swarm of special undercover agents descended on Cleveland looking for suspects behind the killings and bombings. The Treasury's efforts were quickly stifled when the FBI took charge of the investigation. ATF's investigation into Danny Greene's affairs, however, caused him to suspect that someone within his own ranks was responsible.

Greene informed Enos that additional precautions were needed. From now on, he would accompany him as a lookout. The next bomb Enos was scheduled to install was on John Delzoppo's car. Once the proposed victim's car was located, Greene took up a position across the street to make sure he wasn't being watched. Greene waited for Enos to crawl under the vehicle before using a remote control devise. Greene threw the switch, then casually departed the scene.[8]

---

[8] Enos' death was ruled accidental, and the investigation was quietly closed.

*Chapter 9*

## The Fire Storm

CRIME WAS ON A RAMPAGE the year the Carter administration took office. The FBI's year-and-half investigation into Jimmy Hoffa's disappearance was no further ahead than the day it started. The Mafia was firmly in control of the Teamsters, and violent killings were unabated. The new administration held the belief that something had to be done at the national level, but not necessarily by using the time-honored methods of the FBI. Conceivably, another crime-fighting agency needed to be created to investigate these turbulent matters.

Although the FBI's logistical problems were successfully shielded from the public, the agency appeared to be out of control. As usual, the FBI was running amok the morning Geraldine Linhart arrived for work. Her file clerk employment allowed her limited access to the FBI's Secret Files Room. It was a typical day of pulling files, copying paperwork and transmitting sensitive information to the FBI's Washington headquarters. Fingering through a stack of papers, she spotted code names of ten area informants. None of the code names meant anything to her, nevertheless, she had a job to do. She began copying.

When she finished, Geraldine slipped the information into her purse and went about her daily routine. When the noon hour arrived, she left the building among the crowd of other federal employees. And rather than selecting a downtown restaurant, she began her lunch break by driving to a suburban car dealership.

At the dealership she was greeted by a tall gentleman. She rolled down her window, and he handed her an envelope, "There's a thousand here. Would you like to count it?"

Geraldine peeked inside, "No, that won't be necessary," and handed him an envelope. "Here's some information you might find useful."

"If this checks out, there'll be more," he added.

Geraldine nodded, then drove back to the downtown FBI office. Anthony Liberatore got into his car and headed to the Roman Garden Restaurant located in Murray Hill.

◆

Having spent three weeks visiting his mother and renewing friendships from his old Murray Hill neighborhood, Jimmy Fratianno was ready to get down to business. He was eager to complete the indoctrination ceremony before returning to Los Angeles. Fratianno was a man of slight physical stature, but as an underworld figure, Fratianno projected a bigger than life image; his résumé included killing a dozen people and his credentials were indisputable.

*Jimmy Fratianno*

As *consigliere* to the new Mafia don, it was Tony 'Dope' Delsanter's responsibility to see that this invited guest from the west coast received the red-carpet treatment. "Is there anything you need?" Delsanter asked.

"Let's see. I could use a couple broads, a box of cigars and some of your best whisky."

"No problem Jimmy. I'll take care of it right away. Maybe I should have stated it a little better ... is there anything you'll need to conduct the initiation ceremony?"

"Oh, I see. Let me think... Naw, I've got everything I need. Just see that everyone's ready and on time," Fratianno ordered.

"Did Maishe fill you in on the particulars?" Delsanter queried.

"Yeah. Maishe told me you've got permission from the Genovese family to make ten new members," Fratianno responded. "That means you'll have to locate a decent size room."

"There are only four guys for you to initiate. We can use the basement of the Roman Gardens."

"Like I told Maishe, I'll be glad to do this thing under one condition. I want it made perfectly clear that it's the don's responsibility to make sure they're all straight with the organization. Is that understood?" Fratianno demanded.

"Yeah, sure Jimmy, but you know all these guys," Delsanter reminded.

"I know them, but at the same time, I don't know them, at least not personally. I left Murray Hill back in the late '40s, so when we do this thing, I want it understood that I'm not responsible if any of them are not stand-up guys. I'm taking your word that none of them are tight with the feebees."

"Come on. These are all stand-up guys. Hey, one more thing. A couple of them wanted to know if you're going to conduct the ceremony in Italian?"

"Oh! You want me to do it in Italian? Good idea," Fratianno smiled.

"They were hoping you wouldn't, 'cause some of them guys only know a few words."

"Listen, I hardly ever conduct the ceremony in Italian. Half the current members aren't even *gumbas* for Christ sake. Look at Maishe Rockman, you think he's Italian? Tell them to relax. Anything else?"

"Yeah. You remember Lips Moceri?" Delsanter asked next.

"Of course. I heard he got himself whacked."

"Danny Greene has claimed responsibility, and said he wanted to send us a message. The don has authorized a hit on both him and John Nardi."

"Who's been given the contract?" Fratianno inquired.

"That's why we're inducting new members. We thought we could get the new members involved, and have Liberatore handle it. Do you have any ideas on how he should go about doing it?"

"These things have to be well thought out. I'll think of something. For now, I want you to gather as much dope about these two clowns as possible. I'll see Liberatore after the ceremony."

The prospective members filed down the basement steps of the Roman Gardens Restaurant and into a dimly-lit room. Fratianno studied each man's face without saying a word. The group stood in silence with their heads respectfully bowed until Jimmy Fratianno took the notion to speak.

"Do you know why you're here?" Fratianno asked seriously.[9]

Each proposed member responded in the negative as the *consigliere* had previously instructed them to do.

"My name is Jimmy Fratianno. I am a member of *La Cosa Nostra.* Each of you have been proposed for membership in *La Cosa Nostra,* which in English means 'this thing of ours.' We're a secret organization, but before I tell you the rules and regulations, I'll give all of you the option to leave now." Fratianno began strutting back and forth with his hands on his hips. "Once you are accepted into the organization, you cannot leave, so if you have any reservations, I'm telling you to leave this room right now." He pointed toward the exit.

No one moved. Each man had been waiting his entire life for this moment.

"Okay, you were given your chance to leave. By your presence, you have chosen to accept membership and initiation into *La Cosa Nostra.* I will now inform you of the rules and regulations under *sub rosa.* First, you cannot operate a house of prostitution or have any prostitutes working for you. Second, you cannot become involved in narcotics. Third, you cannot fool around with a woman who is married to another *La Cosa Nostra* member. If you desire to become involved in any illegal activity, you must first obtain the don's permission to engage in that activity. But you are not permitted to approach or speak to the don directly. You must first consult with your immediate superior and receive

---

[9] The ceremony was revealed by Angelo Lonardo after he became a registered informant for the U.S. Treasury Department. The U.S. Treasury's official position is that these records have been destroyed.

permission to speak to the don. He will then approach the *consigliere* on your behalf and speak to the don. Is this understood?"

Each man silently nodded his head affirmatively as Fratianno maintained eye contact. "Now, when you are in the presence of other members and someone is with you, your introduction of that person will be ... 'This is a friend of *mine*' ... which means the person with you is not a member. But, if the individual being introduced is a made member, you will say ... 'This is a friend of *ours*.' I now want you to nod your heads and acknowledge to me that you understand this custom."

Once again, each proposed member nodded his head. Fratianno then walked behind a table covered with a dark cloth. In one sweeping motion, he threw back the cloth unveiling a small stack of cards, next to a dagger and a gun. Fratianno picked up and held the dagger, looked toward the ceiling and proudly announced, "From this day forward, you shall live and you shall die by the dagger and the gun. You enter this way and you shall leave this way."

He motioned for Delsanter to give each man a card, which depicted the picture of a saint. He struck a match, and one by one the cards were lit while being held by the member until the cards burned down to ashes. Fratianno then held the dagger in front of each man's face before taking hold of his hand and drawing a drop of blood. "Your blood symbolizes your solemn oath never to reveal to anyone your membership in *La Cosa Nostra*. If you violate this oath, you shall pay with your life. If you are called upon to do so, you must take the life of anyone whom the don has authorized. Now I will embrace each of you." As Fratianno stood in front of each participant, with a kiss he announced, "You are now a member of *La Cosa Nostra*."

*Anthony Liberatore*

As Anthony Liberatore was formally welcomed by Jimmy Fratianno into the Mafia, he leaned forward and whispered, "I have something to tell you right away."

"Yes, of course, and there is something I wish to discuss with you also. I suppose it concerns Danny Greene?"

"No, but it's just as important," Liberatore responded.

"Is it something that can wait?"

"No. I have to tell someone," Liberatore mildly pleaded.

"If it's something that important, I'll listen. See me in the hall after we discuss business." Turning to the others, "I will now turn the meeting over to the *consigliere* who has an important matter to discuss."

The *consigliere* cleared his throat. "As most of you know, we are confronting a serious situation with Danny Greene. He and John Nardi have sworn to kill all of us to gain control over the rackets. I'm informing each of you that the don has personally authorized the death of both Greene and Nardi. I need a volunteer to oversee the planning of their elimination."

All the new members raised their hands. "I will inform the don of your support," Delsanter said. "Now we'll meet upstairs in a private room to discuss this matter in more detail."

As the guest of honor, Fratianno led the procession out the door and toward the stairs. Liberatore brushed past the others to stop Fratianno. "You won't believe what I'm about to tell you." Liberatore waited until the others filed past, "I have a snitch inside the FBI office."

Fratianno smiled. "You're shitting me! Tell me you're putting me on."

"No, honest. I have my own snitch right inside the Bureau."

"Who put you up to this? Was it Maishe? — Lonardo?" Fratianno baited.

"Nobody put me up to anything. I'm telling it to you straight."

"You got the feds to fink on themselves? I don't believe it," Fratianno shot back in disbelief.

"It's a broad," Liberatore interjected, "and she's got direct access to the FBI's informant files. I'll be getting more information any day now."

Fratianno reached up and patted Liberatore on the shoulder, "Man, if that don't beat everything I've ever heard. Listen, we have to get upstairs to discuss what we're going to do about Greene, but if it's not too long a story, tell me how in the hell you pulled this off?"

Liberatore moved closer, "There's this guy by the name of Rabinowitz. The guy's queer for wiseguys. He's not gay, but real strange."

"You mean something like a Mafia groupie?"

The simile lit up Liberatore's face, "Yeah, 'groupie.' Anyway, he's been hitting me up for a loan to make a down payment on a house. He's engaged to some broad by the name of Geraldine Linhart, who wants to get hitched and settle down."

"So what's the big deal?"

Liberatore glanced around, "It just so happens that Geraldine works for the feebees as a file clerk."

Fratianno held up his hand, "Let me see if I've got this straight. This Rabinowitz groupie has agreed to have fiancée, Geraldine, steal shit out of the FBI's files and turn the stuff over to you for a loan?"

"Right. For fifteen grand."

"Swear to God you're not putting me on?"

"No bull. I'm not only getting information from her, I get my money back with interest," Liberatore said with a tone of irony.

"Nobody's *that* stupid ... I don't like it. I don't mean to piss on your parade, but someone has to be setting you up. Who else knows about this?" Fratianno demanded to know.

"No one, other than this broad and her Mafia groupie. You're the first one I've officially mentioned it to."

"Do us both a favor. Go slow on this," Fratianno advised. "It may be just as you say. I'm willing to take your word for it, but I don't want you to do anything equally as stupid."

"I've got the FBI's list of code names. It'll only take a couple days and I'll have their identities in the palm of my hand," Liberatore proudly announced.

"I'd like to stick around for that, but I can't. I'm expected back in Los Angeles to take care of personal business. Just do me a favor ... I want you to keep me posted."

Fratianno returned to Los Angeles with a sense of urgency. He didn't wait long before placing a series of emergency telephone calls in a frantic effort to reach his former FBI handler who had retired to San Francisco.

"We've got trouble! Big serious trouble, and you've got to bail me out," Fratianno demanded.

"What's the problem, Jimmy?" the voice on the other end responded.

"The organization's got a snitch right inside the FBI!"

"What? Is this some kind of April Fool's joke, Jimmy?"

"I'm telling you, the Mafia's got its own snitch inside the fucking Bureau."

"That's impossible. Someone is pulling your leg," the former agent retorted.

"Yeah, right. Well one of our new members, Anthony Liberatore, is in possession of FBI informant code names. You've got to protect me."

"Calm down. In the first place, I'm out of it. I've been retired for two years, remember? Your informant file was sent to Washington. It's probably lost or archived by now. Field agents wouldn't have access to that info unless they specifically requested it."

Fratianno responded abruptly by banging the mouthpiece of the receiver against the telephone. He screamed, "Hello! Hello! I must be speaking to an asshole on the other end of this line!"

"Jimmy! Calm down for Christ sake."

"My life's on the line, and you say '*calm down!*'"

"All right, I'll make a call and see if anyone is still around that I can trust. If not, I'll place a call to Washington, and see that your informant file gets hidden as deep as possible."

Fratianno's ex-FBI handler broke the connection and muttered, "There are some organizations you can't retire from. Fratianno belongs to one of them and I belong to the other."[10]

◆

With the infusion of Uncle Allen's additional members transferred into Jackie's Local 507, the groundwork had been laid. Big Bill announced his formal retirement at the Executive Board meeting, along with a proclamation that his son should take his place on the Board.

Not everyone was enthusiastic with Jackie's undistinguished appointment, so a voice vote was held. A call for the vote, a bang of the gavel and a quick nod—it was all over; Jackie was instantly elevated to vice president of the International Brotherhood of Teamsters. More importantly, the time-honored post carried a permanent trustee position on the Central States Pension Fund.

With this difficult and trying moment of behind him, Jackie gave thought to Uncle Allen. "I'm telling you Tony, he better give up his weekly stipend, or start giving some serious thought about confronting my attorney."

"What's bothering you now?"

"I need that money more than he does."

"But Jackie, a grand a week ain't all that much money."

"It not just a grand a week. He wants expenses. Then there's Liberatore. He's drawing a couple grand a month, not to mention my attorney fees and shit like that."

---

[10] Jimmy Fratianno's FBI informant statue was mutually terminated after his FBI handler retired circa 1975.

"There's got to be more behind this than just a few grand here and there. What do you need the money for?" Tony asked.

"It's that peanut farmer in the White House."

"What does Jimmy Carter have to do with Jackie Presser? He damn sure isn't hitting you up for campaign money."

"That's the whole point. He's not playing ball," Jackie responded. "I've got to find someone who is willing to play on my terms. My ol' man warned me something like this would happen. He said not to wait until the last second."

"Did Big Bill have any suggestions?" Tony asked.

"Yeah, but I think my ol' man's beginning to lose it."

"Oh? What does he have in mind?"

"He thinks we should ... never mind, it's so silly it's not worth mentioning. I think those treatments he's been receiving have started to affect his brain."

"No, tell me," Tony pressed.

Jackie laughed. "Get this. He thinks we should support Reagan."

"The movie actor?"

"Yeah, the actor. I'll have to start making a list of some serious contenders. Maybe I'll call Nixon and see if he's got any suggestions."

"Are you going to ask him about the Gipper?"

"Well, Nixon's got a good sense of humor. Maybe I will add Ronnie's name to my list just to get his reaction."

♦

"Tony, I'm telling ya, it's nothing but one piece of bad news after another," Jackie complained. "First Carter gets elected ... and now this."

"When did McCoy tell you?"

"About twenty minute ago. I was just getting to the point where McCoy and I could trust one another, and now he wants to split."

"Nothing lasts forever Jackie."

"I'll bet the reason he wants to retire is because he can't stand Carter. Well maybe I should retire from them too."

"You think that's such a good idea? Both Greene and Nardi are just waiting to have you popped. You turn in your toys to McCoy, and those two will get you for sure," Tony advised.

In their February 16, 1977 meeting, Agent McCoy took the initiative, "I can assure you Jackie, nothing has changed. In fact, I received word directly from headquarters that you'll be provided with additional protection, including a new code name."

"What's wrong with the one I've got? I kinda like it," Jackie responded.

"Your new FBI code name will be *Alpro*."

"Hey, how do you like that. I get a new agent, and a new identity. Mind telling me what the hell is goin' on?"

"Listen Jackie, not all my snitches are going to be so lucky. We're cutting a few of them loose, so they'll be on their own in this big bad world. We're not going to be around to protect them, so if I were you, I'd be counting my blessings."

"I don't suppose you'll be taking down Greene or Nardi before you leave?" Jackie inquired.

"As a departing gesture, I'll see what I can do, but no promises."

"Level with me damn-it. What's going on?"

"This has all been approved at the highest level. The new director of the FBI, Clarence Kelly himself, has ordered *The Tailor* files permanently sealed and moved to Washington headquarters. And, as an added safeguard, the Assistant Deputy Director Oliver B. Revell, has been informed about your special privileges."

"So what you're telling me is that it's business as usual. I still get to maintain my cover, and keep any money you guys pay me and the stuff that falls through the cracks at The Front Row Theatre."

"That's my understanding. Our original arrangement, which Hoover approved, will remain in force."

"Good. Oh, my attorney wanted me to remind you about getting something in writing. Seeing as how I'm gonna be getting a new man, maybe that's not such a bad idea."

"I'll pass your attorney's request along."

◆

By the time Jimmy Fratianno's information reached the FBI's Washington headquarters and filtered its way down the chain of command, the damage was done. Anthony Liberatore had been steadily receiving installments of information from Geraldine Linhart, ranging from the license plate numbers of undercover vehicles to in-depth field reports on various Teamster locals. With each installment, Liberatore had an envelope of cash ready for her.

Fratianno's FBI connection resulted in camera surveillance being set up to monitor the Secret Files Room. Special Agent Patrick Foran took charge of the operation.

"I'll be damned. Would you take a look at this," Foran motioned for Special Agent Robert Friedrick to join him watching the surveillance monitor.

"What's going on?"

"This broad is snatching information right out of the secret file room," Foran said.

"What kind of information is she looking for?"

"It doesn't matter," Foran responded.

"You want me to arrest her, or do you think we should wait until she steps out of the building?"

"Not so fast. We might be able to turn this to our advantage."

"Are you suggesting we help her?" Friedrick responded in puzzlement.

"Any suggestions?" Foran queried. "Let me put it this way ... if we could get rid of a few headaches, who might that be?"

"Hmm, my choice?" Friedrick pondered. "Personally, I'd like to see someone like Danny Greene or John Nardi taken out of action."

"So would a lot of people. What if someone was to put Nardi's name on our list of informants?"

"He's not an informant," Friedrick responded.

"We know that, but the people she's handing the information to don't know that."

"What about Danny Greene?"

"Greene's nothing but a royal pain. McCoy recruited him back in '69, but as far as I'm concerned, he's been nothing but trouble. And now, he's so hooked on his own junk, he's worthless."

"Why do you think McCoy kept him on the payroll?" Friedrick asked.

"I think he was hoping to use Greene to get to someone important like Angelo Lonardo. He figured that if we didn't get to him first, the Treasury boys would."

"What about this other guy, The Tailor? You think he's worth keeping?"

"That's a damn good question. According to McCoy, The Tailor thinks he has us fooled. McCoy has played along with him over the years, and now it's my turn. And get this, McCoy told me The Tailor's attorney wants the Bureau to prepare some type of written contract, stating that we've authorized his criminal conduct."

"Really?" Friedrick retorted.

"He's serious. Before McCoy retired he put through a request to headquarters. I wouldn't be surprised if a memo comes back down in a couple days."

"Right, probably telling you to tell him to go fuck himself," Friedrick responded. "So, what's the deal. Are you going to keep The Tailor on or cut him loose?"

"I'll have to give it some thought. McCoy said that The Tailor's Achilles' heel is that he's scared shitless about going to prison. And we're the only one standing between him and his fear."

"I take it, the Tailor is into a lot of shit?" Friedrick deduced.

Responding in a deliberate fashion, "You have no idea. McCoy said The Tailor is into telling us only what he wants us to know. Ever since Watergate, he's been operating with his own agenda, but I have news for him."

"Oh? You think he was involved in that?"

"Just before his files were shipped to headquarters, I reviewed them. It's obvious he had something to do with it. Nonetheless, I have no intention of letting The Tailor's agenda become my agenda."

"So what's today's agenda? ... Are you going to arrest Geraldine?"

"Not right now. We haven't played out our hand yet."

◆

The list of code names and files that Geraldine Linhart turned over to Anthony Liberatore were turned over to the underboss, Angelo Lonardo. In turn, Lonardo handed that information to the Mafia don, Jack Licavoli.

One of the more intriguing items included the FBI's file on himself. The next file was on John Nardi and Teamsters' Local 507. Licavoli read the file carefully then commented, "You know what I find interesting in all this shit? There ain't a damn-single word mentioned about Jackie ... not a damn word!"

"I never thought of that," Lonardo puzzled in amazement.

"Yeah, now that you mention it, that is mighty strange," Liberatore added.

Licavoli tossed the files on his coffee table, "How is it the feds can have all this stuff on Local 507, and not know a damn thing about Jackie Presser."

"Yeah, you'd think the FBI would know he's serving as the Local's President and the Vice President of the International," Lonardo added.

"And what about his position on the Central States Pension Fund? They don't even mention anything about that. Are they completely stupid or what?" Licavoli retorted.

Liberatore turned to Lonardo, "I can't imagine why the feds haven't stumbled upon all the crap Jackie and his attorney are into with The Front Row Theatre."

"I just realized something else," Licavoli interrupted. "There isn't anything in the Bureau's files on Big Bill either. You'd think with all the guys he's had popped, they'd have something on him."

Liberatore broke in with, "I heard that Big Bill had something pretty good on Hoover. Maybe he told his agents to stay away from Big Bill's Syndicate. That would explain it."

"Hmm? Anthony, who's that guy you know in Chicago? You know, the one who keeps screaming about Jackie being an informant," Lonardo inquired.

"Ah, Harry Haler. No one has been taking him seriously. He's real pissed at Jackie for cutting him out of the action in the Hoover-Gorvin contract," Liberatore recalled.

"Like the Weasel said, this is all too good to be true. I smell a rat. I think the Weasel is right. The feebees might be just setting us up. Besides, how come all the informants have code names except the two on the bottom, Nardi and Greene." Licavoli looked directly at Liberatore, "Anthony, did you add those two names to this list?"

"No, honest," Liberatore protested. "That's the way the broad gave them to me."

"I find that hard to believe. After all, Danny Greene an FBI informant? Please. What's he supposed to be ... an FBI wet boy?"

Liberatore and Lonardo shrugged. They didn't know what to make of the information or the don's astute remark. The session ended with Licavoli ordering Lonardo to summon Maishe Rockman.

◆

"Jackie, I've just come from seeing the don. Licavoli tells me that Liberatore has some female supposedly inside the FBI office feeding him information on informants."

"Say what?"

"The don is taking it with a grain of salt. He's convinced the FBI is trying to set us up."

"Oh?"

"Well the supposed list of informants includes the names Nardi and Greene."

"That's got to be bullshit. Nardi and Greene, informants? They're the two biggest drug dealers around, and Greene's nothing but a hit man. I suppose me and my ol' man were on the list too," Jackie concluded.

"No. In fact, you and Big Bill's names didn't appear anywhere, not even under the information on Local 507." Even Maishe was puzzled by that, but he elected to keep it to himself.

"I think the don is right," Jackie agreed. "It's just a setup to trap some of our guys."

Jackie privately expressed his concerns to Tony. "Now I know what's really going on."

"What's that?" Tony encouraged.

"McCoy knew all along this was going down and that clever bastard kept me in the dark."

"You think that's why the FBI changed your Tailor handle and moved your files to Washington?"

"What else could it be? Well two can play this informant game just as easy as one."

♦

To aggravate Jackie, Carmen was doing everything possible to disrupt his outward tranquillity. Jackie had the ability to thrive while living on life's edge, but his new mistress, Cynthia Ann Jerabic, was taking up far too much of his time and affections to suit Carmen. She used that as an excuse to exercise her Latin temper and to explode, "You think you can treat me like some damn nigger. I got news for you Jackie. It ain't gonna happen. It ain't gonna happen no way."

"I don't have time for this. What the hell's the matter with you anyway?"

"This new bitch you've been sleeping with, that's what I'm talking about."

"Cynthia Ann? She doesn't mean a thing."

"Don't hand me that shit."

"But Carmen honey, I've slept with a lot of women."

"Don't Carmen honey ..."

"You're a fine one to talk. I got you and mister hot lips on tape, in case you didn't know."

"I've worked too damn hard Jackie. You can't threaten me."

"Now I'm not threatening you, just ..."

"I know too much Jackie, so you just keep that in mind."

"Oh, like what?"

"I know about your friends in the Mafia and the Front Row deals. I know how you launder the money, the Workers' Comp schemes, them ghost employees you got, and all the shit in Washington with Nixon, Mitchell and all of them people from Israel."

"Carmen honey, I think you're overreacting. So I slept with her a couple times. I'm telling you, it was no big deal. I'll come right over and we'll have a long talk." Jackie replaced the receiver and glanced at Tony, "I've had it with that broad. I've gotten rid of wives before, and I can do it again."

"Hell Jackie, you been up to bat so many times you should be a pro at it by now," Tony responded.

♦

The March meeting with Jackie's new Big Brother handler was more than a let's-get-acquainted session. Unlike Agent McCoy, Agent Patrick Foran did things by the numbers and in accordance with the guidelines Hoover had laid down for his special agents. If Jackie wanted to keep his special FBI privileges he would have to perform, which meant he had to deliver the goods. There would be no more wild-goose chases, no more 'I'll think it over and get back to you on that issue.' In short, Agent Foran would not tolerate Jackie playing mind games. It was a new day, and there would be new black-and-white ground rules.

"I want to make sure we get something straight between us. Your special FBI privileges are on the line. The new director thinks you've been playing too many games with us," Foran revealed.

"I don't know what you're taking about," Jackie snapped back.

"I've done a thorough review of the information you furnished McCoy, and quite frankly, I think you've been stringing us along. You either start giving us something of substance, or I'll have to pull your meal ticket. Am I making myself clear?"

"What-n-hell do you want? What did I do?"

"For openers," Foran said, "let's start by you telling me what's going on?"

"I'm not sure what you want. Tell me what you want to know," Jackie invited.

"Okay, let's start with your buddy Frank Fitzsimmons."

"What about him?" Jackie asked.

"No. That's not an answer, that's a question. Here's the routine. I ask the questions, and you provide the answers. Now, tell me about Fitzsimmons?" Foran instructed.

"Fitz is desperate."

"Why?"

Jackie rubbed his chin, "For one thing, he wants Dorfman to give up his control over the $1.6 billion in Central States Pension Fund assets. Fitz is running scared from all the heat you guys have been applying. Word is, he might be willing to cooperate with the Treasury guys in exchange for not going to prison."

"Sorry, that wasn't good enough. We've already surmised that on our own. You'll have to do better."

"What do you want me to say?"

"That's another question. I'll ask the questions. What I want from you is answers, something I can write down that would be worth my time," Foran stated.

"Hey, my time's valuable too. I got a lot of shit to take care of, and Fitz is the least of my worries."

"Now there you go again, dancing around the issue. You still haven't answered my question, damn-it. I don't think we're communicating. Maybe you've got a hearing deficiency. Maybe you should get your hearing checked."

"There ain't nothing wrong with my hearing. You just don't like hearing the truth. Nothing's going on, and you want blood from a stone."

"No, you either start leveling with us or else I pull the plug and watch your life go down the toilet right along with all the other horseshit you've been handing out."

Jackie paused a moment. "Listen, if I start telling you this stuff, you have to promise it won't start coming back on me. I'm the only one who knows this shit, and I'll be dead tomorrow if any of it gets traced back to me."

"Cut the bullshit," Foran ordered. "This better be good, or this could be our first and last meeting."

"Dorfman is going to get rid of Fitz, one way or the other. If he doesn't resign voluntarily, Dorfman's going to have him whacked," Jackie revealed.

"Go on. There's got to be more to this," Foran prodded.

"Only that Dorfman wants either Roy Lee Williams or Harold Gibbons to be Fitz's replacement."

"Why?"

"Dorfman indicated that Chicago can control those two guys. Either of them will jump to whatever tune Dorfman wants to play," Jackie said.

"Okay, that makes sense. Anything else I should know about?"

"Not really," Jackie replied.

"Not really? Oh?" Foran responded. "I'll be the judge of that. Like I said, I catch you playing bull-shit games with me and I'll personally see to it that your ticket gets pulled, punched and canceled."

"Okay-okay. Christ, don't you ever let up?"

"Sounds more like a question than an answer."

"You're going to get me in trouble for this, I just know it," Jackie winced.

"I'll get you in trouble? Sounds like you did most of this on your own time. But I'll tell you what. I'll leave now, file my report, and if anything turns up that I discovered you held back on, I won't be bothering you again. I'll send around a couple of agents to pick up our toys and you can face the music alone."

"All I'm asking is that you make damn sure I'm not directly associated with how you received this information. Shit. I'll be a dead man if it gets out." Foran appeared unimpressed as Jackie threw out the name, "Dan Shannon."

"What about him?"

"He was scheduled to be whacked. Dorfman had to get it approved by Nick Civella out of Kansas City."

"Why?"

"Shannon won't do what he's told."

"You said 'scheduled' as if it's an on-off situation. Give me the particulars."

"It was in the works when Fitz caught wind of it. He got Civella to call it off."

"So what you're saying is that Fitzsimmons has the power to get a Mafia hit called off."

"Being the General President of the Teamsters carries a lot of weight," Jackie replied.

"So why did he call it off?"

"Fitz figured it would bring down too much heat, but Civella got pissed as hell."

"Why?"

"Well, you know ... it takes a lot of planning. Civella put in a lot of time and effort setting the whole thing up so that it could be pulled off without a hitch."

"I see, sort of like when Hoffa got whacked?"

"I don't know anything about that job. You're just like McCoy. He was always throwing that in my face."

"The records seem to indicate you knew about the hit before anyone else. How do you account for that?"

"In my position, I hear stuff. That's what you pay me for," Jackie reminded.

"Any other hits going down I should know about before I read about them in the newspapers?"

That was one question Jackie would have preferred Agent Foran had not asked, but it was too direct. "Well, I've heard some rumors, but that's all, just rumors, mind you. I got nothin' to back it up."

Nodding, "Okay, you *got nothin'* to back it up."

"I heard someone mention something to someone else, and who knows how many times it's been repeated, but a couple of local guys are supposed to be whacked."

"Who, how and why?"

"How the hell should I know!"

"Make an educated guess," Foran ordered.

"Maybe John Nardi, for one. He might simply have an accident. But it's like I said, that rumor has been floating around for a couple of weeks. It's just grapevine talk, so don't quote me on it."

Foran smiled. Adding Nardi's name to the informant's list had obviously reached the right people.

"Anyone else?"

"Yeah, me. I heard someone might have a hit planned against my whole family, but I don't suppose you'll do anything about that."

"I think we've done a pretty damn good job keeping your ass out of jail. As for helping you stay alive, I'll give you a solid piece of free advice."

"Yeah, what's that?"

"Don't fire any of your bodyguards."

Like Jackie, Danny Greene had his own reliable sources for information. Upon learning from the Bureau that John Nardi was scheduled to be eliminated, Greene sent a special messenger to hand deliver a note to Nardi on the morning of May 17th. The message informed Nardi that an immediate attempt would be made on his life, and for him to use extreme caution.

Because Greene did not reveal his source or how he came by this information, Nardi did not take the privately delivered message seriously. He left his office at Teamster Headquarters on East 19th Street at three o'clock that same afternoon. He walked the short distance to the corner where his Olds 98 was parked. Before getting in, he observed Eddy Lee's car parked next to his driver's side. There was nothing for him to be concerned about, so it was safe to approach his vehicle. On the other side, however, there was another vehicle a little farther away. It appeared to be a safe distance. Nardi inserted the key to unlock his car. The distant vehicle's driver's door exploded.

The ear-piercing blast striped Nardi's clothes from his body. Within moments, a small crowd from the Teamsters building began running to the scene still smoldering from the blast. Nardi was still alive. The first man to reach the scene elevated Nardi's head slightly. The noise from the arriving spectators drowned out what Nardi was trying to say. The man holding his head had to lean his ear closer to Nardi's mouth.

John Nardi forced a weak smile then said, "It didn't hurt." He never took another breath.

◆

Danny Greene was not noted for exercising self-control. With his most powerful ally dead, Greene publicly vowed to take revenge. No one ignored the threat, including Jackie, who wasted no time. Without packing or giving the matter a second thought, he picked up the phone and called Inn The Woods travel agency. If a seat wasn't available on the next flight to Miami, then the agency was to charter a private plane.

Even though Jackie had left town for health reasons, Agent Foran insisted that he stay in touch by telephone from Miami.

"What have you heard?" Foran asked.

"I just learned that Dorfman is on the verge of doing something drastic."

"Get to the point. Drastic? How so?"

"Fitz has just canceled Dorfman's ten-year insurance contract covering the Central States Pension Fund."

"Now that's interesting. So what do you think Dorfman will do?"

"Don't quote me on this, but I think Dorfman might have Fitz killed. He might do it himself, if necessary."

Foran continued to take notes as he spoke, "Are there any other hits in the works?"

"I guess you've probably heard by now that Greene has vowed to whack everybody in sight," Jackie relayed.

"Greene's not my problem. Besides, murder is a local issue."

"Christ, that's what McCoy used to say. So what you're saying is that you guys can't do something to stop that crazy bastard," Jackie complained.

"Who knows. He might get careless and kill a U.S. Marshall or a Postal employee. If that happens, we might get called in."

"What does he have to do for Christ sake, use a machine-gun?" Jackie inquired.

"Something like that. What's your point?"

"My point is this, damn-it! How many people does Greene have to kill before someone arrests him? Can't you guys pick him up for questioning or something?"

"On what grounds? Listen, we're not interested in who Greene kills or how many. He's probably whacked a couple dozen guys over the ten years, but look at who he's taking out."

"So what you're saying is that as long as he sticks to killing undesirables, you guys ain't going to do a damn thing. Is that it?"

"There you go again, asking questions. That's my job, remember?"

♦

John Nardi's violent death rekindled the Justice Department's interest in Jimmy Hoffa's disappearance, and a new RICO investigation was initiated at the request of the Carter administration. Jackie was immediately designated as the government's chief informational source, and by June of '77, his insider's information was being routinely disseminated from the FBI's Washington Headquarters to all field offices throughout the country under the new ultra-top-secret Alpro cover.

Jackie presented an endless array of reasons why he had to stay out of town, and Bari Lynn saw that as an opportunity to see her grandfather on a regular basis, especially now that he was retired. Big Bill was concerned for her safety, and suggested it might be better for her to go to Europe, perhaps to take up studying art.

For the first time in her life, Bari Lynn found her grandfather willing to talk about the past. He began speaking openly about his children, whom he felt did not love him. He was particularly annoyed because none of his children had expressed any concern about him going into the hospital.

After disappearing for four months, Jackie returned to his office and a full appointment schedule. It took Bari Lynn a full week to schedule an appointment to see him. She took the opportunity to confront him on several issues, one of which involved the unthinkable.

"Are you going to prison?" Bari Lynn asked.

"What gave you that idea?" Jackie responded.

"It's all over town. Everyone's talking about your possible involvement in Watergate, and some new RICO investigation."

"What in hell are you talking about? What have you heard?"

"I've heard plenty. Everyone has been talking about Jimmy Hoffa's death, and there are rumors floating around that someone other than the FBI may be called in to get to the bottom of it. Well you were so overjoyed about his disappearance, they may be wondering if you could shed any light on it."

"If anyone asks you any questions, you're to keep your trap shut. We didn't have anything to do with that, but if you start running off at the mouth, some people may get the wrong impression."

"Yeah. And I suppose they'll get the wrong impression about The Front Row Theatre and the money from Las Vegas that you've been laundering."

"I see what this is all about. You want to shake me down. Okay, how much?" Jackie reached into his pocket and withdrew a wad of hundred dollar bills. "Here you little bitch," Jackie tossed a small stack of hundred dollar bills on his desk. "It's bad enough I can't get any sleep at night and now my own daughter is holding me up."

Bari Lynn recorded in her journal that night that there were tears in Jackie's eyes when she left. He didn't know how to say good-bye to her. It was obvious from their conversation that Big Bill had talked to Jackie about these delicate subjects, and now Jackie was confronting an emotional dilemma.

◆

"Jackie, I think we might have our first big break in getting Danny Greene off the street," Maishe stated.

"Are you saying what I hope you mean?" Jackie replied.

"Your daughter, Bari Lynn?"

"What does she have to do with this?" Jackie asked.

"Doesn't she take physical therapy over at the Brainard Office Building?"

"Yeah, I think that's where she goes. You want me to tell her to stay away from there for any reason?"

"It might be a good idea for her to avoid that place during the first week of October," Maishe suggested.

"Okay. Now, mind telling me what this is about?" Jackie inquired.

"Liberatore came up with an excellent idea. Remember when you mentioned to me about Greene not using the same telephone to make two calls?"

"Yeah, I seem to remember saying something about that. John Joyce told me about it when I told him to tail Greene. So what's the plan?"

"One of the guys installed a tap on a phone Greene regularly uses. Even though he was clever enough not to reveal his itinerary, we intercepted a message Greene left with a receptionist that he needed to schedule an afternoon appointment to see his dentist. We'll have someone there to greet him when he shows up."

On the afternoon of October 4$^{th}$, a previously parked maroon Chevy Nova was started and re-parked next to a green Continental. Forty-five minutes passed before Danny Greene emerged from the office building and proceeded to his vehicle. He eyed the lot to see if anyone might be watching him. Standing with his back to the inconspicuous Nova, he inserted his key to unlock his driver's door. Raymond Ferrito decided that this would be his best opportunity to throw the switch ...

*Boom!* The explosion was heard for miles. Danny J. Greene's close proximity to the point of detonation caused his limbs and head to be torn from his body. Unlike his compatriot John Nardi, he would have no last words.

*Chapter 10*

## The Pendorf Files

JIMMY CARTER's second year in office raised serious questions as to what role the FBI should play in national politics. There were obvious philosophical differences that had been raised even before the Carter administration took office. For some, the Bureau's dubious track record and covert mission appeared cloudy.

Publicly, the Bureau had proclaimed that anything involving organized crime within the labor movement fell under its exclusive federal jurisdiction. But with murders and bombings among warring factions of the underworld running at a 30-year high, it was equally obvious that the Bureau had allowed such questionable elements to get out of control. The quick-fix solution: Control the media by leaking false cover stories.

For some of the President's domestic policy advisers, it appeared as if rank-and-file special agents with FBI had their own agenda, quite apart from any national interests and policies. Since the 1920s, the Treasury Department had been closely monitoring the activities of organized crime. Over the years, Treasury agents had compiled a comprehensive profile of key individuals, which was published in the Treasury's Blue Book Series. This information, however, drastically differed with the version and information the FBI was furnishing Congressional and White House officials. Both versions of organized crime appeared valid and convincing, but because each was based upon opposing pieces of information, only one of those versions was accurate.

To demonstrate to the Carter administration that the FBI's version was the correct rendition over the one being presented by U.S. Treasury agents, it would be necessary for the Bureau to launch a major investigation and prove the Bureau's scenario. At stake was the justification of the FBI's massive secret budget, some of which was being paid to underworld crime figures for information. That budget had come up for review.

◆

Mafia don John Licavoli ordered Maishe Rockman to inform Jackie Presser that John Nardi's son was to be removed from the Teamsters' ghost employee payroll. For the past eight years, dating back to when Special Agent Martin McCoy first suggested that Jackie "get close" to Nardi, Jackie's private secretary Gail George had been mailing Nardi's oldest son a $300 weekly paycheck. Now that Anthony Liberatore had supervised the successful elimination of the country's most dangerous crime consortium, the Mafia don felt that Nardi's son should pay for the sins of the father.

To reward Raymond Ferrito for his successful efforts in eliminating the threat that had plagued both the Mafia and the Syndicate, he was given full Mafia membership. Greene's assassination, however, created new problems for law enforcement agencies, as well as new opportunities for capturing the available drug-trade business. The North Coast Dirty Dozen, a branch of Hell's Angeles, moved in to cover the void, and within the next 36 months, 19 more deaths would follow.

No one knew when the killings would stop, least of all Jackie's daughter. Bari Lynn's journal entry reflected her tension, as well as the suspicion that Jackie was taking out his frustrations with Carmen and the Carter administration on her. She felt that perhaps her father was hoping that he could get to Carmen through her. Jackie had cut off Bari Lynn's income just as easily as he had Nardi's son, and she was down to her last twenty dollars.

With pressure mounting at home, criminal investigations into his background turning up everywhere, access to the Carter administration non-existent, and rumors about a new hit contract on his own life being let; Jackie felt the need to leave town until things settled down.

He pressed the intercom. "Gail, contact Inn The Woods Travel Agent. And while you're at it, send in my private bookkeeper."

Moments later Cynthia Ann gently knocked twice before stepping in. "Yes, Mister Presser, you wanted to see me?"

"It's Jackie, to you. Forget that Mister Presser crap."

"Yes Jackie." Cynthia Ann glanced across the office in Tony's direction.

"Listen, the reason I called you in was to see if you're available."

"I'm not sure I know what you mean," Cynthia Ann responded.

"Are you available to make a trip? Before you say 'no' let me tell you where we're going. —Vegas. Are you interested?"

"It's awfully short notice. When were you planning to leave?" Cynthia Ann inquired.

"My plans are for us to leave as soon as possible, and that includes you too Tony." Turning back to Cynthia Ann, "So how soon can you be ready?"

"I suppose it would depend upon finding someone to watch over my two children. May I ask what this is all about?"

"Strictly business. I'm going to inspect some prime real estate held by the union in downtown Vegas."

"Who will be going?" Cynthia Ann asked.

"What difference does that make?"

"Hey Jackie, women gotta know what to take," Tony suggested.

"Oh. Well I'm not taking Carmen, if that's what you mean."

"I'll have to give it some thought," Cynthia Ann replied.

"What the hell is there to think about? Gail's coming, my attorney is going, as well as my two kids. There might even be one or two others. So, are you in or out? I got to know now. Gail is making the arrangements. You better tell her one way or the other." Jackie turned his attention to Tony to signal Cynthia Ann the meeting was over, and she quietly left.

"You got balls, I'll say that much for you," Tony stated.

"What do you mean?" Jackie asked.

"Leaving for Vegas with another woman right when all this stuff is going down."

"Like I said, it's strictly business," Jackie responded.

"Sounds more like monkey business if you ask me," Tony injected.

"When I want your advice I'll ask for it."

"Hey, I was just thinking of your interest. You still have to be careful that Carmen doesn't take the notion to stick you in your sleep. Just keep in mind, I can't watch you every minute of the day and night."

"That's what makes my life so exciting. I never know from one minute to the next when I'll get it."

"You're crazy, you know that."

"Listen, Carmen is the least of my worries." Jackie was back on the intercom to Gail, "Hey sweet lips, did you get in touch with the travel agency?"

"Yes Jackie. Have you decided how many are going yet?" she inquired.

"That depends. Let's see, there's me, you, John, Tony, the two kids and Duke Zeller. Did Cynthia tell you she was coming with us?"

"Yes Jackie. That makes eight," Gail calculated.

"Oh, one more thing. I want me, you and Cynthia Ann to have adjoining rooms."

"Of course," Gail automatically responded.

Once Jackie was off the intercom Tony asked, "You think you should pick up some extra muscle in case you can't handle two at once?"

"Naw, I can always watch."

"You can't be going all the way to Vegas just for recreation. What's really going down?" Tony inquired.

"I thought I might kill a couple birds at one time. I'm going to have a talk with Duke Zeller, and set him straight about a few things."

"Oh? You having problems with the Hoover-Gorvin agency?" Tony asked.

"No and I want it to stay that way. He's got to keep his mouth shut about how I'm laundering campaign money."

"I thought John Mitchell covered that up for you before he left office."

"He did, but now a couple of bastards are looking into it again," Jackie responded.

"Who? What are they hoping to find?" Tony asked.

"Keep this under your hat. I've been tipped off by Rotatori that Carter has formed some secret strike force for the purpose of looking into my business dealings. They're even going to be looking into Uncle Allen's affairs. Christ, they start looking into his stuff, there's no telling what they might turn up."

"Such as?"

"Such as the second half-million in cash to Nixon."

"I see. Well with John Mitchell gone, you've got to be extra careful. You don't need another Watergate investigation."

"You got that right. These special investigators may start asking questions about the Hoover-Gorvin agency. That's why I have to warn Zeller to keep his trap shut," Jackie revealed.

"You don't need to take your attorney along to do that. You must have something else in mind," Tony ventured.

"Another reason for going to Vegas is to have a sit-down with Senator Howard Cannon. He wants me to do him a little favor involving some land deal."

"And what do you want in return?" Tony asked.

"I want him to fix Jimmy Carter and Ted Kennedy's wagon real good. We've got to get those two out of office."

"You still pissed over the Master Freight Agreement?" Tony inquired.

"Like my ol' man says, better to get even than get mad."

"How do you plan to do that?"

"We have to get our man into the White House. While I'm there in Vegas, I'm going to ask Cannon if he's got any good ideas on who he thinks the Teamster Executive Board should endorse. Maybe we can discretely pump a little cash into someone's primaries."

"Any ideas?" Tony probed.

"I'm telling you Tony, I think my ol' man's got rocks in his heads," Jackie mused.

"How's that?" Tony asked.

"He thinks we should make an all-out effort to support Ronnie Reagan. I'll suggest it to the Executive Board, but first, I'll have to check out this actor. You know, see if Reagan's willing to play ball on my terms."

"How are you planning to do that?" Tony queried.

"Cannon can do that for me. If this actor wants to play king-of-the-mountain, the guy better know my terms. What I say goes, and that's that."

"I hear Senator Cannon might be tight with Allen Dorfman. He may want the Teamsters to support someone else," Tony speculated.

"That's what I'm concerned about. I can't have Dorfman and his Chicago crowd running the show. There's got to be some way I can get the feebees to put more heat on that guy."

"You sure that's such a good idea? You start messing with Dorfman and he could cause you a heap of serious trouble," Tony advised.

"That all depends on the way you look at it. Suppose Dorfman was out of the picture?"

"I guess you'd have a lot less problems with the Pension Fund," Tony concluded.

"Right. More importantly, he wouldn't be sticking his nose in and competing with me for presidential favors."

♦

At the Las Vegas meeting with Senator Cannon, the strategy was simple: Get on the bandwagon early and make a serious financial campaign commitment. The time to stand up and be counted was before the battle was won—not after the votes were tallied.

"So we'll be making a decision on who the Executive Board should endorse. Now don't laugh, but my ol' man seems to think Ronnie Reagan can be gotten to."

"That may not be a bad selection," Senator Cannon responded. "Keep in mind he projects the right media image."

"Yeah, but are you sure the folks down on the farm are going to go for his anti-Communist theme," Jackie inquired.

"The voters eat that stuff up," Senator Cannon stated.

"Yeah, I know. I've used it myself," Jackie reflected. "I just hope he isn't serious about the anti-big government idea."

"You have to tell the voters what they want to hear or you're dead in the water."

"Is there any way you can check this movie actor out to see if he's willing to play ball with us? If so, I can put my money where my mouth is during the primaries."

"That's the name of the game. Money certainly talks."

"Tell me Senator, how well to you know Allen Dorfman?"

"Mister Dorfman and I go back a long way. I knew his father, Red Dorfman, very well back in the late 40s. That's when I met your father and Mister Luciano. Together, we put Las Vegas on the map. I've always valued our friendship. Why do you ask?"

"Nothing in particular. It's just that now that I have my ol' man's seat on the Central States Pension Fund, we'll have to start working a little closer, that's all."

"Well you can count on my support just like your father did."

◆

Upon Jackie's return from Las Vegas, he found his calendar filled with union-related engagements, and he used this as the perfect excuse for avoiding his weekly Big Brother meetings. By early June, he was unable to put Special Agent Patrick Foran on hold any longer.

Unlike his former FBI handler, Martin McCoy, he took his work far more seriously. Whereas McCoy knew how and when to bend the rules, Foran honestly believed in the Bureau's mission, even though that mission had become blurred from time to time. He still felt he could make a difference and valuable contribution.

The two secretly met just before the June meeting of Joint Council 41 to discuss the situation, and put things back on course.

"Look Jackie, it's a whole new ball game, and I for one, don't think you're getting with the program."

"I don't know what you're talking about. I've kept you guys abreast of everything." Jackie blew his smoke in Foran's direction.

Waving off the smoke, "Why do I get the impression that every time we meet, we both have totally different agendas?"

"Like I said, I don't know what you're talking about," Jackie responded.

"The stuff you've been blowing at us is borderline superficial. We need far more detailed information. If you can't or won't provide us with what we need, I think it's time we terminate our relationship."

Jackie sat a moment collecting his thoughts. "Why all the heat?"

"I just told you, it's a whole new ball game."

"Rotatori tells me that my Uncle Allen and me are going to be watched by some newly formed organized crime strike force. I'm suppose to be on your side, remember. All I ever seem to get is one piece of static after another. I got other problems to deal with. It was never this way with me and Marty. So tell me, what gives? —Huh?" Jackie pulled a deep drag on his cigarette.

"Let me clear up some of the smoke. The current administration is taking a dim view of your extraordinary criminal activities."

"You mean the Carter administration. I think we ought to be calling a spade a spade," Jackie inserted.

"Put it anyway you want, but that's not the issue. The Carter administration is not pleased with your ongoing criminal escapades with the Syndicate and Mafia."

"J. Edgar Hoover approved the whole deal," Jackie remind him. "McCoy told me the new FBI director would be informed of my special privileges, but I guess you guys don't communicate among yourselves so good."

"Nonetheless, the administration is of the opinion that you should be prosecuted, not protected," Foran concluded.

"I knew I should have had something in writing," Jackie retorted.

"I don't know how Robert Rotatori found out about the Strike Force's investigation, but he's correct."

"How come you didn't tell me? Huh?" Jackie demanded.

"It just came down. The Carter administration didn't consult us on the decision."

"Great!" Jackie smirked. "So what the hell is this all about anyway?"

"The administration secretly set up this special unit called the Presidential Commission On Organized Crime Strike Force. It was so secret, they didn't even tell us about it."

"That makes me feel a whole lot better," Jackie said facetiously. "What the hell's going on? What are they looking into?"

"Apparently the administration wasn't satisfied with our investigation into Hoffa's disappearance. We pointed out that the Treasury boys didn't do any better then we did, but that still didn't satisfy Carter's people."

"So what does that have to do with Jackie Presser?"

"That's what has us more than a little concerned. Instead of setting up operations in Detroit, they came here looking for answers."

"Why here?"

"That's the sixty-four thousand dollar question. Fortunately, at the moment there are only two undercover agents running it, plus a third guy handling the legal paperwork. They're in town right now looking into your affairs, starting with your Front Row Theatre project."

"That's off limits. McCoy promised me the Bureau would protect me if I cooperated, so you have to throw up some road blocks. Besides, my Front Row deal had nothing to do with Hoffa."

"As far as we're concerned, they're on a wild-goose chase. We might be able to slow them down, but their investigation will probably lead them to Vegas, searching for answers, information and evidence as to Hoffa's disappearance."

"Oh really? And how would it look to Washington if everyone found out that the Bureau had been authorizing my so-called criminal activities? Huh? What about that?"

"Let's not get off the subject," Foran insisted.

"Like it or not, the way I see it, we're stuck with each other. So we're just going to have to make the best of it, ain't we?" Jackie turned to gaze out the window.

"Don't push your luck. You've received more money and gotten away with more shit than any informant in U.S. history, and we've got to get something in return." Agent Foran was not budging an inch.

"You want insider's knowledge on things, and all I get in return is this shit. John and I worked our asses off to negotiate the Master Freight Agreement, and now I hear that prick in the White House is going to void the whole thing. You have any fucking idea how much money that's going to cost me? Well I'll tell you! Plenty. More money than you'll see in your whole damn life!" Jackie picked up his ashtray and flung it across the room.

"Feel better?"

"This shit ain't going nowhere. I getting the hell out of here before I do something one of us might regret."

"That approach isn't going to work with me. I think you have the wrong set of priorities, and you better start getting some of them straight," Foran warned.

"Listen, I told you the last time we talked that Roy Williams is on the take. You have any idea the enormous kickbacks he's receiving? You guys were supposed to be investigating him, and now I find out that you're spending all your time worrying about the Master Freight Agreement. What the hell's going on?"

"So who is Roy Williams getting kickbacks from?"

"Who do you think—Dorfman out of Chicago."

"We know where Mister Dorfman resides. Our Chicago office keeps a pretty close watch on him."

"Yeah, but Dorfman's shrewd. I told you guys before, Dorfman is running everything now that Hoffa's history. He knows how to cover his tracks legally," Jackie noted.

"I'm sure Dorfman's attorneys are every bit as good as the one you've got."

"Leave my attorney out of this," Jackie fired back.

"Listen, if you don't start putting some solid answers on the table, maybe you should start bringing him with you."

"If you promise me you'll tag Roy Williams for me, I'll tell you how to nail his ass good," Jackie offered.

"We're not going to serve as your personal hit squad. My job is to gather information and report our findings. What Washington does with that information is not my concern."

"If that's all you're gonna do is file some report, we can skip the whole matter and move on to something else."

"I can't make such promises," Foran responded.

"Hey baby, that's the way it has to be. I do something for you, you have to do something for me."

"If you've got something solid, you have my word the Bureau will move on the information."

"Now we're making some progress here. Okay, here's the deal. Williams is scheduled to have a secret meeting with Dorfman in a place called La Costa," Jackie revealed.

"What's La Costa?"

"It's a resort out in southern California. Their meeting will probably have something to do with the McCormick Inn."

"The one in Chicago?"

"Right. The McCormick Inn by the way is Dorfman's base of operations."

"Hmm. I wonder if our Chicago office knows this," Foran reflected.

"I kind of doubt it. Dorfman's a lot smarter than you think."

"I'll telex Chicago and suggest they put a tail on him," Foran said.

"Bad idea. Like I said, Dorfman's smarter than you think. I suggest you do whatever you have to do to bug those two places," Jackie suggested.

"That's not as easy as you might think. If we plan on using any of the information in court, we'll have to get a federal judge's authorization, and sometimes it's better to avoid that."

"Do whatever you have to, but if you follow my advice, I guarantee you'll tap yourselves into a mother load of information."

◆

Jackie's tip on the La Costa meeting proved to be an invaluable piece of information. Although the initial intent was to capture Roy Williams accepting a kickback from Allen Dorfman, the FBI managed to intercept and record a telephone conversation between Senator Howard Cannon and Allen Dorfman. To the Bureau's surprise, it was discovered that Jackie and the Teamsters' Executive Board were planning to bankroll Ronald Reagan's campaign for the White House.

The fortuitous interception of that single telephone conversation between Senator Cannon and Allen Dorfman revealed a labyrinth of powerful and influential individuals stretching across the industrial midwest to the west coast and back to DC. As a result, Agent Foran set up another meeting with Jackie to focus on that issue. To avoid a confrontation, Foran would avoid mentioning anything the Bureau had discovered about Jackie's political influence peddling.

"I want to thank you Jackie for that tip on Roy Williams. There seems to be a lot more people involved in this than the Bureau initially anticipated. I want you to know that there is the distinct possibility that we may have to pull in some additional agents on this."

"So you're going to get Williams for me?" Jackie asked.

"We've assigned the project a code name, so I think it's fair to say we're moving in that direction."

"What code name is that?" Jackie asked.

"We're calling it the *Pendorf* operation."

"Ah, short for pen-it-on the Dorfman crowd. I like that," Jackie mused.

"Actually, it's short for penetrate Dorfman, but you're nomenclature works just as well. This could very well turn into one of the Bureau's most massive operation since the Lindbergh Kidnapping case," Foran revealed.

"It don't make any difference what you call it as long as you nail Williams before the next Teamster election."

"Let's not get into that right now. I have a bunch of names here to run past you. If you know any of them, just fill us in on any details."

"Yeah-sure. So who you got?" Jackie continued.

"One guy is Don Peters."

"Yeah."

"Another one is a guy by the name of Sidney Korshak."

"Yeah."

"And what about some other guy by the name of Bramlett?" Any of these individuals ring a bell?" Foran asked.

"Ooh, this is good. No, this is great!" Jackie responded.

"Then you know them?"

"After all these years, you guys are finally plugging into what's happening."

"Look, stop horsing around. Just tell me what you know. Who are they?" Foran prodded.

"Now we can start doing some serious stuff. Okay, let me outline it for you so that you have a more complete picture." Jackie walked across the room to pick up the ashtray and lit another cigarette. He stood holding the ashtray and smoking while he continued, "About ten years ago, Don Peters set up a deal through the Central States Pension Fund. The loan was supposed to allow Dorfman and Korshak to purchase a secret ownership in the McCormick Inn."

"Are you sure about this?"

"Yeah, I'm sure. Both my attorney and Nixon told me that the whole thing was done in violation of this Taft-Hartley Act."

"So Nixon knew about the deal?" Foran inquired.

"I think we might have discussed it over a golf game or two. Anyway, the way I figure it, Nixon ought to know, 'cause he's the one who worked on writing that Act. Right?"

"I understand you know the ex-President personally." It was a casual inquiry and Agent Foran hoped it would not take Jackie too far off the subject.

"Yeah. Dick and me are tight. We're scheduled to have a golf game the next time I get to La Costa. What's the big deal?"

"That's where Frank Sinatra lives, isn't it?"

"Frankie lives in Rancho Mirage, but that's close, so he sometimes joins us."

"Your attorney Climaco, does he usually join you?" Foran inquired.

"I've made a few introductions. So what? That ain't got anything to do with you guys nailing Williams."

"Fine. Let's drop it."

"Where was I?"

"Climaco and Nixon told you the McCormick deal violated the Taft-Hartley Act," Agent Foran reminded him.

"Yeah. Well anyway, since that loan was made, Dorfman has practically controlled the pension fund moneys from various Teamster locals."

"How's that?"

"It all has to do with Dorfman writing overpriced insurance policies, and collecting huge profits. Those profits come from my union members, and this is nothing but a bunch of crap."

"I see."

"Like hell you do. If you'd have known about this stuff, you'd have been asking for more details years ago. Like I said, this stuff's been going on right under your noses for at least ten years."

"You made your point. Now, what about the profits?" Foran asked.

"Okay, the profits are then channeled back through the Dunes Hotel in Vegas, and split up by Korshak, Bramlett and Dorfman. But keep this in mind ... Dorfman don't trust Bramlett."

Agent Foran continued to write down the information as fast as possible, "Let me catch-up here. ... You said that Dorfman doesn't trust Bramlett. Why's that?"

"You college boys think you're so smart. You can't put anything together," Jackie added smugly.

"You've made your point ..."

"Dorfman doesn't think Bramlett can take any heat."

"From us?"

"Hell-no. None of those guys are worried about the FBI ... it's the Treasury boys and the Department of Labor's Inspector General's office they're worried about."

"Hmm? I think I see what you're driving at," Foran concluded.

"Well let me tell you something you don't see and couldn't figure out in a million years. The back-room talk is that Dorfman has asked Nick Civella, the boss of the Kansas City family to have a couple of his men take Bramlett out of the picture."

"Just to keep him from talking to the Treasury," Foran clarified.

"Yeah. So what's the trade-off?" Foran nodded as Jackie continued, "In return for Nick's efforts, Dorfman will look after Nick's financial interest."

Leaning forward, Foran inquired, "Which are?"

"You don't know?"

"Come-on Jackie, if we knew I wouldn't be asking."

"Yeah, well the next time you start threatening me about canceling my special privileges, you just keep that in mind. You can't pull this off without Jackie Presser.

What I've known for all these years, you and ten thousand agents haven't been able to uncover."

"You always seem to have an interesting viewpoint," Foran responded.

"Damn-right."

"Now don't go flying off the handle on this, but if this 'stuff' as you call it has been going on for ten years, why is it that none of this information ever appeared in Agent McCoy's field reports?" Foran inquired.

"I'll tell you why. It's because all you guys were always looking for the Hoffa connection. The real power guys like Dorfman in the Syndicate and Civella in the Mafia have been laughing their asses off, watching you guys chase your tails. Hey, now don't go flying off the handle just because you got a little pig shit on your face," Jackie retorted.

Agent Foran knew that Jackie was right, however this was not the time to play hardball. He needed Jackie's information, and if it meant eating a little crow for the moment, so be it. "You can save us a lot of time on this. Maybe the present administration is completely wrong about you. But listen, I can set the record straight. You know, show them the error of their ways."

"Now you're talking my kind of lingo," Jackie said. "I was beginning to feel like Rodney Dangerfield. Okay, now that we're going set the record straight, what were we talking about?"

"Nick Civella's financial interests."

"Right. Okay, let's see ... he's got a piece of the Dunes Hotel, the Stardust and that Spanish joint."

"The Hacienda?"

"Yeah, that's the one, the Hacienda. Listen, I got to be going. Is there anything more you have to know about? If so, make it quick. I got things to do."

"No, Mister Presser, I think that will keep us busy."

Tony was waiting for Jackie as he left the hotel room, "How did it go Jackie?"

"Better. It's about time those bastards started showing me more respect."

"I take it Foran has stopped calling you 'fat boy,'" Tony remarked.

"Yeah. He's calling me Mister Presser."

"Oh? You must have given him some pretty good information? You better be careful you don't start saying too much. What did you two talk about?"

"Damn, I just realized I shot my mouth off about Nick Civella."

"*Aah Jackie*, you shouldn't have done that. If Civella starts catching heat, he'll have his wiseguys whack a couple dozen guys just to plug up leaks."

"Yeah, you're right. Maybe mentioning Civella's name was a mistake."

"You better hope like hell none of that shit gets traced back to you. If he takes the notion to have you whacked, I might not be able to protect you."

"Damn-it Tony, I let my guard down just once, and see what happens."

"What the hell happened?" Tony asked. "How could you let something like that slip out?"

"All I wanted Foran to do was to have the Bureau go after Williams and Dorfman. That's all he had to do."

"I see. Foran couldn't figure out what was happening, so you had to show him up. I'll bet you rubbed his face in it, didn't you?"

"Something like that," Jackie responded. "Why did I have to mention the others?"

Suddenly Tony stopped the car, "You didn't say anything about the Genovese family or anyone from the New York Commission, did you?"

"Oh God no. I ain't that stupid for Christ sake."

◆

Their next secret meeting fell back into a familiar routine, one in which Jackie felt it would be safer to say as little as possible, but appear to be fully cooperating with the Bureau.

"Let me begin by telling you Mister Presser, you've grown twelve notches with the Bureau."

"That's nice. I was beginning to have my doubts."

"My last field report has put the Pendorf operation into full swing, and we've got you to thank for it." Agent Foran was hoping to maintain an air of mutual cooperation.

"Yeah, well I'm real glad for you. Now maybe we can get something done. Has there been any progress on nailing Roy Williams?"

"To be perfectly candid with you, Williams is only going to be a secondary target."

"Ah-shit. I knew something like this would happen. I just knew the moment you started asking about the others you'd get sidetracked."

"Now before you get worked up over this, let me finish. The Bureau will probably take Williams down when we get Dorfman's group."

"Yeah-sure. I'm happy for you."

"That Nick Civella tie-in, however, was a real eye opener. With that, we're going to be able to tie-in all of them. I think where we want to focus our attention is on any local ties between organized crime and Civella's people."

"This is not good ... not good at all."

"What do you mean?"

"Are you sure you're going in the right direction on this? I keep telling you, nail Roy Williams and you'll wind up with the whole enchilada. He's the one you have to get, damn-it. What do I have to do to get through to you. You're going off on some wild tangent."

"My mission is to find a local connection. Who do you know inside the local crime family that might be tied in with Civella's group?"

"Give me a moment. I'll have to sort a few things out. Civella is dangerous."

"What about Anthony Liberatore?"

"He's becoming a pain in the ass, that's for sure." Jackie began to ramble, "I wouldn't mind seeing him get sent up the river. ... I'm still pissed about that Harry Haler fiasco. ... In fact, I'd love to see a bug up his ass."

"Mister Presser? Is Liberatore connected with either the Chicago or Kansas City crime families?

"No, not directly, at least not that I'm aware of."

"What about 'Babe' Triscaro? Would he have any direct contact?"

"Absolutely not."

"Okay, what about a guy by the name of Milton Rockman?"

"Maishe! Now wait a minute! You've got to leave certain people alone, Babe's one of them and Maishe is the other."

"Oh? What's the deal with Babe Triscaro and Maishe Rockman?"

"Look, I've got someone better, and it's a good one too. You check it out and I guarantee you'll find the connection you're looking for."

"What's his name?"

"Skippy Felice. He's president of Local 293, the Teamsters' Beverage Drivers. He also serves on the Joint Council."

"Very good."

"There's only one small problem. You'll have to cover me good on this one," Jackie insisted.

"Oh? What's the deal?"

"Listen, because of Skippy's position on the Joint Council, the others might start getting suspicious. Besides, all them other names you mentioned are nothing more than a long list of bad options. You'd just be wasting your time."

"No problem, Mister Presser."

"No problem, Mister Presser, no problem. All I got are problems from one end to the other. If it ain't my wife Carmen, it's Uncle Allen. If it ain't Uncle Allen, it's one of my kids getting into trouble. And if it's not my kids, it's some asshole like Skippy trying to whack me. One word from Skippy to the don, and my ass will be sitting on the bottom of the lake. ... So, you think you'll be able to cover me?" Jackie asked.

"We'll do our best."

"No, damn-it, you have to do better than that. Can I count on you or not?"

"What specifically do you have in mind?" Foran asked.

"I got your answer. What you're telling me is that I better not hold my breath on this, so I better be prepared to take matters into my own hands."

"I told you we'll do our best. What more can I say?" Foran responded.

"I'll just casually mention during the meeting that I heard some rumors that the feds were going to begin targeting some individuals on the Joint Council. That way I can always say, 'Hey! I'm the one who warned you guys.' Yeah, that'll work. If they really press me on details, I can always say I heard it from Leftowitz or Climaco. After all, they got contacts inside the Attorney General's Office. Them guys will buy that."

◆

For the FBI, Jackie was finally coming of age. In the last seven years dating back to 1970, the *Tailor Files* were little more than a thin folder of odds and ends, pared with spotty rumors and false leads—especially if it involved the Genovese crime family or Jimmy Hoffa. Overnight, as *Alpro*, Jackie had turned into a treasure chest of information, and with so many FBI agents following up on his leads, it was impossible to keep everything secret.

One well-concealed secret the Bureau was able to maintain involved the trucking deregulation bill before the Senate Judiciary Committee. With Senator Edward Kennedy serving on the Committee, the Bureau saw no value in sharing its information with that Committee.

While the Senator from Massachusetts was working with the Carter administration to develop and introduce the bill, Senator Howard Cannon was working equally as hard to defeat it.

Allen Dorfman had instructed Senator Cannon to kill the bill before it went any further. Senator Cannon's suggestion was to put it in committee where it would die a natural death until the next congressional season. It was a small favor, and one Senator Cannon was happy and willing to perform, seeing as how trucking was not a big issue in his home state of Nevada.

◆

Dorfman's decision to have the trucking deregulation bill killed caught Jackie in political crossfire. In a meeting with his attorney, he looked for some way out of the quagmire that had been created.

"You're blowing this whole thing out of proportion." John could ill afford to have his celebrity client creating problems where few existed.

"Easy for you to say. Your ass isn't the one on the line. I'm on record for having supported the bill, and now Dorfman and Cannon are pulling this shit on me."

"If you want to take five seconds and listen, I'll show you how to get out from under," John responded. John's strongest asset was advising him on where to stand politically, and this was one of those issues.

"What's your idea?" Jackie inquired.

"My suggestion is that you tell Dorfman what he wants to hear. Tell him you're behind him one hundred percent. In other words, you simply tell each side what they want to hear. It's that simple. Now stop losing sleep over this."

"Not a bad idea. I just tell Dorfman what he wants to hear. Why didn't I think of that? ... I know why I didn't think of it ... I've been thinking too much about Williams and Fitz. The more I think about it, the more I've come to realize that both Williams and Fitzsimmons are becoming a real liability for us."

"You should do something about that. There has to be some way you can mend that broken fence. If you don't get them on your side, you'll never get enough support to make a bid for the presidency of the International. As far as I see, that's a bigger problem than Dorfman at the moment."

"I have an idea. I think I can kill two of them birds with one stone."

"What's your idea?"

"Suppose I was to tell Fitz that Dorfman was going to have him whacked," Jackie posed.

"That's an interesting idea. Coming from you, he'd believe that. Dorfman has to be pretty hot under the collar about Fitzsimmons' decision to cancel his insurance contract," John concluded.

"Yeah, and Fitz would be scared shitless!" Jackie mused.

"But he'd be grateful as hell you warned him. He might even feel he owed you one. In fact, they would both owe you. Fitzsimmons will owe you for saving his life, and whether or not Dorfman gets his insurance contract back, you can always say you were the one pushing for him," John advised.

"Right. Now here's the good part. I leak this stuff to the feds, and Dorfman's got more heat than he can handle. ... Did I mention that this Pendorf operation the

Bureau is working on is going be the biggest sting operation in history?"

"You told me," John reminded him. "Why don't you call Fitzsimmons now and get the ball rolling?"

Jackie's call to Frank Fitzsimmons informing him about Dorfman's plans to have him hit resulted in Fitzsimmons making a 180 degree about-face. With Jackie's enthusiastic support, Dorfman was awarded a no-bid, three-year insurance contact to cover the Central States Pension Fund.

◆

In appreciation for that support, the least Dorfman could do was to have Maishe Rockman deliver a personal message. "I can't begin to tell you Jackie, what this means to the organization."

"We all got to do our part, Maishe."

"I don't know what you did, or how you managed to get Fitz to change his mind, but whatever you said on Mister Dorfman's behalf has made life a whole lot easier."

"What are friends for?"

"He wanted me to personally relay his appreciation to you."

"The way I see it Maishe, we're all in *this thing of ours* together. I look out for his interests, and he'll look out for mine. Right?"

"You've got the right attitude, Jackie." Maishe turned to being reflective, "I remember when Big Bill retired. Some of the boys weren't really sure you could handle the job, but I have to hand it to you ... you've come a long way, and you're doing one hell of a fine job.

By the way, speaking of your father, how is Big Bill doing?"

"Not so good. He gets tired easily. You know the ol' man, he's not one to complain, but I think he's in a lot of pain. He's been going in for check-ups every few months now, so he's not in too good of shape. So ... is that about it?"

"Well, there is one other little matter Mister Dorfman wanted me to mention. There's a little parcel of land that's being held by the Teamsters in trust."

Jackie leaned forward, "Which little parcel of land are we talking about?"

"About 5.8 acres in Nevada," Maishe revealed.

"You're not talking about the same 5.8 acres of prime real estate in Vegas by any chance?" Jackie knew that Maishe was leading up to something. *I'll bet Dorfman is going to snatch that land for himself.*

"As a matter of fact, I believe we may be talking about the same piece of property. The point is, it's going nowhere, lying vacant and totally unproductive. You're merely paying taxes on it, and getting nothing in return."

"What's Mister Dorfman's offer? You have to understand, it wouldn't be my decision alone, but I can certainly present a reasonable offer to the Board on his behalf."

"That's not exactly what Mister Dorfman had in mind. He wants the Teamsters to transfer their ownership to Senator Howard Cannon so that it can be privately, as well as productively developed."

"My attorney has already explored that possibility. He told me that as long as its held by the pension fund, it can't be developed for private use. John's very familiar with them federal laws. So what are we suggesting here? We transfer the property into the good Senator's name, he uses his influence with the Gaming Commission to develop it for recreational purposes?"

"I have to say Jackie, you've got your act together on this."

"I guess that only leaves one remaining issue. What's in it for Jackie?"

"I'm sure we can work something out. Something reasonable, of course. Do you have anything in mind?" Maishe inquired.

Jackie paused, pretending to ponder the situation, but he was three-steps ahead. He and John had already decided what they wanted, and yes, it was reasonable. "Tell you what... You set up a sit-down between me and the good Senator Cannon. Tell him to bring his legal mouthpiece."

"Consider it done. Just assure me that you'll be reasonable."

"Should I take a blood oath? You have my word, I'll be reasonable."

"That's all we ask. That's all we have ever asked of you Jackie. Listen, say 'hello' to Big Bill for me, will you?"

Jackie started to pick up the phone to call his attorney as Maishe left, but was interrupted as Tony entered the office.

"Everything go okay, Jackie?"

"Everything is going great."

"What did Maishe want to see you about?" Tony inquired.

"He wanted me to be reasonable. Damn straight I'm reasonable. In fact, I can be down right reasonable when I have my own way."

"You've always been that way."

"I feel good enough to celebrate."

"What do you have in mind?"

"I think I'll have Gail break out some of Rubin's new porno flicks and set us up a little office orgy."

On January 10th, 1979, a meeting was set up in Senator Cannon's office. While Jackie met with the Senator, John Climaco and the Senator's attorney met in the outer office to work out the details for transferring the Las Vegas property. The unwritten terms of the agreement included a promise from the Senator that he would secretly tie up the deregulation of the trucking industry in his Commerce Committee.

Ten days later, and before Senator Kennedy was scheduled to introduce his deregulation bill, President Jimmy Carter met with his domestic policy adviser, Stuart E. Eizenstate. Eizenstate informed the President that the administration should openly support the bill Senator Kennedy would be proposing. The domestic policy adviser had been ill-informed by the FBI about Jackie's hidden agenda, and in turn, he informed the President that the Teamsters would not oppose the bill with any measure of vigor or interest.

As part of the Pendorf operation, the FBI had documented the Dorfman-Cannon meetings, as well as the deal that had been struck between Jackie and the Senator. The Bureau made a judgment call and decided it would not be in the national interest to share its information with the President or any of his allies in the U.S. Senate.

Within two days of Senator Kennedy's introduction of the deregulation bill, Senator Cannon delivered on his promise. He put the bill into the Commerce Committee, where it died.

The following week, January 29th, the Pendorf operation had officially grown into the largest single legal wiretapping and surveillance operation in U.S. history. Thirteen separate wiretaps were installed on Dorfman's insurance offices located in the western suburbs of Chicago.

Jackie and his attorney were unaware of how much the FBI had obtained during its surveillance operation, not only on their individual operations, but on their intentions to finance and install their own man in the White House. Such power meant that Jackie would then be able to have the one thing he wanted more than anything else—to be a respected member of the overworld.

*Chapter 11*

## The Alpro Connection

THE CLOSER the Carter administration looked into what the FBI was doing, the fuzzier the picture. And with Danny Greene no longer available as a prime informational source on organized crime activity, the FBI turned its attention to *Alpro* for obtaining that information. To keep the information away from prying eyes, the sensitive Alpro files were cross-indexed to *Probex* in Cleveland, *Pendorf* in Chicago, *Strawman* in Kansas City, *Watergate* in Washington, and of course, *Jimmy Hoffa* in Detroit. Curiously, the Alpro files were missing Jackie's involvement with the La Costa resort in California, the various casino operations in Las Vegas, or any reference to the Genovese crime family based out of New York.

Nonetheless, FBI offices coast-to-coast were busy. Alpro kept the Bureau inundated with fresh leads—often in an effort to eliminate anyone who might pose a threat to his becoming General President of the International Brotherhood of Teamsters.

Each communication carried the highly classified cover sheet, warning the appropriate SAC office not to discuss or even admit the existence of Alpro outside the Bureau, which included federal judges, law enforcement agencies and federal investigative units, such as the newly created President Commission on Organized Crime. The President would be advised only on a need-to-know-basis, but seeing as how Jimmy Carter had opted to by-pass the Bureau and form this independent Commission, it was obvious that the President did not have blind faith in the Bureau.

Mounting pressure for fresh leads and more information made its way from the Bureau's Washington headquarters down to the various FBI offices. Alpro's handler, Special Agent Patrick Foran, was instructed to squeeze out every drop of information from Alpro. Agent Foran applied one of the Bureau's more effective tourniquets to accomplish that objective.

"Let's hope it's all over," Agent Foran baited.

"What's all over?" Jackie puzzled.

"This memory lapse you've been suffering from for the past eight years. Let's hope it's over, and that your memory has fully recovered."

Not amused, "Ain't nothing wrong with my memory," Jackie responded. "This is all I need, another smart ass in my life. So, what did you want to know?"

"It's hard to say where to begin. There's so much to cover. At the rate we're moving on the Pendorf operation, it's almost impossible to keep up. Headquarters has assigned more special agents to the Pendorf investigation."

"If you got so many agents assigned to this, how come you're not investigating Skippy Felice? I thought you guys were going to do that for me."

"We're on it," Foran reassured him.

"What does that mean?"

"Just what I said, we're on it."

"This informant stuff is not as exciting as I was led to believe. You guys should have stayed with chasing Communists and small-time hoods. I think you're in over your heads when it comes to investigating the serious stuff."

"Now who's being a smart ass," Foran retorted.

"Did you look into that new food chain I told you about?"

"Yes, we're looking into the Riser Food Chain."

"That's all a front," Jackie smirked.

"Maybe so, but we don't see how it ties into Allen Dorfman. You, as Alpro, have identified Dorfman as Jimmy Hoffa's replacement, now it's my job to find the Dorfman connection."

"Yeah, well maybe he's not directly, but his attorney is involved."

"How so?" Foran inquired.

"This new contract takes in all the trucks, warehousing operations and retail clerks in all food chains. These food chains will be the main sweetheart contract covering all that stuff with the Teamsters. The reason why it's being done this way is so the new Riser Corporation won't have to deal with the various IBT locals. It'll all be handled at the national level. This is how it's going to be done for the whole country."

"That still doesn't answer my question. How will Dorfman make money off this?" Foran repeated.

Jackie began grinding his teeth, but managed to flash a faint smile, "It's all smoke and mirrors."

Foran was not amused, "I don't have time for shit like this. Are you going to give me a straight answer, or not?"

"I told you, it's being done through the attorney fees."

"That doesn't make any sense," Foran surmised.

"Hell, I know, 'cause that's how Angelo Lonardo and my attorney handle it with Blue Cross."

"Blue Cross? What's your involvement with them?"

"Look, damn-it, you already got more on your plate than you can handle now, so let's just skip it, okay."

"Okay lets get back to Dorfman," Foran invited.

"Look, there are always legal fees involved in all this stuff. That stuff is all considered legitimate overhead and the government never questions it. So the attorney bills the outfit, and in this case, the food chain for high legal fees. A large percentage of those fees get kicked back to guys like Dorfman and his pal, Korshak."

"And this was all set up at the national level?" Foran pondered whether he should ask Jackie why he hadn't brought this to his attention earlier, but then decided against it.

"Of course. It comes right from the top," Jackie assured. "You ever heard the saying that 'shit rolls downhill?'"

Agent Foran began snapping the button on his ball-point pen as he asked, "You have any proof of this?"

"Shit yeah. I ought to know. Hell, I was there. I saw Fitz and Dorfman in La Costa at the Invitational Golf Tournament. Look, it's like I keep telling ya, Dorfman's into everything. Take that large housing project on the north side of Chicago. Who you think owns seventy per-cent interest in that joint? Red Strada gave Dorfman his thirty percent. Dorfman has promised all the Mafia members sitting on the Pension Fund a percentage if we financially back this project."

Again, Foran wondered why Jackie had withheld this information. "Does this mean you're going to make money off this housing project?"

"I have to maintain my cover. I might pick up a half mill out of the deal if I was to sponsor the loan."

"That much from one deal?" Foran asked.

"There's a lot of money to be made in these HUD projects, but I doubt if I'll see much of it under Carter's administration, that's for sure."

"Is there anything else you can tell us about Dorfman's illegal activities?" the agent probed.

"Like I told you, the guy's into everything. He even has his own massage parlor operated by his girlfriend," Jackie volunteered.

"This massage parlor, do you know where it's located?"

"It's in Vegas. He operates the place as a silent partner, just like his silent ownership in the Dunes Hotel."

"Dorfman owns that!" Agent Foran responded.

"Not all of it. His silent partners include Joey Auippa and Nick Civella. Hey, forget about Civella. He's not my problem, and I don't what him becoming one either."

"That could turn into some very incriminating evidence. Is there anything else in Vegas that Dorfman might be involved in?" Foran pressed.

"Sure. He's got some guy running Slots of Fun for him in Vegas, but I don't know the guy's name."

"Where does Dorfman get all the money for this?"

"Amalgamated Bank out of Chicago handles a lot of it. I told you before that Dorfman's tight with Don Peters, and Peters is an officer with that bank."

"You think Fitzsimmons knows about all this?" Foran inquired.

Folding his arms and smirking, "Of course Fitz knows. He's into the Vegas scene as much as Dorfman, for Christ sake."

"Is Fitzsimmons working through Dorfman on this?"

Gesturing, "Sometimes, but not always. He's in tight with the main man in Vegas."

"Who's the main man in Vegas?" Foran asked.

Jackie couldn't disguise his contempt, "You don't know? You don't know who runs Vegas?"

"Well we've heard rumors, of course, but none of them have ever panned out."

"You got agents from one end of that town to the other. I'm dealing with a bunch of damn morons. How the hell did I get myself messed up with you clowns?"

"Just answer my question," Foran ordered.

"I don't know what to say. I guess I better start with the basics. Have you ever heard of an organization called *La Cosa Nostra*?" Jackie inquired.

"Stop being a smart-ass. Just give me the name of the guy in charge."

"The guy's name is Moe Dalitz," Jackie revealed.

"Who?"

"He is the main overseer in Vegas for the various crime families around the country. Everything goes through him if it involves casino operations. It all started way back when Jimmy Fratianno left Murray Hill. For awhile, Fratianno was the local liaison with Bugsy Siegel and a couple other guys."

"The guys who started The Flamingo," Foran clarified.

"Well, with a little help from my ol' man."

"How so?"

"Hey, big projects require big money. My ol' man was in-charge of the Teamster's Central States Pension Fund. He set up the deal and got the loan approved. After that, Dalitz started buying up all the land at fifty and seventy-five cents an acre for guys like Lansky, Hughes and Luciano."

"As in Meyer, Howard and Lucky?" Foran asked.

"Who did you think I was talking about? But you'd have trouble getting anything on Moe."

"Oh? Why is that?" Foran inquired.

"'Cause he owns the sheriff in Vegas. ... I think the sheriff's name is Lamb, or something like that. Yeah, Sheriff Lamb, that's his name. Anyway, Lamb provides Moe with all his protection."

Foran was still puzzled, "But I still don't see the connection between this Moe Dalitz and Frank Fitzsimmons."

"That's because you were always looking for Hoffa. You guys have been handing out the same line of bullshit for so long, you've begun to believe it yourselves. If you want to keep believing that Hoffa ran the show, that's okay by me."

"So you think that we were staking out a phantom?"

"While you guys were wasting your time watching Hoffa in Detroit and following him around Washington,

DC, the guys in charge were setting up operations elsewhere. Some of us ain't as stupid as you think we are."

"Hmm." Foran paused.

"I guess we set up shop and must have forgotten to invite you guys. And I'll tell you something else. You ain't going to get invited unless you got lots of money, connections and influence."

"Oh?"

"Now you take a guy like me. I got connections. That's why you need me, 'cause they ain't going to invite you to none of their parties." A slight smile crossed Jackie's lips as he paused to watch his cigarette smoke. "Moe, he gets invited. Fitz takes him out to La Costa, and believe me, you couldn't afford the cover to get in a joint like that."

Foran searched his memory, "What you're saying is very interesting, but I believe the Bureau's records show that a guy by the name of Allen Glick is in charge of Las Vegas operations."

"Well I'm here to tell you them records are wrong. Allen Glick's just a front man, ... a patsy. He does what he's told."

"You sure about this?" Agent Foran pondered the issue of whether some of the other government agencies also had misinformation.

"I'll tell you a little story." Jackie watched Foran's face. "Once, back in the beginning, Glick became hot. Guys were coming into his casino and taking money out of his place by the suitcase. One day, Glick stops some guy and says, 'Hey, what are you doing here? What's going on?' The guy didn't respond. He just leaves without saying a word. Anyway, Glick keeps this up, constantly stopping these people carrying out all these suitcases of cash. Finally, one day some guy tells Glick to stay in his office and not to come out until he leaves the casino. But Glick don't listen so good. That's when Glick got picked up and taken for a ride to some abandoned warehouse to see Nick Civella. Glick is throwing a fit, but Nick, he don't say nothing. Next thing you know, they just bring in some guy, and sit him down in a chair. Then, one of Nick's men pulls out a gun, puts it to the guy's head and lets him have it. Of course, the guy slumps forward and the body just falls out of the chair along with his brains splattered all over the place. Glick finally stopped talking. Mind you, Nick still ain't said a damn word. He nods and two of Nick's goons sit Glick in the same chair. Nick tells him, 'I'm only going to say this to you once. I want you to go back to Vegas and stay in your office. If you don't understand what I'm telling you, say so now so I can cancel your contract.' The same guy who shot the other poor bastard now puts the gun to Glick's head. Glick got the message. Bottom-line is, the organization don't have no more problems with Mister Glick."

"So this Allen Glick, does he take his orders from this Moe Dalitz?"

"Naw, Glick answers to Morris Schanker. Morris is Civella's front man in Vegas. What you guys don't seem to understand is that each part of Vegas is under a different crime family's control."

"Hmm. ... How so?"

"Let me see if I can remember who made that introduction. It was a guy by the name of Irving Cohn ... yeah, some big land developer in California. Irving is close to

Morris, and it was Morris who introduced Glick to Nick Civella and Allen Dorfman. That's how it really happened."

"Any idea why they did this?" Foran inquired.

"You're just testing my memory, right? You think that just because I don't write none of this stuff down, I don't remember so good. Well I remember plenty."

"Don't let me stop you," Foran prodded.

"It all came about because of some real estate deal. When Glick finished college ... I think he graduated from Ohio State, he went to California and got into real estate out there. He was setting up some real estate deals that involved Dorfman. Dorfman liked the way Glick was able to package the deals, so naturally, Dorfman put Glick in touch with Sidney Korshak."

"The guy they call Super Jew," Foran interjected.

"Right. Anyway, Korshak got Glick into Vegas. ... I think it was Korshak that introduced Glick to Lefty Rosenthal, and it was Lefty that officially placed Glick in charge of Argent Corporation."

"This Argent company, what's its role in all this?"

Jackie flashed a grin, "You guys make me want to laugh. I got to hand it to you college guys. You get yourselves fancy degrees and come out dumber than dogs." Jackie held up his hand. He didn't want to hear Foran's comments or remarks. He wanted to have the last word. "Okay, Rosenthal's running the skimming operation of the slots in Vegas for the Chicago family. If you want to get Rosenthal, all you have to do is put the IRS guys on him."

"That's always a possibility," Foran commented.

"I was told you guys do that a lot. It didn't work with Hoffa because he wasn't into this stuff like we are."

"So, Allen Glick, he's merely a front man for both Kansas City and Chicago. Dorfman gets all his money from this bank in Chicago, or how does that work?"

"Sometimes it's totally legit. When they told Glick he could remodel the Hacienda, I think he went to Aetna Insurance for the money. I'm telling you, the guy really knows how to package deals. I wasn't impressed with my percentage, so I queered the deal. That's why Glick was forced to go elsewhere."

"Any idea how much Aetna loaned him?" Foran asked.

Scratching his chin, "If I'd have gotten involved in the deal, I'd know exactly, but like I said, I wasn't going to get much of a cut, so I wasn't interested. But the deal would have had to have been somewhere in the thirty-to-forty mill range."

"What was the problem?" Foran inquired.

"The cheap bastards were only willing to give me fifty or sixty grand, so I made them go elsewhere for their bread."

"Are you telling me you turned down an opportunity to make fifty or perhaps sixty thousand dollars tax free?" Foran responded in disbelief.

"Sixty gees ain't nothing. That's peanuts. I'm entitled to at least two percent from each party. You start doing crap like that, and first thing you know, everyone and his brother wants me to cut him a similar deal. I'd be shooting myself in the foot."

Foran quickly calculated, "That would come to $1.6 million! Is that what you're making on these transactions?"

"Well, you got to remember, I got expenses coming up."

"Such as, ..."

"Such as the million bucks a year to my attorney."

"Is that what you're paying Climaco?"

"That's just his retainer. I got expenses up the ass. Take them politicians for example. They're always hitting me up for private contributions, and it ain't just four or five of them either—it's damn near all of them. Who do you think bankrolled Mayor Voinovich's campaign? Next thing you know, he'll be running for Governor. Then there's the charities and crap like that to keep up appearances. I don't want to get into it."

"Fine," Foran responded. "We were talking about Las Vegas before we got off the subject. How is it set up?"

"That's all done through couriers, you know, bagmen for the various Mafia families. Some of them are picked for the job, but in most cases, they ain't got no choice."

"Oh? How is that?"

"Some of them are chosen because they're in debt to one Mafia family or another, or the family has got something on them. So the guy's got no choice, like I said." Jackie didn't want Foran to press him on this issue for fear he might mention Maishe Rockman's name. "You got to stop this routine of challenging everything I say, okay? If I tell you something, you can make book on it. I don't appreciate having my word questioned."

"I wasn't questioning your word on this. It's just that we don't know how their handling these types of transactions."

"You got that right, 'cause if you did, you wouldn't be paying me for it. Okay, here's how it works. These couriers walk into a place that's secretly owned or controlled by some family. He's given some chips to play with. It goes like this. Say the guy buys fifty bucks in chips. But they don't give him fifty, it's more like fifty gees. He mingles with the crowd. After he's been there a while, he cashes in all the chips. The pitboss usually tells the dude who to deliver the money to. So you see, the money comes right off the floor. It never gets to the counting room where the IRS and Treasury guys are watching everybody. Sometimes, they're carrying so much bread, they gotta use suitcases."

"Does any of that money find its way back here?"

"Don't be asking me that question. Sure I get some of the money 'cause of my position and connections. I don't want you guys messing with my bread. That's strictly off limits."

"Okay, we'll leave that one alone, but you have to tell us who to stay away from." It was a left-handed ploy Foran had been waiting to use.

"I got your word on that?" Jackie clarified.

Foran held up his fingers in a Boy Scout salute, "Scout's honor."

"Okay. You have to stay away from Babe Triscaro, Maishe Rockman, Angelo Lonardo and my attorney."

"Consider it done. Now, how is Las Vegas operated?"

"Caesar's Palace and The Flamingo stuff is split up between New York and Cleveland. The Hacienda bread is split with Kansas City and Cleveland. ... Let's see, the Dunes take gets divided with Kansas and Chicago, and so does the Marina and Circus Circus. The Sands, their stuff goes strictly to New York, just like Slots-of-Fun goes strictly to Chicago. The Tropicana, ... let's see, that's controlled by Detroit and St. Louis. And the Aladdin is under Detroit's control."

"You forgot one. What about the Shangri-La?"

"That's LA's turf. So there, you got yourselves the whole picture. Now I've told you all there is to know."

"How do you get your money from Las Vegas?" Foran inquired.

"Damn-it! I told you, that's off limits."

"I have to know. Washington has to believe you're playing it straight with us, or they will pull the plug. You may have gotten away with this in the past under Nixon and Ford, but the Carter administration wants to see you and organized crime families in prison."

"I need that bread. That's part of our deal. Besides, if I stop collecting my share of the take, everyone's going to start getting suspicious."

"I want the name of your courier," Foran insisted.

"Maishe. He bagged for my ol' man until he retired. When Hoffa found out about it, he went through the roof. He threatened to have us both and Fitz thrown out of the Teamsters. Fitz was sure that Hoffa was serious. That's why the organization had him whacked."

"Maishe, did he know about all this?"

"Now goddamn it! You can't be messing with Maishe. He's got to be left alone. Besides, you start messing with him and he'll run. If he even starts getting nervous, I'd be in deep trouble with the New York, Cleveland and Chicago families. I can't deal with them guys directly. I need Maishe as a buffer. You hassle with him, and that's it. You'll cut me off from all my information."

"We certainly wouldn't want that to happen. Okay, is there anyone else we should be looking at in Las Vegas?"

"Did I mention Ash Recznik, Dick Thomas or the Delhaney brothers?"

"We know about Recznik and Thomas, but who are the Delhaney brothers, and how do you spell their name?"

"Don't be asking me stuff like that. What do I look like, a telephone directory or something? I don't know their first names, and no, I don't know how to spell their last name either. Anyway, them two brothers are bidding on taking over the Stardust. I'll probably be asked to finance the deal through the Pension Fund."

"Is there anything else you can tell me about these two?" Foran asked.

"Not really. Wait, I just remembered something. They secretly owned the Tropicana once. But the Stardust Casino is controlled by Lefty and Ash at the moment. Now that I think of it, maybe you should go soft on the Stardust, 'cause I got a personal interest in that joint. Why not just stick with Dick Thomas and his land developments. He's tight with Moe."

"Dalitz?" Foran clarified.

"Yeah. Don't you see the connection? Christ, I got to do everything including your thinking for you."

"Enlighten me," Foran prodded.

"Thomas was the go-between for Moe and Civella. He was Civella's bagman before they promoted him."

"I'm beginning to see how this all ties together. Listen, not to change the subject, because I find this all very fascinating, but headquarters wanted me to touch base with you on the Master Freight Agreement."

"Well if you want to get some shit started, that'll do it. Why don't we just change that subject." Jackie crushed out a half-smoked cigarette.

"What's the problem?"

"Jimmy Carter's the problem. That son-of-a-bitch gets reelected and someone's going to shoot him."

"Does the Master Freight Agreement that's going to be signed in April have anything to do with what we've been discussing?"

"Naw, he's just gonna fight this inflation crap at my expense, that's all. Carter wants us to follow his guidelines on salary increases and benefits. If that peanut farmer thinks he's going to fight inflation at my expense, well I have a big surprise in store for him."

"I know what you mean," Foran reflected. "The Carter administration is trying to do an end-run on the Bureau by bringing in the Department of Labor to target Dorfman and your Central States Pension Fund."

"Hey! They got to keep their damn hands off my bread! I knew that bastard was up to something like this, I just knew it. Someone's got to set him straight on a few things."

"That's the problem. Carter isn't exactly listening to us. When the administration found out about Dorfman's control over the Central States Pension Fund, they went off half cocked. That's probably the reason why they've set up this President's Commission On Organized Crime. They should be letting us handle it our own way. We can take out selected individuals without upsetting the whole apple cart."

"I hear ya," Jackie agreed.

As an afterthought and without any specific reason, Foran asked, "By the way, do you know where the Teamsters will be negotiating the contract in DC with the various trucking firms? For some reason they've been keeping it a secret."

"Sure, at the Mayflower Hotel." Jackie waited for Foran to write it down before continuing, "You know why it's being kept a secret?"

"We haven't a clue."

"It's because of them dissident bastards, that's why. We figure they're going to try and disrupt our negotiations."

"The dissidents, by that you mean the splinter groups, such as PROD, TDU and FLASH?" Foran clarified.

"You're finally putting things together pretty good. We figure after it's a done deal, them groups will call a strike. Hey, you want to make some serious bread on it?" Jackie asked.

"Technically, we're not supposed to benefit personally or financially on stuff like this, but I'm interested in hearing you out. How are you planning to make money off a labor strike?" Foran inquired.

"You keep telling me you see the big picture, but you don't. I'm putting my money on them truckers striking, and I hope the dumb bastards do just that."

"I take it by that you're going to make some money on it if they do. I just can't see how. Isn't that going to cost you money in strike fees, union dues and everything else?"

"You ever hear of commodities?"

"Of course," Foran responded.

"My attorney tells me it'll be the easiest five mill I ever made in my life. So here's the tip. Put all your money in commodities and you'll double or triple your wealth. Personally, I'd put my loose change in steel. Anyone holding steel when you can't get your hands on it will make a fortune when demand goes crazy. In the meantime, Carter is going to be made to look like a fool."

"Does anyone outside the Teamsters know this will be going down?"

"Sure. Both Nick Civella in Kansas and Joey Auippa from Chicago plan to make an extra quick mill on the strike. Us guys on the Executive Board and our attorneys should all make out pretty good. ... See, here's how it works. Them drivers think they got us over a barrel, but for that kind of money, they can strike us all they want." Jackie's grin turned to laughter.

♦

On April 4$^{th}$, 1979 FBI Supervisor Patrick J. Foran set up another Alpro meeting. He had uncomfortable news from the director of the FBI that had to be relayed personally. Foran hoped Jackie wouldn't cause a scene.

"Okay, lets get this stuff out of the way, quick. I got a date and don't want to keep this broad waiting too long. She might get cold on me. So what's the emergency?"

"Remember that contract agreement you wanted?"

"Yeah," Jackie responded with suspicion.

"It finally came through. Headquarters has asked me to review it with you."

"Is this going to take long?" Jackie asked. "All this time I thought you were going to ask me something about Skippy Felice. What gives? How come you ain't doing anything about that?"

"I can't get into that right now. Skippy will have to wait. This is more important. The director of the FBI ..."

"Huh-uh. He's that Carter appointment."

"As I was saying, the director wants me to review these ten items with you personally, and to make sure you understand certain conditions."

"What conditions? We already have an understanding. That's all you had to do was write it down. What's this crap about 'certain conditions?'"

Foran looked down and began reading from the list of items in a two-page memorandum from FBI headquarters. "Item one: As an informant, you are being advised that your assistance is strictly voluntary."

"Voluntary my ass. McCoy blackmailed me into this, and now you're telling me I'm fuckin' myself voluntarily. That's bullshit!"

"Item two: As an informant you are being advised that you are not and cannot consider yourself to be an employee or undercover agent with the FBI."

"More bullshit. Hoover sent me in to check out the Watergate leaks, remember?"

"Item three: As an informant, your relationship with the Bureau will be held in the strictest confidence, and will not be divulged to anyone."

"Thank you. I really appreciate that."

"Item four: As an informant, you are assured that the Bureau will take all possible steps to maintain your confidentiality. Item five: As an informant, you are instructed to report positive information as soon as you obtain it to ensure that the information is as accurate and complete as possible. You are also instructed that this information should only be furnished to the FBI." Foran looked up to see if Jackie was paying attention. "What that means is that you're to keep your mouth shut. We don't want you blabbing this stuff to the Treasury boys or the Labor Department, or any other government agency, including the State Department, CIA or Secret Service. Is that understood?"

"You don't expect me to sign this, do you, 'cause I ain't."

"I'll take that to mean you understand. Item six: Informant has been instructed that when carrying out assignments he shall not participate in acts of violence or use unlawful techniques to obtain information for the FBI or initiate a plan to commit criminal acts."

"Now look who's calling the kettle black ..."

"Item seven: Informant has been instructed that when carrying out assignments, he shall not participate in criminal activities with persons under investigation except insofar as the FBI determines that such participation is necessary to obtain information needed for purposes of federal prosecution."

"Yeah, right." Jackie looked toward the ceiling. In a very low tone, he began humming to himself, but just loud enough for Foran to hear him.

"Item eight: Informant has been advised of FBI jurisdiction in criminal matters and where applicable, domestic security matters. Stop making that noise. It's damn annoying. Item nine: Informant has been advised that any compensation received for his services must be reported as income when filing federal income tax returns or other appropriate tax forms."

"This is all bullshit."

Foran looked up, "That means that the government wants you to begin paying taxes on your skim money, loan kickbacks, ghost employees and influence peddling pay-offs."

"How am I suppose to maintain a good cover if you tie my hands with crap like this. I got expenses," Jackie complained.

"And finally, item ten: Informant has been advised of the FBI policy against the obtaining of information relating to defense plans and strategy of persons awaiting trial."

"You through?"

"That's it. Headquarters insisted that I read each of these items to you in person. I'd like you to sign this acknowledgment form, but if you'd like to talk it over with your attorney first, that's okay."

"Damn right I'll do that. He may have a few items to add to that list. Give me a copy of them, so he'll know what we're talking about. But I gotta tell you right now, I ain't too happy about this."

The following day, the realities of Jackie's new restrictions set in, and he discussed the matter with Tony on his way to see Agent Foran.

"So what are your plans?" Tony asked.

"I'm telling you Tony, this has really got me upset."

"You have to decide if you're going to let them call the shots."

"Well I'm going to start using these bastards to my advantage. Okay, if that's the way they want it to go down, that's the way it'll go down."

"Just what do you have in mind, Jackie?"

"When my man gets in the White House, I'm going to get this contract rewritten, and that's a fact."

"You're not still thinking about bankrolling Ronald Reagan?" Tony clarified.

"I sure an hell am."

"Come-on Jackie, he ain't gotta chance. I think you're just wasting your money. I think someone like George Bush has got a better shot at it."

"Don't worry. I'm hedging my bet. If he gets the nod from the Republicans, I'll back him. ... Did you know that he was tight with Nixon?"

"How so?"

"My man Nixon appointed him Ambassador to the UN. Then I think it was Ford who appointed him to run the CIA?"

"It's like I said Jackie, he's the type of guy you need in the White House."

◆

"My attorney wants to know one thing. Is this retroactive, or what?" Jackie demanded to know.

"No. My understanding is that it only took effect after you were informed, so you're slate is clean as far as we're concerned. Anything that may have transpired prior to yesterday, never happened."

"Okay, then as far as we're concerned, I'm straight with the Bureau?" Jackie asked.

"As far as I'm concerned you are. Now, maybe we can move forward. So, have there been any new developments with Dorfman or Fitzsimmons?"

"Ted Kennedy is in for a battle over deregulating the trucking industry. Dorfman has seen to that. He's going to make his life a living hell."

"How so?" Foran smiled.

"The guys on the Executive Board feel that his bill will be detrimental to the Teamsters if it passes."

"Are you referring to the Teamster members or the executives?" Foran asked.

"Dorfman told both Williams and Fitz to lean on Senator Cannon to have the bill end up back in committee. Williams had his Washington attorney request Cannon hold hearings. Cannon will use them hearings to kill the bill. According to Williams ..."

"You mean Roy Lee Williams, the IBT vice president from Kansas City?" Foran wanted to make sure who Jackie was referencing.

"Yeah. Anyway, according to Roy Williams, Senator Cannon wants a favor in return. He wants Williams to handle a land deal for him with the Central States Pension Fund. The Teamsters own 5.8 acres of land next to his land in Vegas. Senator Cannon was going to have his son-in-law purchase the Teamster parcel, but the first deal fell through."

"Why?" Foran asked. Once again Foran pondered the question of why Jackie had been withholding this information all these years.

"The little shit wanted it for practically nothing. We'd have made out better donating it to a church and taking a tax write-off for Christ sake. Dorfman forced the issue, so we had to sell it to him. They got it for a half mill' under its real value."

"What are they planning to use it for?"

"Senator Cannon is going to build some condos and a golf course on it. But here's the good part. It wasn't until after the deal that Williams found out that Cannon is tight with Dorfman. In fact, Dorfman gave Cannon three-hundred thou of his own bread to cover the down payment. How do you like them apples?"

"Very interesting. So, is Roy Williams upset about all this?"

"Upset? Try pissed! He's mad as hell with Fitz, and he's been running around bad-mouthing Fitz every chance he gets, especially to the organization."

"The Mafia," Foran clarified.

"Who did you think I meant? My guess is Williams is going make a bid for the presidency of the International. If Williams can get the support he needs from the Chicago family, and that includes Dorfman and Auippa as well. See, Williams takes all his orders from Civella, so he's got that tied up and in the bag. But Chicago wants Fitz to stay in as president of the International, so Williams' only hope is to chip away at that support. Get the picture?"

"What support from the Mafia does Fitzsimmons have besides Chicago?"

"Let me tell you, it's on shaky ground. He went to Florida for a month trying to drum up support. He met with Kelly Mannarino, the underboss for the Pittsburgh family and Sammy Provenzano from New Jersey." Then Jackie added, "Word is, a bunch of guys might go into the government's Witness Protection Program and start testifying against him."

"Any idea who these individuals might be?" Foran asked.

"Sure. Chuckie O'Brien, Hoffa's so-called adopted son may be ready to open up. And they are real worried that Frank Sheenan will not be a stand-up guy and may testify against Fitz and some other individuals. Then there is Jimmy Tamer, he's involved in that Aladdin deal, and they're concerned he might talk."

"You mentioned Sammy Provenzano. The Bureau is always interested in the Newark and Philadelphia families. Anything going on there we should know about?" Foran asked.

"Nothing you don't already know. Sammy's brother Tony Pro, is in Attica on some minor shit. I hear he's getting out soon."

"That's impossible. He is scheduled to pull another four or five years. We couldn't nail him on the Hoffa thing, because he had an air-tight alibi."

"I don't know a thing about the Hoffa hit other than what I told McCoy and Garrity. I do know that Sammy has a judge who is willing to spring his brother for the right price. You know, now that I think about it, how come you guys never go after judges? Oh brother, that was a dumb question. I know why you guys don't go after judges."

"You know the judge's name?" Foran inquired.

"I can't start asking questions like that. They want to share what they got, that's one thing. I start asking a question like that and the first thing they'll want to know is, why I'm so interested in stuff like that," Jackie complained.

"Okay, you're right. It's not important." Foran paused. "Have you heard anything else that might be going down in Chicago?"

"Maishe just got back from Mexico. He was on a hunting trip. He stopped off in Chi Town before returning to Murray Hill. He tells me the Stardust Casino deal in Vegas might be nixed by Donald Peters. Now there I can press him for details 'cause I got a piece of that action."

"Good. Stay on top of that," Foran suggested. "Anything else?"

"I hear you guys might be looking for some guy by the name of Gil Davis?"

"As a matter of fact, we have a fugitive warrant out on him."

"He's tight with Dorfman, you know. He's supposed to be on the move. I heard he's living in some mobile home. Anyway, he crossed into Canada. You might be able to find him in London, Ontario. Thought you might like to know."

"Great. We'll notify the Canadian authorities. Have you heard anything else on what's been happening?" Foran pressed.

"Let's see, ... oh, Jesse Carr, he's out of Anchorage, Alaska. He's been trying to stay away from the organization since Hoffa disappeared, but he hasn't been having much luck. Not if the Super Jew gets his hands on him."

"Dorfman's attorney?" Foran confirmed.

"Right. Dorfman and Korshak have been putting the squeeze on him, and he hasn't got ol' Jimmy Hoffa to protect him anymore. He's been trying to build some condos in Palm Springs, on the west coast. Dorfman and Korshak want a piece of Carr's action."

Foran continued to take notes without looking up, "Don't stop now."

"Let's see. .. Oh, here's another hot news item. Joe Morgan is worried as shit. His buddy, some guy by the name of Udell ... Larry Udell. He's real sick and in the hospital. Anyway, this Udell guy is Morgan's buffer between the Mafia and himself. He's worried that if the guy dies, the outfit is going to have him whacked."

"Why?"

"Why what?" Jackie thought it was a dumb question. "Morgan's weak. Morgan and Udell have been involved in numerous scams together using Teamster money right under your noses."

"How?"

"They buy up trucking companies, make land deals and scam loans from pension money throughout the east coast. Now, you take Tony Pro, . . ."

"Provenzano?"

"Yeah. He may be in the joint, but he can damn sure let out a contract. You guys should pay Morgan a visit. You put half as much heat on him as you do on me and he'll open up."

"What do you know about Tony Provenzano?"

"Nothing. I don't know nothing, and I'd appreciate it if you'd stop asking me about it," Jackie stated.

"Are you aware that Tony Pro answers up to the Genovese crime family in New York?"

"Don't be asking me no more questions about Tony Pro," Jackie ordered.

"Look, we've known since day one that Provenzano sent three wiseguys from New Jersey to Cleveland and then on to a small airport north of Detroit Metro. We know damn near everyone involved in the assassination. We know that your friend Frank Fitzsimmons asked for the hit contract. We know who worked on planning the assassination. In other words, we know damn near everything, so what's the big deal. If you know something, you better come clean about it."

"All I know is that Tony Pro served time with Hoffa at Lewisburg. That's why the organization must have felt he could get close to Hoffa. I don't know anything else. End of subject. *Finito!*"

"Why did the hit team fly into Hopkins International before flying to Detroit area?"

Jackie sat there in silence, refusing to say another word until Special Agent Foran came to the conclusion he was getting too close to home. He knew that Jackie obviously knew more about Hoffa's assassination than he was willing to discuss.

♦

FOR THE NEXT FIVE MONTHS Alpro inundated the FBI with detailed information on every organized crime family throughout the country, save one: As long as the Bureau carefully avoided all reference to the Genovese crime family out of New York, Jackie was willing to cooperate.

Still it was not enough. The FBI's lack of progress or willingness to share information about Jimmy Hoffa's assassination had worn thin with the Carter administration. To exacerbate the matter, the FBI also refused to move against Roy Lee Williams, and it now appeared to the administration that one major criminal would be replaced by another to head the International Brotherhood of Teamsters.

Without notifying the FBI, two special agents with the President's Strike Force on Organized Crime began setting up their surveillance operation. From their offices on the upper floors of the Keith Building, Special Agents Jim Thomas and George 'Red' Simmons could keep constant observation of Jackie's arrivals and departures. From an office located at Cleveland State University's Law Library, however, the view of Jackie's backdoor entrance and parking lot offered a better vantage point for observing the steady line of private visitors seeking favors, loans and deals.

It soon became apparent to both undercover agents that they were not alone. By the end of the first week, it was obvious that the van regularly parked and sitting quietly on the street was occupied by Treasury Agent, Dale Wiggens who was assigned to ATF. At the other end of the street, another unmarked vehicle began regularly appearing from the Justice Department. Although they could not visually detect it, the two undercover agents felt they were being watched by the FBI.

Special Agent Simmons turned to his partner. "I think we're going to be fighting a lot more than just a couple of organized crime figures. We may have stumbled upon something much bigger than we anticipated."

*Chapter 12*

## The New Man

AMERICA ENTERED a new geo-political era when a dark-horse candidate entered the New Hampshire presidential primary. In his "I paid for this microphone ... It's mine!" speech, Ronald W. Reagan set the tone—not only for his presidency, but for the rest of the decade. That announcement signaled the end of Jackie's four-year hiatus from national politics.

In addition to his overseas connections, his trilateral effort to use the FBI, the Mafia and the Teamsters to jackpot the Carter administration was about to pay off.

The key element, however, consisted of pouring four years of accumulated cash into a former California governor's coffers to finance primaries which would tip the scales of presidential access in Jackie's favor. If Ronald Reagan won the presidency, he would owe him, above and beyond the special privileges, money and equipment bestowed upon him by the FBI.

Jackie shared many things in common with the former Hollywood movie actor, one of which included political ideology. Jackie knew the value in promoting anti-Communist rhetoric to gain national popular support. He understood the concept of surrounding himself with talented handlers who could comb a positive image. Most importantly, it was the former governor's social, economic and labor-management beliefs that attracted his attention and financial support.

Like Ronald Reagan, Jackie believed that the best way to protect the assets of wealthier Americans from the extremes of liberal government was to get government off the backs of enterprising individuals such as himself. Perhaps the country could once again return to those Victorian principles that J. Edgar Hoover stood for and promoted during his era.

Likewise, the five New York crime families making up the largest *La Cosa Nostra* Commission were not unhappy about Ronald Reagan's decision to enter the presidential race. Not since the reign of President Nixon had the Commission found anyone they could enthusiastically support. Collectively, they felt that if Reagan could capture the White House, the country could return to a business-as-usual agenda. And just perhaps, Reagan could be persuaded to curtail the federal heat being applied to organized crime activity.

Nonetheless, Ronald Reagan's candidacy appeared to be a long shot. He would need massive amounts of public exposure, good script writers and several early primary victories to stay in the race. Jackie felt that what Reagan really needed was an endless supply of cash, and he volunteered to pass the hat among his underworld associates.

Jackie's political message got through.

Senior-level bureaucrats within the FBI sensed that Jimmy Carter's presidency was vulnerable, and it would only be a matter of time before a new President appointed a new FBI director. This was not the time to offend those with rising political influence unless they were willing to expose their own careers to unnecessary risk. If a change in the national administration occurred, Bureau administrators reasoned that Jackie's first order of business would be to set fresh ground rules, and perhaps get his FBI contract either equitably modified or thrown out. The Bureau had to be prepared for that political reality.

The pressure the Bureau had been systematically applying on Jackie would have to be stopped. The best way to handle the situation would be to promote Agent Patrick Foran out of harm's way, and assign Jackie someone who was less assertive, less demanding and less threatening. The Bureau found those specific attributes in Special Agent Robert S. Friedrick.

♦

"So, Big Brother has decided to assign me a new man."

"Patrick Foran has been promoted to supervisor," Agent Friedrick immediately replied. "Naturally, I was advised of your special status with the Bureau."

There was something about Friedrick that Jackie liked. Perhaps it was because he didn't look or act like Agent Foran, but whatever it was, Jackie perceived a subtle lag in his demeanor. Perhaps he could be corrupted, if not by money or sex, then perhaps by the intoxicating aroma of real power and influence.

The years he had spent living on the edge, battling enemies, flirting with death, masterminding transactions and surviving one criminal investigation after another meant only one thing: This agent was out of his league, and no match for someone who had the street-savvy to outwit them all.

"Let's get something straight between us. The job is to protect me and my people. Is that understood?"

"Well my instructions are somewhat along that venue," Friedrick responded.

"Carter's days are over."

"I have every reason to suspect that might be the case, Mister Presser."

"Listen. My people tell me there's going to be another crisis engineered. There's going to be a stink made over those Iranian hostages. It will ensure that the peanut farmer from Georgia won't get back in."

"The general consensus at the Bureau is that if the opposition can put up a strong candidate or a three-way race develops, we predict that we'll see a new man at the helm."

"Yeah, well Ronnie is strong enough. In case you didn't know, he's my main man. I'm backing him all the way. Whatever it takes. Look, I like you. I don't know why, but I do."

"Thank you, Mister Presser. The Bureau thinks that mutual trust is very important."

Jackie used silence as a dramatic pause, "... The real question is, can I trust you?"

"Well I certainly hope so." Agent Friedrick understood the basic procedure: Establish trust before attempting to exercise control over the subject. What he did not realize was that Jackie, having been educated by two domineering handlers, knew how the Bureau's mind-control game was played.

"If I share something with you, can I trust you to keep it to yourself?"

"Sure Mister Presser."

"There's going to be another oil crisis. Maybe not as severe as the one in '74, but it will be enough to shock the market. I suggest you put everything into oil futures. You do that right now and you'll retire rich. A barrel of oil is gonna hit seventeen dollars, perhaps as high as twenty-two." Jackie lit up a cigarette to let his words sink in.

"Christ, the country would go broke at those prices. How did you find this out?"

"I got contacts and connections with a foreign government, and know what I'm talking about. Don't say I didn't give you a solid tip. This hostage thing in the Middle East is far from over. Also, there's going to be another major flare up and Carter is not going to be able to survive the political fallout."

"Speaking of international affairs, we understand you've been in direct contact with some general in the Israeli government." It was a polite inquiry, based upon a report filed by the State Department.

"Damn. I can't do nothing without every son-of-bitch and his brother knowing about it."

"I don't know if you're aware of it or not, but that's in direct violation of federal law. If the Carter administration catches wind of this, you could get yourself into serious trouble."

Leaning forward, "Let me repeat myself, Carter won't see a return engagement. I'd start planning on getting a new boss if I were you." Friedrick nodded to this possibility. "I also suggest you get some of this heat off me. I can't take a crap without someone knowing about it. Pretty soon, they'll have as many agents watching me as they did Hoffa."

"We're trying to keep a lid on things for you."

"Yeah, well the Bureau ain't trying hard enough," Jackie returned.

"There are two special undercover agents we're primarily concerned about."

"Who's that?" Jackie inquired.

"They're with the President's Strike Force on Organized Crime. In case you didn't know, they have you under heavy surveillance. One plays the heavy, and the other plays the nice guy, but don't let either of them fool you."

"Whatever gave you the impression Jackie Presser is easy to fool?"

"I didn't mean it like that."

"So what's with this 'heavy surveillance?'"

"They're using everything. They've set up shop over at the Keith Building. We suspect that they're using wiretaps and camera surveillance to watch you."

"That don't surprise me none. Don't worry, they're not sharp enough to catch me using those methods. I've been followed by a half dozen agencies during the past ten years, and none of them have ever caught me napping."

"That's not what has us concerned."

"Oh?" Jackie responded.

"What we're concerned about are the direct personal interviews they've been conducting."

"Hmm ... I see."

In a rapport-building gesture, Friedrick added, "If you want, I can have your office swept for bugs."

"Naw, that won't be necessary, but I appreciate the offer. I got my own guy who handles that."

"You have someone who handles bugging?" Friedrick responded

"Yeah. The guy's the ex-chief of police from Beachwood. He's pretty good. He caught my wife screwing around and video taped it for me. It's so good, I've toyed with the idea of turning it over to Rueben Sturman."

"Isn't he the porno czar? You know him?"

"Sure, I know Rueben. He's been a friend of the family for years. Before Carmen and I got married, I had him over to my place all the time." Jackie paused. "Are you into those kinky flicks? I got plenty of the good ones from Rueben's private collection, so if you're interested, just say the word."

"I have to be careful. We have to take lie-detector tests, and they sometimes ask us about stuff like that."

"Just thought I'd ask. ... Is there anything else you can tell me about these two guys on my tail."

Friedrick thought a moment. "The IRS tipped us off when they requested copies of your tax returns. Naturally, we told them to deep-six their request."

"You mentioned something about these two interviewing people. Who have they been talking to?"

"We put a tail on the heavy, Jim Thomas. He's been contacting at least a dozen people. He talked to someone by the name of Nate Dolin at The Front Row Theatre, but I don't think he got very far."

"He won't either. The Dolins are my people. They'll keep their traps shut. Anyone else I should know about?"

"Let me think .... There's some guy in Chicago they've tracked down. I can't remember his name, probably because he uses so many aliases."

"Oh for crying-out-loud, you're talking about Harry Haler! Talk about pissing in the wind!"

"Is he someone we should be worried about?" Friedrick asked.

"I thought you guys had him locked up. I knew I should have asked for a contract on him. Okay, let me have it. What's he been saying?"

"Haler's been telling the Strike Force agents how you and he set up some phony ad agency to channel illegal payments to Nixon. He also claims that you're a government informant."

"Lucky for us no one believes him."

"What about Anthony Liberatore?"

"Don't worry about Liberatore," Jackie shot back.

"Any idea on where he is? It seems like he's gone into hiding."

"So I've heard. Hey, why don't you put him on your Ten Most Wanted List—or are those kinda guys still off-limits?"

"We might do that, Mafia member or not. The Bureau's really annoyed with Liberatore for setting up the hit on Danny Greene, not to mention the little matter involving Geraldine Linhart lifting our files."

"Listen, Liberatore did everyone a big favor. I'll bet if he had been working for you guys, he'd have gotten a promotion. I've squared things with the crime family, so as far as Liberatore is concerned, I'm in pretty good shape. ... So tell me, what's the Bureau's position on all this?" Jackie asked.

"Well, you know, you can trust us to keep a lid on it. Our role in this wouldn't look too good if that were made public, so it looks like we have no choice but to protect you as much as possible."

"See that you do. ... Okay, now that we know where we stand, how can I help you?"

"I understand that you want the Bureau to move on some guy by the name of Roy Lee Williams."

"You're all right. I got a good feeling about this. To show you how much I appreciate your cooperation, I going to share something with you." Jackie paused to structure his thoughts. "Look, if you can take Williams out of the picture, I've got a good shot at becoming the next General President of the International. To do that, however, we have to nail Williams."

"I'm not sure what you're driving at. What is it you want the Bureau to do?"

"No, you're not listening. I want you to take him down."

"You mean, as in 'set him up' so that he'll take a fall?"

"Right. So here's my deal. I'll tell you anything and everything you want to know. In return, you have to get the Bureau to lean on him until he falls."

"How do you suggest we do that?" Friedrick inquired.

"Now listen carefully. This guy Williams has been real sick. He just got out of the hospital. There's a ninety-nine percent chance he's going to make a bid for the International anyway. I want you to throw up some roadblocks." Jackie lit another cigarette, then continued, "It's like I told Agent Foran, Williams is tight with Allen

Dorfman out of Chicago. Between the two of them, they got my access to certain pension money tied up. I'll need better access to that money if, let's say our next President has special projects he'd like funded."

"Now it's my turn to share something with you."

"Yeah?" Jackie invited.

"I don't know how to explain this to you, but ..."

"Listen, I ain't stupid so just say it," Jackie ordered.

"We're not in this thing alone. We have to compete against other investigative agencies for cases."

"Such as ..."

"Such as the Treasury Department. Except for working with IRS, we're practically in this alone."

"So, what's this got to do with me or targeting Williams for that matter?"

"The Treasury has zeroed in on Williams, and it's fighting us for jurisdiction over the case."

"Now you listen. I don't care which agency brings him down so long as he takes a fall," Jackie responded in annoyance.

"That's what I'm driving at. The Treasury wants to develop him as one of their informants. If that happens, they'll be protecting him just like we've been protecting you."

"Now I'm beginning to understand what's been happening."

"That's why we've been forced to switch the focus of our investigation from Williams to Dorfman. So far, the Treasury hasn't caught wind of our Pendorf operation, or we'd be faced with fighting a war on two fronts. I think that's why Agent Foran probably stalled you on moving against Williams."

"Yeah, I think you're right. — Damn."

"Why? What's the problem," Friedrick asked.

"I overheard a conversation between Willams and Dorfman. They're planning on appointing Tom Duffy as Executive Director of the Pension Fund."

"Is that going to cause you a problem?" Friedrick inquired.

"By rights, I should be the one getting that appointment. Dorfman owes me."

"How so? For what?"

"Fitzsimmons canceled his insurance contract, and I fixed it so that he was able to get it back. But it seems like Dorfman's got a short memory. Well I have both a good memory, and a long one."

"I'm sure you do, but do you have any idea on how we might zero in on their plans?"

"Sure. You do as I tell you and I'll make you a star," Jackie invited.

"Mister Presser, that won't be necessary."

"No, I mean it. Anything you want. If it's for sale, I can buy it. But I only do that for my friends. Say, you like foxy broads? Huh? How many would you like?"

"I appreciate you thinking of me like this, but I can't."

"Hey, you don't have to give me your answer right now. Just think about it, that's all. No crime in thinking about it, is there?"

"No, of course not," Friedrick responded.

"I like to show people my appreciation, that's all."

"Please, just tell me what you think we should do."

"Fine. Okay, let me see where was I? ..."

"Williams and Dorfman are planning to appoint Duffy."

"Oh-yeah, this guy Williams has a suite of private rooms at the Sheraton O'Hare in Chicago. The rooms are either on the fifth or sixth floor. You won't have any problem locating his office because it's on the eastern wing."

"Like I said Mister Presser, the Treasury boys are already watching Williams pretty closely."

"Forget them. Just install a bug in Williams' office. You do like I'm telling you and I guarantee you'll catch him discussing stuff with Dorfman and the Chicago Mafia."

"If that's the case, we've got Dorfman's offices already bugged," Friedrick added.

"Damn-it. You're not paying attention to what I just told you. Dorfman's not stupid. Chances are he already knows you've got his phones bugged. ... You want to catch Williams, you got to bug Williams. You can bug Dorfman for the next fifty years and you'll be wasting your time."

"I think it's safe to say the Bureau's got better things to do with its time."

"And something else. All calls to Williams go through the switchboard. I wrote the phone number down, it's here someplace. ... Yeah, here it is."

As Agent Friedrick carefully jotted down the number, he interposed, "We understand from a newspaper article that Frank Fitzsimmons is dying of cancer."

"That's bullshit. All he's got is a small tumor in his stomach. You guys got to stop believing all the junk that gets leaked to the media. You only need one source for the real information. Me."

"We were told that that's the reason why the Teamsters' Executive Board meeting will be held in Palm Springs, Florida this year."

"More bullshit. I don't know where you're getting this crap, but you're listening to the wrong people. When you really want to know what's going down, just come to *The Tailor*. I'll iron-out the wrinkles."

"Okay, if you say so."

"Now listen, our guys operate pretty much like you guys. We leak phony cover stories to the media to throw up a smoke screen."

"I wouldn't know anything about that."

"Yeah, right," Jackie responded. "The real meeting is going to be held where we always hold it, in a place called La Costa on the west coast."

"Are you saying that we'd be heading in the opposite direction?" Friedrick exclaimed.

"That doesn't surprise me none. Listen, I never told Foran or McCoy about this because I didn't completely trust them."

"I appreciate your confidence. Do you have any idea when this meeting is going to take place?" Friedrick asked.

"They're keeping that a secret until the last minute. All any of us know is that it will be sometime after Fitz finishes his radiation treatment." Leaning in and lowering his voice, "He's supposed to announce that he's going to take a vacation, and that's our signal to secretly go to La Costa."

"This is fantastic. This stuff will blow the brass's minds."

"Okay. Now you know what I know," Jackie assured him.

Half thinking to himself, "Foran is going to be pissed."

"Yeah, well me and Foran never hit it off. Like I told you ... it's a new ball game when my man's in the Oval Office. You help The Tailor, and The Tailor helps you. Foran never understood those terms."

"May I tell you something off the record?" Friedrick whispered.

"Shoot." Jackie leaned back in the chair.

"Now don't take this the wrong way. Remember the Israeli situation we were discussing?"

"Yeah?"

"Well if I were you, I'd keep a low profile on that while Carter is still in office. If anything even smells like it might disrupt the Camp David Accord, his people will come down on you heavy."

"I hear ya."

"Just between you and me, we did not have this conversation."

◆

"How did it go with the new man they've assigned you?" Tony asked.

"I've got him eating out of my hand," Jackie responded proudly. "God I love this shit."

"Sounds like it went well. I take it you two hit it off?"

"The guy's no Agent Foran, that's for sure. But I got to tell you something Tony, the FBI's real fucked up."

"How so?"

"I don't think they know what they're doing. I mean to tell ya Tony, the stuff they were asking me about was real basic—you know I mean?"

"Like playing with only half a deck?"

"Yeah. It was the kinda stuff they should have known about for years. I got the impression that they've been operating in the dark for the last twenty years. It's a wonder they ever solve anything."

"You got to be careful Jackie that you don't educate them too much. What did the new guy what to know?"

"Dorfman."

"What about Williams or Fitz?" Tony asked.

"I'm telling ya they're out-to-lunch. It's partly my own fault. Awhile back I was trying to motivate them to target Dorfman, figuring that they'd take him down and that would get him out of the Central States Pension."

"So what did you say?" Tony inquired.

"I told them that Dorfman was in charge now that Hoffa was out of the picture."

"Oh-brother. So now they want to go after Dorfman like they went after Hoffa, which probably means they're not interested in Williams or Fitz. Right?"

"Something like that. They're leaving all the serious stuff up to the Treasury Department. I told this new guy to bug Williams' office in Chicago, and he starts handing me crap about bugging Dorfman instead."

"Hey Jackie, there's no accounting for poor taste and bad judgment. All they've been interested in is chasing Communists. ... So, you think this new agent will follow your lead?"

"I've got a good gut feeling. I think Big Brother has finally sent me someone I can work with. ... And I'll tell you something else ..."

"Yeah?"

"You may have just said the magic word. 'Communists.' If I can convince this guy that everyone except me in the Central States Pension Fund is a Communist, that just might light a candle under Big Brother's ass."

◆

FBI Agent Robert Friedrick could not contain his zeal. "I don't know how we can thank you enough, Mister Presser. Because of your information about bugging Williams' private offices, our Pendorf investigation is about to explode. This time, we're going in like Gang Busters."

"I thought the Bureau had given up on that," Jackie reflected.

"Hell no! Your last tip changed the whole focus of our investigation. At least a dozen guys will take a fall. We might even be able to nail Dorfman himself."

"I'm real happy for you, but there's some problems," Jackie interjected in a lazy tone.

"Has something new developed?" Friedrick asked.

"I got someone else for you to target."

"For a moment, I thought you had bad news."

"The bad news has a name, ... Joe Morgan."

"Who is he?" Friedrick encouraged.

"He's vice president of the Southern Conference."

"What's the problem?"

"Morgan might make a bid for the International presidency. If he does, that will make it a three-way race. All of them have to be moved out of the way. Fitz has been in there too long. My people don't trust Williams, and Morgan would be real bad news. I want you to take them all down."

"If we do that, the Teamsters won't have anyone to run for the office."

Jackie smiled, "Yeah, I know. ... Look at it this way. As the General President of the International, I can help you guys get rid of all the Communist conspirators."

"Thank you."

"You're welcome. ... What did you thank me for?"

"I may have mentioned this before, but we're in a battle royal with the Treasury over jurisdiction. You've just handed us our jurisdiction. Now we can take charge and kick the Treasury boys off the case."

"Just make sure your superiors understand the importance of fighting the Communists."

"That's not going to be a problem," Friedrick assured him.

"Maybe I should have mentioned this sooner, but I just assumed you guys knew that Moscow supports these guys. That's what helped them to get to where they got."

"Exactly." Leaning forward, "I know I can share this with you without it going any further, but the talk inside the Bureau is, once Reagan is President, our budget to fight the Communists will be doubled, perhaps tripled in size. We'll have enough men to fight the Communists man for man, anywhere. So, what can you tell us about Morgan? You think he's one of the Communists?"

Jackie paused a moment to reflect on what he had done. "Okay, let me put this in simple terms. ... Morgan has aligned himself with Tony and Sammy Pro, and Joe Territolla from the Eastern Conference. Their plan is to use their group to prevent Williams from becoming the next boss of the Teamsters."

"Will the Communist be supporting Williams?" Friedrick inquired.

"Hey, don't you have all that stuff in the files?" Jackie retorted.

"It's probably there someplace, but your files were sent to headquarters. Only someone like Oliver Revell has access to that info."

"Who's he?"

"He's the Bureau's Deputy Director. Most of what I know comes second-hand from Agent Foran. He filled me in on some material, but it's hard to keep all this information straight when no one has access to those files."

"Hmm, I see. ... Listen, give me a moment to speak with Tony." Jackie stood up and walked to the window were Tony was keeping vigil, "Can you believe this?"

"You got him started, Jackie. Now they're going to get sidetracked looking for the Kremlin connection."

"All I did was mention Communists and they go nuts. It's like passing smelling salts under their nose. I wonder what kind of music these guys listen to?"

"What's your point?" Tony asked.

"Point being, I've never known anyone who could get things so screwed up. It's a wonder they ever get anything done, let alone get it straight." Jackie returned to his chair, "Okay, let's see if I can bring you up to speed. Williams is supported by the Central, Western and

Canadian Conferences, which means he's got the Chicago Mafia behind him."

"And by that I take it you mean Allen Dorfman and Sidney Korshak?"

"Close enough."

"If that's the case," Friedrick concluded, "Williams should have things pretty well locked up."

"Not necessarily. The Treasury has got some of them guys in Chicago running scared. Word is that if the Treasury indicts Williams, Dorfman has got some guy named Lauren Robins waiting in the wings."

"Another Communist?"

"Look, let's not complicate things too much. The point I was making is that nobody's heard of him, so he don't have a chance."

"Frank Fitzsimmons, you think he'll stay in the race?"

"Hell yeah. He ain't going to resign no matter what. He's forming a slate with Ray Schlossling. But you do like I'm telling you ... target Williams and the whole thing falls apart. I told this to Foran a thousand times, but he wasn't paying attention. He spent too much time listening to the wrong radio station."

"That won't happen with me. I think were going to make a great team, Mister Presser."

♦

ON THE MORNING of July 3, 1980, Jackie's office intercom came on. Something in Gail's tone of voice signaled him to be on-guard.

"Jackie?"

"Yeah Gail, what is it?"

"You have someone here to see you. Are you free or busy?"

"I'm busy for the rest of the day. What's up?"

"The individual says it will only take a few moments," Gail replied.

"Does the individual have an appointment?"

"No."

"In that case, see if you can fit something in. My calendar should have sometime available early next month."

A moment of silence passed with each interchange. "He says he's with the U.S. Treasury Department."

"In that case, tell him to see my attorney, John Climaco."

"He says this is not an official visit."

"What's that suppose to mean?" Jackie fired back.

"He says you might want to hear what he has to say."

"Okay, send him in. But get Tony in here also." Jackie waited for the intercom to fall silent before rationalizing his decision, "I ain't talking with any of these guys without a reliable witness."

Without waiting for Tony to arrive, Gail ushered Treasury Agent Steven Wells into Jackie's office. She walked over and whispered privately in Jackie's ear, "Tony's on his way."

"So what do you want to see me about?"

"My name is Agent Wells. I'm with the U.S. Treasury Department." He reached into his pocket to produce his credentials.

"What do I need to see that crap for? Gail told me this was supposed to be informal."

"Right you are. I'll keep it strictly informal."

"Good, because I got nothin' to say."

"We suspect that some of your telephone lines may be tapped, so I thought it best to see you in person. Mind if I sit down?" Agent Wells asked.

"I don't mean to be anti-social or nothing, but you ain't going to be here that long. Just state your business."

"We understand that you're working as an informant for the FBI."

"Are you asking me or just making with conversation?" Jackie turned to gaze out the window.

"We've had you under surveillance for awhile," Wells revealed.

"Is that supposed to get me worried? So what?"

"So, we think you've teamed up with the wrong crowd."

"What's that crack supposed to mean?"

"You know damn well what it means," Wells retorted.

"Like I told Gail, I'm busy. State your business or get out."

"There's only so much the Bureau can do to protect you. We know more about your operation than they do. They haven't been watching you like we have. All they know is pretty much what you feed them."

"I don't know what in the hell your talking about. No, I take that back. You don't know what the hell your talking about."

"The FBI hasn't had you under surveillance, but we have. They have a track record of not watching their informants, so they're not up to speed on how you've been stringing them along."

"You know what I think? I think you're pissed because the Bureau's taken complete charge of your Allen Dorfman investigation."

"If it makes you feel any better, you're absolutely correct. We are pissed, to turn a phrase. We had him nailed to the cross and were in the process of arresting him when the Bureau moved in claiming some bullshit about him being in cahoots with communists. I wonder who put that idea in their heads?"

"So, is that it? Is that what's so important? If so, thank you for sharing it with me. Now if you don't mind, there's the door."

"As a matter of fact, there is something else. Have you informed the FBI just how deeply you're involved with New York's Genovese crime family?"

"I got no business with nobody from New York or the Genovese family. So I got nothin' to say."

"As for this new agent they've assigned you, Robert Friedrick, I have to hand it to you. The way you have him eating out of your hand is quite a feat. But it won't last. Sooner or later, we're going to come down on him, and when we do, we might just take Jackie Presser down with him."

"You finished? I hope so, 'cause I ain't interested in anything else you have to say." Jackie reached over and pressed the intercom, "Where in the hell is Tony?"

"He's walking in right now," Gail responded.

A split second later Tony Hughes entered Jackie's office. "I got here as fast as I could, Jackie. What's going on?"

"This guy says he's with the U.S. Treasury. He thinks I'm some sort of FBI informant or something, but I think he's gotten himself lost. Show him where we put the door."

As Tony approached, Agent Wells continued, "Let me state my other reason for this unofficial visit. I wanted to ask you if you knew an individual by the name of Joe DeRose?"

Jackie raised his hand slightly to signal Tony to wait a moment. "Maybe. I don't know him personally of course, because he's nothing but a hoodlum. I think he's from the Youngstown mob, but I got no business with him. Tell him Tony."

"Mister Presser has no dealings with Joe DeRose, I can testify to that." Tony kept his eyes fixed on Jackie waiting for the signal to usher the special agent out the door.

"He has just picked up a contract to have someone from this place hit. But seeing as how you don't seem to know this guy, we must be mistaken." Wells turned in Tony's direction, "Don't trouble yourself. I can find my way out."

Jackie and Tony waited for the sound of Agent Wells' footsteps to fade, "What the hell do you think that was about? He says they've been watching me."

"Beats me, Jackie. You think you should contact someone?"

"Yeah, let's fight fire with fire. I want you to contact Curly Montana for me. Have him get in touch with DeRose and find out what this is really about. Then, take me over to see Friedrick. In the meantime, I'll contact Climaco and see if he's heard anything from his sources inside the Justice Department. The Treasury may be just trying to stir up some shit."

Sinking into his chair and biting his fingernails, Jackie pulled open a desk drawer, scattering the bottles while fumbling for something to take.

◆

WITHIN TWO DAYS of Treasury Agent Wells' unscheduled visit, Jackie set up an urgent meeting with Special Agent Robert Friedrick. A downtown motel that had been previously used was selected. Tony kept vigil from the window overlooking the parking area, while Jackie continued to pace and smoke waiting for Friedrick.

"It's about time. What the hell took you so long?" Jackie wasn't expecting a status report.

"Christ, we're swamped. The Bureau has practically every division involved in setting up wiretaps and making a case against Dorfman. Not to mention the surveillance operations we have set up in Detroit, Atlantic City, Miami, Kansas City, Los Angeles and Washington. I've been smothered in paperwork ..."

"Don't bother me with that stuff. I've got my own hide to worry about."

"What's wrong?" Friedrick asked.

"Some guy from the Treasury Department paid me a visit."

"I hope you didn't tell him anything. When did this happen?" Friedrick responded in an alarming tone.

"A couple days ago. What's going on? I thought you guys were going to watch my backside. Can't I trust you guys to do anything right?"

"What did he want?" Friedrick asked.

"He tells me that DeRose out of Youngstown has a contract to have me whacked."

"Do you have a name to go with this Treasury agent?"

"I think he said his name was Wells ... is that right Tony?"

"Yeah. Wells ... Steven Wells. I think he is with ATF," Tony added.

"What did you tell him?" Friedrick inquired.

"What do you take me for? Some kinda moron. I didn't tell him jack-shit," Jackie repugnantly responded.

"Let me rephrase that. What exactly did Wells have to say?"

"I think he's trying to get me to switch sides. The hit thing may be just some clever Treasury scam. What do you think, Tony?"

"It's possible Jackie, but I don't think you should take any chances. DeRose ain't no one you should be taking lightly."

"Just the same, it would be a good idea for you to stay away from those guys," Friedrick suggested before adding, "They'll lock you up and tell you it's for your own protection. Remember Joe Valachi?"

"Yeah," Jackie responded.

"That's what they did with him. You don't want that happening to you."

"Hell no! I ain't going into no Witness Protection Program. How about you, Tony?"

"No way. I'd rather take my chances. But it might be just like Jackie said. It might be just a scam," Tony added.

"You're probably right. If something like this were going down, the Bureau would have heard something about it."

"Right," Jackie replied.

"Nonetheless, I think you did the right thing."

"With the presidential elections right around the corner, I don't need this," Jackie reflected.

"Listen ... if Wells keeps bothering you, we'll have the deputy director intercede on your behalf. The last thing we need is to have some Treasury agents beating our action."

Jackie turned to Tony, "Hey, get a load of this guy. He's beginning to talk like us. ... 'Beating our action.' I like that."

"Seeing as I am already here, is there anything going down you want to update me on?" Friedrick inquired.

"Let's see," Jackie reflected. "Fitz is sick as a dog. He's lost a bunch of weight and his hair is falling out 'cause of them cancer treatments. And, oh yeah, we're all going to be holding the real meeting in La Costa about the thirteenth of July."

"All?"

"Yeah, you know, as in *all* the key players. But you got to keep that real quiet, 'cause if anyone finds out, all hell is going to break loose."

"Sure, I'll keep a lid on it. Anything else?" Friedrick asked.

"Let's see ... Fitz is going to be staying at his condo, ... and oh, I just remembered what I wanted to tell you. ... Remember a guy by the name of Shonder Birns?"

"Wasn't he one of the guys Enos blew up in his car?"

"That's the one. Well Shonder had a couple enforcers working for him. Danny Greene was one of them, but he had another guy working the Black neighborhoods by the name of Don King."

Agent Friedrick snapped his fingers a couple times, "The boxing promoter? The guy with that crazy hair-do?"

"That's the one. Anyway, this guy King is in tight with Tony Pro's brother Sammy on the east coast. And get this, he wants Sammy to set him up with a Teamster charter for professional boxers."

"Oooh. The guys upstairs love rumors like this. You got any particulars?"

"Nothing much because I didn't know if the Bureau was interested, but I take it you want me to see if I can get more particulars on this?" Jackie inquired.

"Sure."

"Okay. All I know about it so far is that he's got a scheme for milking the Teamsters' medical coverage, but I'll let you know as things develop."

"I appreciate that." Agent Friedrick jotted down the information. "Anything else going on? What about the Detroit area?"

"Hmm? ... Yeah. Awhile back I told McCoy and Foran about a guy by the name of Chuckie O'Brien. You know who I'm talking about?"

"The kid Hoffa adopted." Friedrick continued writing.

"Well he's now working for Joe Morgan. Remember, I told you about that." Jackie took a drag from his cigarette before adding, "Anyway, it was Tony Pro's idea. I guess it's in payment for ...." *What the hell am I saying!*

"Yes? Go on ..."

"Nothin'. It flew out of my head. It probably was in payment for something, that's all." Jackie made eye contact with Tony while Friedrick wrote.

"Wait a minute. How can Chuckie hold a union position? Wasn't he convicted a few years back for his illegal union activities?" Friedrick remembered.

"Yeah. I guess the federal judge who imposed the sentence had a sudden change of heart," Jackie concluded.

"Oh?"

Tony added, "I think what Jackie is trying to say is that the judge got a telephone call from Tony Provenzano. ... Get the picture?"

"Are you shitting me?" Friedrick retorted.

"Not really," Jackie said. "The judge wrote Chuckie a letter saying it was okay for Morgan to hire him as a Business Agent. Hey, what can I say ... money talks, even with federal judges."

"We're going to have to look into this."

"Listen, we're getting away from the important stuff. We should be talking about Roy Williams. You guys were gonna take him out of action for me before the election. What gives?"

"There might be a slight problem with that."

"I don't what to hear no shit. Just take him out. Shoot the bastard, if you have to," Jackie demanded.

From across the room Tony interjected, "That might not be so easy for them to do, now that Danny Greene's been taken out."

Friedrick ignored the side-bar, "It's not that simple anymore. Besides, I don't know anyone in Black Ops. I really wish you wouldn't say or even suggest such things in my presence. It makes me nervous when you guys talk like that."

"I still don't understand your problem. Williams is still receiving big kickbacks, and you're telling me you can't move on that?" Jackie complained.

"Like I say, it's just not that easy. We intercepted a conversation between Senator Howard Cannon and Allen Dorfman in La Costa about Williams," Friedrick responded.

"So, you guys finally got that place bugged. It's about time," Jackie stated.

"We discovered that an individual by the name of Bill Joyce, a general organizer out of Chicago will be serving as Williams' contact."

"That creep," Jackie muttered.

"You know who this individual is?" Friedrick responded. "I don't remember you mentioning his name before."

"I don't know this button-man personally, mind you. I may have heard something about him working for the Chicago Mafia don."

"Dorfman?"

"No, Dorfman's with the Syndicate. I was referring to Dominic Senese."

"Jackie," Tony interrupted, "maybe you shouldn't be putting too much on this guy's plate."

Jackie nodded, "Listen. Now that I think about it, it might be better if you just left that one alone. Just stick with Dorfman, it's a lot safer for all of us. Okay?"

"What's the problem?" Friedrick asked.

"Look, damn-it, that bastard is dangerous. Do I have to spell it out for you. I ain't going near Senese or Bill Joyce. Period. Now, let's change the subject."

"Okay-okay." But Friedrick couldn't resist the temptation to give it one more subtle try, "I only mentioned it because I thought I remembered reading something about him in the local papers, that's all."

Tony turned away from the window, "I think he's got the two Joyces mixed up Jackie. The Joyce he might be thinking about is your ex-chief of police."

"Oh. Yeah, you must be thinking about my man, John Joyce. I got him employed in Local 507 working for me on some special projects."

"How come he resigned from the police force?" Friedrick asked.

"'Cause there wasn't any future in it. He can make more money in one day working for me than putting in a full week with overtime, chasing speeders and handing out parking tickets, that's why." Jackie glanced around the room, then to Tony. "Say, you want to go down and get us a few cans of pop? You know what I like."

"Sure Jackie," Tony responded.

Upon Tony leaving the room, Jackie became more forceful, "Listen. I want you guys to go after Skippy Felice. Since he's gotten out of the joint, he's back at Local 293 practically every day. He wants me to put him back on the Teamster payroll."

"And?"

"And I ain't going to do it! Skippy's got contacts that stretch all the way to Chicago. The Bureau's got to nail his ass again. I don't want him running around behind my back, stirring up trouble for me. And believe me, Skippy can do it."

"I'll see what we can do, but I can't promise anything. We're running short on manpower at the moment. If you pick up anything solid that we can use, we'll move on it," Friedrick assured him.

Jackie exploded, "Jesus Christ! There you go again."

"What's wrong?"

"What's with you guys? You're always wanting me to do your work. Ain't I got enough to do as it is? I was going to tell you about Glenn Pauley and Joe Callo hitting me up to charter a computer workers union, but as it stands, that can wait. If I give you guys too much to do, not a damn thing will get done. That's it for today. I've had it."

The meeting had broken up before Tony returned, holding three cans of soft drinks. With Friedrick gone, Tony said, "I didn't want to say nothing in front of Friedrick, but you didn't tell him anything about what's gonna happen to Scripts-Howard's Press newspaper, did you?"

"Hell-no, and I ain't going to either." Jackie gulped his drink before adding, "You know my policy. I don't ever say nothin' to these bastards until it's too late."

# *Chapter 13*

## Presidential Connections

RONALD REAGAN'S advisers skillfully crafted and established the campaign issues, and on November 4th the American voters agreed: The Republicans were heading back to the White House after a four-year absence. The combination of American hostages being detained in Iran, the perceived threat of world domination by the Communists and domestic inflation seemingly out of control worked to President Jimmy Carter's demise.

Perception was more valuable than truth, and those advising the President-elect were acutely in tune with that reality. Behind the scenes the perception of the hostage situation, the Communists and inflation had influenced the electorate into believing that the truth was the lie, and the lie was the truth. George Orwell's prophetic *1984* had arrived well before its Gregorian calendar date.

Even though the world had entered the Information Age, information was viewed as a commodity that had to be carefully controlled. The new age came with its own vocabulary. Words like *new world order* and *global economy* would be embraced as politically correct terminology for those who sided with the new administration's ideology.

The newly appointed transition team moved quickly to implement new policies that would eventually restructure the country's entire social fabric. In the process, America's high-ranking standard of living would begin a long, slow and agonizing descent. Hope for a brighter future and a higher standard of living would be eventually replaced with pervasive despair, not seen since the Great Depression.

But there was one key difference between the Great Depression of the '30s and the Economic Recession of the '80s: President Ronald W. Reagan was no Franklin D. Roosevelt. This time, there would be no effort to salvage America's working middle class. This time, there would be no massive effort to rebuild America's aging infrastructure. This time, there would be no hope for a brighter tomorrow, for tomorrow's reality had arrived.

Aside from the master strategy, there were of course political and campaign debts that had to be repaid. Not everyone was looking for a cash reimbursement for their investment in President Reagan's victory. Some were willing to settle for presidential access, power and influence. Such special favors would accrue to wealthier individuals who had wisely invested their financial resources in making the transition to the new world order and global economy.

"Jackie, I have some bad news," Agent Friedrick announced.

"What?"

"Word has it that President Reagan is planning on appointing you Secretary of Labor."

Jackie laughed, "How's that supposed to be bad news? Besides, Reagan owes me big time."

"The bad news is that the folks inside the Department of Labor don't like the idea," Friedrick revealed.

"Tough. You tell 'em for me that life's a bitch."

"You remember that special investigative unit that was set up by the Labor Department?" Friedrick asked.

"Yeah, so what? I wouldn't be too worried about those guys because once I get my appointment, I'm going to put those guys out of business."

"Unfortunately, they've already launched a massive investigation into your background, connections and business activities."

"Who cares?"

"They found out that you received six million dollars in connection with the acquisition of the Aladdin Hotel and Casino. They claim the money was laundered by the Continental Corporation. I don't remember you telling us anything about that," Friedrick politely reflected.

"Well blow me down! I must have plum forgot! Foran always said I had something wrong with my memory."

"This is serious Mister Presser. It's oversights like this that could make me and the Bureau appear as if ..."

"Go ahead, say it," Jackie order. "It might make it look like the FBI is protecting a gangster. Well I am a gangster and always have been, and everyone knows it—warts and all. So what? That's what makes me such a valuable commodity."

"That wasn't what I meant. We have to know about these things so that we can protect you. You're leaving us and yourself wide open when things like this happen. When HQ is not prepared, they go ballistic."

"Now you listen. I mentioned this crap to McCoy several years ago. I can't help it if he never wrote nothing down. Let's see, if he did write it down, they would have placed it in *The Tailor Files*. Maybe you should take a peek in that file. I'm sure you'll find some mention of it."

"No one is allowed to see that file. It was sealed and moved to our Washington headquarters after that gal Linhart started leaking information to Anthony Liberatore. I start asking questions and the brass will come down on me like shit."

"Well that's where it must be. I told him all about it, but that was a long-time ago. How am I supposed to remember about a loan that matured back in January of '77. By the way, now that you mention it, whatever happened to that Linhart broad who stole all that stuff from your files?"

"Come-on Mister Presser. Let's not get into that."

"No! I want to know. What happened to her?"

"We put her into the Federal Witness Protection Program," Friedrick sheepishly revealed.

"See, ... what are we talking about here? You help protect one criminal who steals your own shit right out from under your noses, and bitch to me about laundering a few million. So what's the big deal?"

"The big deal is that it took us by complete surprise. In Linhart's case, we knew what she was taking and could control what was being removed."

"I'll be damn. Liberatore was telling the truth!"

"What are you talking about," Friedrick puzzled. "Truth about what?"

"Both the Mafia don and Big Ange Lonardo accused Liberatore of adding Nardi and Greene's name to your informant's list. I'll bet you guys did that yourselves." Jackie leaned forward, "Level with me ... was Danny Greene working for you guys?"

"What in hell ever gave you that idea?" Friedrick responded.

"'Cause he never got arrested for any of them guys he whacked."

"Greene was a very cautious individual," Friedrick replied.

"Ah bullshit. You want to keep our relationship going you better start doing better than handing me that crap. ... So is that it?"

"Not quite. This team of undercover investigators claim, among other things, that you violated the Hobbs Act. I guess they made the Bureau appear pretty stupid," Friedrick confessed.

"Well that ain't the first time that's happened. You said, 'among other things.' What other things?"

"The Labor Department also claims that your attorney has set up a series of various business investments in York Penn, and that you've been moving substantial amounts of money around the country in an effort to hide huge cash reserves."

"Hey, my attorney is doing it all legit. Besides, I didn't write them loopholes into the commerce rules and regulations. You guys should be taking that up with the chairman of the Commerce Committee."

"Senator Howard Cannon?"

"Yeah. You want me to schedule you an appointment?"

◆

EARLY ON THE MORNING of January 20th 1981, special undercover agents Jim Thomas and George

'Red' Simmons entered Jackie's office without calling for an appointment. They wanted to be there to greet Jackie's Uncle Allen when he arrived.

The two agents carefully avoided notifying other law enforcement agencies, including the Attorney General's office. As a result, their presence took everyone by surprise when they produced a secret federal arrest warrant for Uncle Allen's embezzlement of union funds under the RICO Act.

Jackie ordered a joint meeting with his attorney and Agent Friedrick. "I suppose you've both heard by now that those two undercover clowns busted my uncle." Robert Friedrick and John Climaco looked at each other without words. "Well don't just sit there looking stupid."

"What is it you want us to say?" Friedrick asked.

"My ol' man wants him off, and I have to inform him of want you're going to do about it. You're both attorneys, so let's hear something. I want to know how you're going to get him off."

"This is going to be a little difficult," Friedrick remarked. John nodded in agreement.

"I don't want to hear that shit."

"But Jackie ..."

"No 'but Jackies.' I know me and Uncle Allen ain't been getting along so good, but I promised my ol' man you two would get him off. My ol' man is practically on his death bed. As a dying wish, he don't want him doing no more time on my behalf. So I told him it would be taken care of. Now, let's hear something constructive."

Friedrick attempted to be the voice of reason, "If he gets convicted, I can see that he gets sent someplace decent, ... maybe that federal country club in Texas."

"I'll see if we can cut a deal," Climaco added.

"What kind of deal?" Jackie demanded.

"I don't know exactly, but I'm sure I'll come up with something."

"So we're talking pie-in-the-sky crap. It that it?" Jackie responded.

"Look Jackie, I can't promise we'll be able to cut a deal with this special prosecutor they've called in. If not, I'll pull some strings with the federal judge to see that he serves only a minimal sentence," Climaco assured him.

"That still ain't good enough. You have to do better than that."

"But Jackie ..."

"No-buts. You guys don't seem to understand what's at stake here, so let me spell it out for you. If Uncle Allan starts thinking that we didn't work hard enough to keep him out of the joint, he might start talking to the Treasury boys." Turning his attention to Friedrick, "And we certainly don't want to open up that can of worms now, do we?"

"You've made your point," Friedrick responded. "I'm sure the Bureau will intercede if he gets convicted."

"Now he hasn't been convicted of anything yet. We have a few other legal strings we can pull before it gets to that point," Climaco concluded.

"No! Let me make a point. What everyone seems to have forgotten is that my ol' man had Uncle Allen delivered that extra half million to Mitchell for the defense of them guys on the White House staff. You do remember Watergate, don't you?"

John leaned back as he reflected, "That's an excellent point." Turning to Friedrick, "When you stop and think about it, that could be a real *oh-shit* in front of a federal jury if that came out." Turning to Jackie, "I think you've just given us the perfect ammunition we need to get your dear sweet uncle, off the hook."

"Good. Then it's settled."

Climaco turned to Friedrick, "Now you see why he'd make an excellent Secretary of Labor."

"That reminds me," Jackie said, "we've got a White House reception to attend in March." Jackie wanted to make sure Friedrick knew he had presidential connections.

◆

AT THE MARCH reception in the White House for major campaign contributors, Jackie and his attorney were causally approached by one of the President's administrative aides. "Mister Presser, I wonder if I might have a private word with you and your attorney for a moment?"

"Sure." Jackie and John followed the aide to a small sitting room down the hall from the main dining room, away from the other invited guests. "Remind me some day to tell you about the first time I was here," Jackie reflected.

Leaning closer to Jackie's ear, John whispered, "Are you sure you're the one on the 18-minute gap? I heard that Henry Kissinger confessed to that."[11]

"Yeah, sure. Did Henry also confess to whacking Hoover or giving Nixon the million-plus bucks?"

---

[11] There has been much speculation about the 18-minute gap that Nixon ordered erased from his Oval Office tapes. The author formally requested a copy of the White House Visitor's Log for the evening of June 20, 1972, but was informed that it no longer exists.

The aide opened the door and briefly surveyed the room to make sure it was unoccupied before ushering them in. As soon as the door was closed he began explaining, "I was asked by, ... well let me put it this way, I was asked by someone on the staff to bring something of a delicate nature to your attention."

"Oh?"

"A source close to the President wanted me to inform you that the Labor Department was going to have you indicted in connection with its ongoing RICO investigation of your Local 507. I don't want to get personal, but are you related to a Mister Allen Friedman?"

"He's my uncle."

"Did your source have any suggestions on how this might be avoided?" John inquired.

"As a matter of fact, there is someone who may be able to help you in this matter. If you'd like, I can introduce you to him this evening," the aide responded.

"What's his name?"

"His name is Vince Mirada, and he may be able to provide you with some special assistance with the forthcoming indictments."

A blank look came over Jackie. His attorney leaned forward to whisper, "Vince Mirada owns Mr. Coffee."

Jackie nodded, "This Mister Mirada? What might I suppose he wants from Jackie Presser?"

"Oh sir, I wouldn't know anything about that. You best take that up with him. Shall I introduce the two of you?" the aide inquired.

"Sure, but give us one moment," Jackie requested. "We'll be along directly." As the aide left the room, he continued, "Hell, I'll bet I know what he wants."

"What?"

"If I'm not mistaken, Skippy Felice controls the Mister Coffee union contract," Jackie said.

"So you think Mister Mirada wants to dump Skippy and work directly with us for a soft union contract?"

"The only contract I'd like to put out is on Skippy. Come on, let's go meet this guy, Mirada."

Reaching for the door, "You think Skippy is going to make any trouble for you, Jackie?"

They strolled their way back to rejoin the other guests. Jackie carried a luminous smile, and spoke through his teeth. "I'll see that Friedrick takes him out of the picture." Happily acknowledging guests with nods, "I wonder what would happen to ol' Skippy if rumors started about him using nose candy. That'll fix his ass."

At the Teamsters' Convention in Las Vegas during

*Jackie and Cynthia Ann Jerabic*

the first week of June, Jackie was accompanied by his attorney, his bodyguard, and his mistress, Cynthia Ann.

From across the room, Jackie spotted the crime boss of the Chicago Mafia. He turned to Tony, "Listen, first chance you get, I want you to talk to Dominic Senese for me while we're here."

"You want me to see if I can find out what's going on in Chicago?"

"Yeah, but I also what you to see if you can feel him out about Skippy. Just see if he's found out anything."

Tony returned within a half hour, "Jackie, I got some interesting feedback from Dominic."

"What do ya got?"

"He's apparently very upset with Skippy over his Local. He's not too pleased about Skippy's inability to take care of problems in the Local."

"Oh-really? Any other good news?" Jackie asked.

"Now this part ain't so good. Apparently Skippy's been spreading rumors around that you're an FBI informant. Skippy asked Dominic to approve a contract to hit you and me both."

"It sounds like we're dealing with a Joey DeRose and a Harry Haler all rolled into one," Jackie responded.

"What do you think we should do, Jackie?"

"If that's the way he wants to play the game, he's in for a couple of real nasty surprises."

"Is there anything you want me to do?" Tony asked.

"No. I'll take care of it."

"What do you have in mind, Jackie?"

"I'll call John Joyce the moment I can find a clean line. I'll have him tail Skippy. Then I'll give Friedrick a call and have him tip off the ATF and DEA boys. By the time Skippy gets back to Murray Hill, he'll have more heat on him than he could ever imagine."

"What are you suggesting? You think the Bureau will set him up to take a fall on some phony narcotics wrap?"

Jackie looked directly into Tony's face, "Anyone who gets in my way from now on is going to be taken out of action."

"Jackie, you're talking crazy. I don't think Dominic is going go along with Skippy. I'll bet he thinks Skippy is just blowing smoke."

"And I'm telling you, it's a whole new ball game, Tony. You must have forgotten who the President invited to the White House. ... And whether you know it or not, the Bureau now dances to my tunes."

♦

THE FOLLOWING MONTH, the man who had nominated Jimmy Hoffa as the General President of the Teamsters, established the largest labor local, ordered the deaths of at least a dozen people, held silent ownership in the Yellow Cab Company, and operated the largest music and vending company, quietly passed away.

Among his major lifetime accomplishments was the financing of a little crossroads town in Nevada that would eventually become the most profitable entertainment facilities in the world. Another achievement included building the largest organized crime Syndicate in the country. His enterprises were considered so successful and respected that J. Edgar Hoover had ordered *his boys* not to interfere with any operation involving the man known throughout organized crime as Big Bill.

Big Bill Presser had accomplished more than most men could have accomplished in six lifetimes, yet he successfully managed to live a modest lifestyle, never flaunting his enormous power and wealth. Since the '40s, he had quietly built and maintained an active liaison with each *La Cosa Nostra* crime family. Over the years he had earned each crime family's confidence and respect. That reputation opened the door for his son.

And although Jackie did not inspire the confidence and trust of his late father, it was assumed something had rubbed off along the way. Why else would Big Bill appoint Jackie to permanently replace him on the Central States Pension Fund? But whatever reservations senior-level members of organized crime may have had about Big Bill's son, it was Jackie's direct access to President Ronald Reagan that erased any lingering doubt.

Aside from the underworld community, the Organized Crime Unit with the Department of Labor noted Big Bill's passing. Undercover agents Thomas and Simmons logically assumed that organized crime families from across the country would either be present or send a high-ranking representative to pay their final respects. Anticipating that this would occur, the two agents set up surveillance to record the event. It came as a mild surprise to agents Simmons and Thomas to discover that all other branches of law enforcement were likewise present to capture Big Bill's funeral on film.

The funeral and the lengthy procession that followed was the largest ever attended in Ohio's history. Jackie however, saw things from a different vista. Turning to Tony, "I hope none of these people think that by attending the ol' man's send-off that that's gonna entitle them to a piece of my ol' man's estate, 'cause it ain't."

"Jackie, you shouldn't be thinking about things like that at a time like this."

"Oh? And what should I be thinking about?" Before Tony could respond, he continued, "Me and Climaco are going to see the ol' man's attorney first thing in the morning and get things straightened out."

"What kind of things, Jackie? I'm sure your father left a will, didn't he?"

"Wills don't mean shit. That's just for little people."

"But Jackie ..."

"No buts. The ol' man left me in charge to administer the estate, and that means that what I say goes. As far as I'm concerned, none of them deserve a damn nickel ... except maybe the ol' lady. I'll see she gets something because she's the only one that ever took my side."

Interrupting, "But Jackie, you gotta go by what it says in the will."

"I don't have to do no such thing. I own Judge Tally, so he's going to do what I tell him to do."

"You think you can get Judge Tally to break the law?" Tony inquired.

"Break what law? I'm the law as far as Judge Tally's concerned. Besides, you think some two-bit probate judge wants to fuck with someone with presidential connections? No way ... not unless he's stupid or something."

The following day, Jackie and his attorney met with Gerald B. Chattman, Big Bill's private attorney. They had mutually agreed to a private reading of Big Bill's last will and testament. No one else was allowed to be present.

After their meeting, Jackie declared himself the sole beneficiary. He informed Probate Judge Tally that it would be in his best interest not to release the contents of the will to anyone, including immediate family members. Judge Tally agreed with Jackie's decision, and permanently placed Big Bill's will under a court-ordered seal. This would ensure that the nosy public and curious heirs would not interfere with Jackie's silent administration of the will.

◆

BY AUTUMN, the Reagan administration's efforts to appoint Jackie to be Secretary of Labor fell through. Presidential advisers were repeatedly warned that if Jackie's appointment was formally presented to the Senate Conformation Committee, an all-out effort would be made to expose the full extent of Jackie's ties to organized crime. It would be pointed out that key individuals like Senator Ed Kennedy from Massachusetts and Senator Sam Nunn from Georgia could tie-up the appointment indefinitely.

Jackie's nomination was quietly withdrawn.

Nonetheless, the White House felt that something had to be done to reward Jackie for his early-day financial support. The White House had decided that the best way to conceal the pay-back would be through a series of lucrative HUD projects for senior citizens. The administration selected Samuel R. Pierce, Jr. to negotiate the deal. In turn, the White House suggested to Jackie that he should select some trustworthy individual to administer these multi-million-dollar HUD projects.

Jackie scanned the list of people to whom he owed favors. Two names came to mind, but only one of them was available to handle the assignment—John Joyce.

Jackie set up an emergency strategy meeting with the other individual. "I want to thank you for getting Uncle Allen off. The ol' man went to his peace, knowing Uncle Allen wouldn't have to do no time."

"It was the least the Bureau could do," Agent Friedrick responded. "But I have to tell you, it wasn't easy. We had to really flex our muscle and influence with the Justice Department to get them to drop their case against your Uncle Allen."

"Like I told Tony, that's it. I don't owe him no more favors. My debt to him has been stamped, paid-in-full. From now on, he's on his own."

"I'm glad we could help."

"Well we still got to do something about those two sons-of-bitches with the Strike Force," Jackie announced.

"You must mean Jim Thomas and George Simmons."

"Yeah. Those two even had the nerve to set up camera surveillance at my ol' man's funeral. Can you believe that," Jackie complained.

"I'm afraid they weren't the only ones with cameras. Several Treasury agents were there too. The State Department and the Secret Service also sent agents."

"Well no one ever said getting to the top was easy," Jackie remarked. "What the hell do you suppose they were hoping to film?"

"I have no idea, but you can bet they weren't there to protect your interests."

"Look, let's just focus on the important stuff," Jackie ordered. "Your job is to protect me, and the best way you can do that is to take out those two clowns with the Strike Force."

"Believe me, we've tried. Nothing seems to work. Those two are like a couple of Philistines," Friedrick commented. "I thought maybe you or your attorney could come up with something."

"Oh," Jackie mused. "What exactly do they have on me?"

"First, let me explain the situation as we see it. These two undercover agents have been digging into your past. Some of the things they've been looking into are beyond the legal statute of limitations."

"Am I supposed to have a problem with that?" Jackie smiled.

"While most of it falls beyond statute limitations, some of it doesn't."

"Such as?"

"Such as the six million you skimmed from the Aladdin for openers. They also dug up something on the illegal kickbacks you received from Hoover-Gorvin and Associates."

"That dates back to Watergate for Christ sake. Hasn't the statute run out on that stuff yet?"

"It all depends on how they approach it. Simple theft, sure. But suppose they take the approach that this was long-term embezzlement? If they take this approach, different statutes apply."

"Okay-okay. Is that it?"

"Not quite," Friedrick added. "They know about the ghost employees you had on the payroll of your Local 507."

"Yeah, well that was McCoy's idea. Is that it?"

"Now they're looking into some HUD grants. One in particular involves several million the Reagan administration is funneling to you through some project in Columbus, Ohio."

"Is that it?"

"No, not quite. The Department of Labor has prepared an LM-II report, and has requested a Program 10 report from us. Now *that* we'll be able to help you out with. My understanding is that our director himself will have to approve it. I'm sure the director will have no problem turning down their request. In the meantime, the Bureau has requested copies of the Labor Department's O.I.G. reports. That should slow them down, but if not, it will at least give us a good idea on where they might attack."

Jackie rolled his eyes, "Go on, anything else?"

In mild shock, "Christ, isn't that enough! We don't have that much crap on Allen Dorfman, Nick Civella and Roy Williams, combined!"

"It ain't as bad as it could be. I'll have my attorney check on the statute of limitations. I'm sure he can get a couple of those items squashed before any of it gets off the ground."

"What about this guy of yours, John Joyce? You think you can trust him to keep his mouth shut about the HUD deal?" Friedrick inquired.

Smiling, "Of course. He signed the paperwork for that stuff. So if any of it goes south, he's the one who has to take the fall, not me."

"The sixty-four thousand dollar question is, should we be told about anything else so that the Bureau can head-off any other criminal investigations? I shouldn't have to remind you Jackie, ... the Bureau doesn't like surprises."

"If it's all the same to you, I'll take my chances," Jackie concluded.

"What do you mean?"

"Look ... suppose I start telling you everything. Next thing I know, you'll have too much on your plate, and nothing will get done. Besides, if you ain't found out about them, then there's a good chance those two bastards won't find out about them either."

"But Jackie, we don't watch our informants. You're supposed to get our permission to engage in any type of illegal activity."

"That sounds like something taken from the Mafia oath," Jackie retorted, "... get permission to engage in illegal activity."

"There has to be a degree of mutual trust. If the brass finds out that you've been holding back, or they get caught off guard because more surprises crop up down the road, they're not going to like appearing foolish or stupid."

"Trust? Is that what this is all about?" Jackie asked.

"Yes."

"I didn't get to where I am trustin' people. I only trust one guy and that's Jackie Presser."

"All I can say is that if these two special investigators zero in on something and we get caught with our pants down, we may not be able to protect you. They're taking their findings to a special prosecutor who's not willing to play by our rules."

"All right. Let's do it this way. I'll throw out some items. You tell me what they've got."

"Okay."

"Did the Strike Force mention anything about the Forge Restaurant?" Jackie inquired.

"They've looked into that too, but as far as we've been able to determine, Simmons and Thomas came up empty-handed. What's the deal there?"

"There's a Workers' Comp case that might not wash with the claim we filed."

"Would that have anything to do with your daughter, Bari Lynn?" Friedrick asked.

"Just leave it be. What about the deal I got set up with Blue Cross?"

"What deal is that?"

"Never mind," Jackie continued as he mentally checked off items from his list. "You answered my question. What about Traveler's Insurance?"

"No, their name hasn't come up in their investigation."

"Good. What do they know about my building lease business?"

"What's involved?"

"Leave it be. Again you've answered my question," Jackie responded.. "Okay, here's a big one. Are those two looking into my Pick-N-Pay grocery-chain deal?"

"Not that we're aware of. Christ, when do you have time for all this?" Friedrick puzzled.

"If you're trying to make a point, make it. Stop trying to pull my chain," Jackie demanded.

"You know what I mean. You're serving as President of Local 507, you're Vice President position with the International, your position on Joint Council 41 and you're a senior trustee on the Central States Pension. Between that and meeting with the President of the

United States, when do you have time for all these other, shall we say, outside activities?"

"I got to keep up appearances," Jackie retorted. "Like I told you, I'm a very busy man."

"That's a hell of an understatement."

"What's that wisecrack supposed to mean?"

"I meant to say, you've got be awfully careful. ... I don't want to get personal or anything, but ..."

"But what?"

"Your private lifestyle has the Bureau a little concerned."

"How so?"

"Well, among other things, these two agents may have obtained secret authorization to bug one of your apartments. Do you have a mistress living with you?" Friedrick asked.

"Now listen, if you guys would stop spending all your time looking into people's sex lives, you might have something to show for your efforts. Ain't you got anything better to do?"

"The way we see it, you can tell a lot about an individual from his extracurricular sex activities. That's always been one of our top priorities."

"Enough of this crap. I want you to work on the important stuff. I want you to nail Williams. If you'd have done like I told you in the beginning, Williams would never have become President of the International."

"We've tried, believe me, we've tried."

"Well obviously you didn't try hard enough," Jackie complained.

"Since becoming the International's President, Williams has been keeping a real low profile. He hasn't been in direct contact with Civella in several months. My guess is that he figured out that we have guys watching him around the clock."

"We've been over and over this stuff a million times. And I'm getting tired of repeating myself. If I've told you once, I've told you a thousand times, you've been watching the wrong people. You want me to tell you everything that's going down, and when I do, I find out later that all you've been doing is peaking into bedroom windows."

"Now Mister Presser, I thinks that's a slight exaggeration."

"Like hell it is."

"If you've got a fresh lead for us, I'll see what we can do to zero in on Williams for you."

"All right... I had a meeting with Sam Arcana."

"Who's he?"

"He's Civella's main go-between. My guess is that Williams is going to align himself with the Chicago Syndicate."

"Why do you think this might be significant?" Friedrick inquired.

"The talk going around is that the Chicago is planning to move the Teamsters' headquarters from Washington to Chicago."

"Oh?" Friedrick invited.

"Yeah. If that happens, the Chicago Syndicate will be staffing the place with their people. You know what that will mean, don't you?"

"That means Allen Dorfman, Sidney Korshak and Don Peters will have complete control over the pension fund money and the Teamsters right from their base of operations."

"Exactly."

"There is absolutely no way the Bureau can allow that to happen."

Jackie crushed out his cigarette, "Now you're using your head."

*Chapter 14*

## Coupe De Grâce

THE 1982 ECONOMY hit the wall of reality and began falling apart faster than the Federal Reserve could hold the pieces together. The Reagan administration's euphoric plan for getting government off the back of private industry, trickle-down economics, and labor policies immediately began being felt in the marketplace. If the rapidly deteriorating conditions continued, Washington insiders believed that President Reagan would not last beyond one term.

The President's advisers had other plans, and moved quickly to put a positive spin on the situation, along with a strategic political game plan. While chastising the Carter administration and blaming the nation's economic problems on the previous administration, the Federal Reserve was quietly working with the new administration to mortgage the future of the next two generations.

Key individuals with knowledge of the administration's master strategy would be able to financially protect themselves as well as handsomely profit from a close relationship with key individual. One individual close to President Reagan was able to capitalize on his direct relationship with the Chief Executive.

◆

Jackie leaned back in his office chair, "I'm telling ya Tony, this is the way it's supposed to be. Reagan has got the right idea."

"I hope you're right Jackie. We don't need to return to the dark days of the Great Depression."

"That's not going to happen, and I'll tell you why." Not waiting for a response, he continued, "Part of Reagan's plan is to take care of us guys at the top of the economic ladder. That way, we'll be in a better position to take care of ourselves in the event of an economic downturn."

"Ain't you forgetting something? What about the large middle-class?"

"Fuck 'em. ... What did the middle-class ever do for Jackie Presser? Huh?"

"Well their union dues provide you with a pretty good salary, not to mention the sizable pension and retirement you'll get. All I can say is that it's a good thing Reagan didn't want to appoint you Secretary of Health and Human Services. Poor people wouldn't be getting nothing," Tony reflected.

"Your damn right. Besides, they're nothing but a drain on the system, always wanting things handed to them, never working a damn day in their lives, having kids they don't care nothing about. Someone has to put a stop to it."

Muttering under his breath, "Christ, you're a fine one to be talking."

"How's that?" Jackie shot back.

Raising his voice, "I said, 'Christ, you're going to be able to set a good example.'"

"You're damn right," Jackie replied.

"Too bad about the Secretary of Labor position. I know you really wanted that appointment."

"I could have handled it. No big deal though."

"I have to say Jackie, you're taking it real well."

"I've been informed that the President will keep me in mind for something else after the heat settles down. In the meantime, I got other fish to fry."

"Oh? What's on your mind?"

"The first thing I got to do is get Friedrick on the stick. Is this guy slow in the head or what?"

"What's the problem Jackie?"

EARLY SUNDAY morning meetings became the weekly routine. This day, a private suite at Howard Johnson's Motor Lodge was selected. Agent Friedrick greeted Jackie in an upbeat mood. "Hi Jackie. What's going on?"

"Not a damn thing."

"We all feel bad about you not getting the Secretary of Labor position."

"The hell with that crap."

"Is there a problem?" Friedrick asked.

"Roy Williams is the problem. He's the same problem I've had since day one. When are you guys going to move on that bastard?"

"That's an interesting point."

"No, that's bullshit," Jackie responded.

"Let me explain. The Bureau has been kind of forced into a holding pattern on that issue."

"Explanations are for losers. I don't want to hear explanations. I want to see bottom-line results. In case you haven't noticed it, we're moving into a new era, not just politically, but socially, economically and informationally. All decisions from now on will be made at the top. Everyone else's job is to carry them out—right or wrong. Is that understood? There is to be no more of this questioning routine."

"What are your immediate concerns?" Friedrick asked.

"I just told you, damnit. —Williams! He's been by-passing me on every damn appointment being made. He's screwing-me-over every chance he gets, and I want it stopped."

"What do you want us to do?"

"Just do your job. Whack the son-of-bitch."

"Please Jackie, don't talk like that, not even in jest."

Smiling, "Oh? You think I'm making a joke?"

"No, that's the problem. I'm sure you're not."

"Then there's no problem."

"What you don't seem to understand is that from time to time, we have to take lie-detector tests."

"So what?"

"They ask us all sorts of questions, including stuff about potential crimes in which we may have direct knowledge. What am I supposed to say if they ask me a question like that? Christ, my polygraph reading would be falling off the damn chart," Friedrick complained.

"Great. I'm supposed to trust you guys, and you don't even trust each other."

"That's not really the issue. I'm under an enormous amount of stress lately. All I've been filing for the past several months are rewrites of old field reports. Even Foran has spotted it. He's got an eye for that sort of thing and has been asking me about what you've been up to.

All I've been able to tell him is that you've been busy with the President's advisers. Now that your nomination has been withdrawn, I can't keep feeding him that line."

"Are you through? Because if you're not, I'm tired of listening."

"Please Jackie, why don't you forget about getting Williams for the time being. I guess what I'm trying to say is that the Treasury's involvement in the matter has made it a dead issue."

"This 'dead issue,' as you call it, is kicking the shit out of me and John. I want something done and done now! Even if you think it's wrong, but for the life of me, I can't see how you guys would know the difference."

"All right, what do you have in mind?"

"Discredit him like you did Hoffa. Leak some stories to the press that he's a homosexual." Jackie snapped his fingers then pointed, "Better yet, spread rumors about him molesting little boys. That'll fix his ass. If that don't work, take him for a boat ride."

Friedrick raised an eyebrow, "You're really serious about this, aren't you?"

"You're damn right I'm serious. Take him out on the lake four or five miles and push him overboard. He'd never make it back to shore."

"I can't put a request like that through channels. Back during Hoffa's era while Hoover was alive, it was different. All our orders came from the top down."

"And that's how it's gonna be again."

"What I meant to say was, if an idea like this doesn't originate from the top, it isn't going to happen."

"The way I see it, and John agrees with me, the only way I got a shot at grabbing the presidency of the

International is if Williams is taken out. Now there's only a few ways we can do that. So what you're telling me is that you need some orders from your top brass to light a torch under your ass. ... Make it happen or I'll have my man in the White House talk to your man."

"Could we change the subject?" Friedrick knew they had reached an impasse. Jackie nodded his willingness. "I received a telex from headquarters. Like I said, my field reports haven't exactly been up to par lately, and I'm catching heat on this. My guess is that HQ is confused about how all the information we've developed over the years ties together."

Jackie shook his head in disgust. He slowly stood up and walked over to Tony who had taken up vigilance near the window. "Can you believe this shit? After all this time, these assholes still don't have the foggiest idea what the fuck is goin' on."

"I know Jackie. What do you want me to say?" Tony replied.

"It's no wonder they keep chasing after their tails. They must have a ton of this shit, and they still can't put the pieces of the puzzle together."

"Maybe their in over their heads. I can't help you. Maybe you should speak John." Tony advised.

Jackie turned away from Tony, walked back to Agent Friedrick and took a seat. "I don't know what more I can tell you, I swear to God I don't. I've given you the low-down on every crime family in the country. I've told you who all the major players are, their plans, where they meet, and who they're going to fuck. In some cases, I've even told you how much they're going to make off a deal. I don't know what more I can say."

"I'm being constantly pressured to show my superiors how the local crime family ties into this whole thing. We've done a number on Felice like you asked, but that's where it ends. It seems like this crime family is totally isolated from all the others."

"What in hell are you talking about?" Jackie demanded.

"Don't take this the wrong way, but some of the guys up stairs are beginning to think that you've been protecting certain individuals."

"That's not true. The local outfit hasn't been involved in much, other than working a few Vegas deals. The biggest thing the outfit was involved in during the past five years was to contact Fratianno. He worked with Liberatore to have Ferrito take-out Danny Greene. ... Now that I think of it, how come you guys never went after crazy bastard yourselves."

"We've already been over this. I've told you, we had nothing to do with Greene's criminal activities. He was strictly operating on his own."

"Yeah, well I ain't buying it. No one can kill that many people and live to brag about it like Greene did. He must have killed at least twenty people himself." Turning toward Tony, "What would you say Tony?"

"Twenty would be very conservative, Jackie. It had to be many more than that."

Back to Friedrick, "See what I mean? How come you guys never tried to stop Greene?"

"I wasn't assigned that detail, so I don't have an answer for you. But that's history. We've got to focus our attention on the local Mafia."

"Listen, the local Mafia ain't my problem, it's the Chicago Syndicate. Look, I'll explain it to you for the umpteenth time."

Friedrick took out his notepad from which he would prepare his January 17th field report, "Ready."

"Anderson answers directly to the Super Jew."

"Sidney Korshak," Friedrick clarified.

"Right. Korshak holds the same kind of position as Don Peters. Both them guys answer up to Dorfman, and the whole damn bunch have to answer up to the Chicago Mafia don, Dominic Senese. Got the picture?"

"Got it. Does anyone locally report to Chicago?"

Jackie suddenly stopped, rose from his chair and walked over to Tony. Using a lowered voice, "If I bull-shit him on this and he's writing it all down, I got to be careful what I tell him. What do you think?"

"I don't know Jackie, I'm only your bodyguard, not your attorney. All I can tell you is that you have to keep this guy on your side. Maybe you should discuss it with John first."

Walking back to Friedrick, "Listen, I've decided you can't write any of this shit down."

"I'll need to put something in my field report," Friedrick responded.

"You're not listening. If I tell you the important stuff, it's got to be strictly off the record." Friedrick closed his notepad and put his pen into his pocket. "The Genovese crime family in New York controls cities like Cleveland, Buffalo and Newark. Cities like Detroit and Kansas City report to Chicago. The whole network of organized crime is linked together with personal liaisons who travel between the various cities and keep the major players informed as to what's going on."

"Off-the-record, who's your liaison with the other crime families?"

"... Maishe, ... Maishe Rockman."

"And this Maishe Rockman handles all the communications with the various families?"

"Not totally. Primarily, he's the go-between for Chicago, Cleveland, Pittsburgh and New York. Here's how it works. ... Say something is going on in California. Anderson sees that the Chicago don is informed, and Maishe carries that information from there to here, and on to the east coast."

"No wonder we've never been able to find a group of them meeting," Friedrick concluded.

"You mean like the meeting in upstate New York back in '57?"

"Yeah. We figured that after that bust, the Mafia stopped meeting altogether."

"Like hell we did. That's why we built our own private meeting place. If something real big was going down, then all the big shots like myself head for a place called La Costa. But like I said, you can't be putting this stuff or Maishe's name in no field reports. Fill the space with something else."

Special Agent Robert Friedrick blinked his eyes in disbelief. For the moment, he alone was the only special agent in the FBI who understood how the system of organized crime actually operated.

♦

THE BUREAU'S lack of progress in driving a wedge between Roy Williams and the Teamsters resulted in Jackie contacting Maishe to enlist the services of the Genovese crime family. He was obliged to use proper channels, and Maishe was the proper channel.

"Maishe, I've got to ask you to do me a personal favor."

"If it's something that I can do Jackie, I'll see what can be done. What is it?"

"I've tried everything I can think of to have Williams removed from the picture. If I could, I'd take a gun and blow his brains out myself."

"Don't tell me you want to ask for a hit contract on Roy Williams? That is not a good idea ... not just now. It would bring down too much heat from the Treasury. Besides that, it's too close to the IBT election, and neither Chicago or New York want that kind of federal heat at this time."

"I see," Jackie responded. "Okay, what about delivering a special message?"

"This message, ... is it going to cause me any problems?" Maishe wanted to cover his backside, and carrying the wrong message at the wrong time was something he had skillfully avoided.

"Okay, let me put it this way. I'd like you to convince New York that Roy Williams is destroying the International. That would be the truth."

"How so Jackie?"

"Williams is going to turn over all operations to the Chicago Syndicate and Dorfman's people. New York is going to be left out of the picture. I'm willing to work with New York, you know that. I can't see how I'm going to be able to do that if Williams is allowed to call all the shots."

"Hmm? ... Okay, I'll bring your concerns, shall we say, to their attention. In the meantime, I don't want you to do anything rash. If they decide something should be done, let it be initiated at their end, not from you. Is that understood?"

Jackie forced a smile, "I know you'll do right by me. I'm not going to forget this favor."

◆

WITHIN 72 HOURS, Maishe Rockman delivered Jackie's concerns to Fat Tony Salerno with the Genovese crime family. In turn, Fat Tony set up a meeting with Sammy Provenzano from New Jersey to double check the facts and see if Jackie's accusations about Williams were true. Sammy confirmed that since Civella's incarceration, Williams was gradually switching his allegiance from the Kansas City crime family to the Chicago Syndicate and Allen Dorfman.

Armed with that information, Fat Tony booked a flight on the next available plane to Chicago for a sit-down. Fat Tony met with underboss Jackie Cerone, who setup the meeting with Dominic Senese. It was a circuitous route, but like the Bureau, proper channels were required. In this case, it would have been an act of disrespect to do it any other way.

As a result of this sit-down, a meeting of the IBT General Executive Board was ordered. For security purposes, the details as to the place and time would be announced only at the last moment.

The Bureau had picked up rumors about the secret meeting that had begun to circulate. Special Agent Robert Friedrick dispensed with the usual formalities for setting up a meeting and contacted Jackie by telephone.

"Jackie, I know this is awfully short notice, but both our divisions on the west coast and mid-west have picked up rumors that something big is going down."

"You're not supposed to be calling and talking to me like this on the phone," Jackie responded.

"I realize that, but this is an emergency."

"So what's so damn important it can't wait until Sunday?"

"The Bureau has learned that a top-secret meeting of all the high-ranking officials is to be held. Have you heard anything about this?" Friedrick inquired.

Jackie paused a moment to calculate if it was too late in the day to cause any serious damage? "Yeah. As a matter of fact, I just got word on it today."

"How did you find out?" Friedrick asked.

"What difference does it make?"

"I had to inform the brass about La Costa. We'll have the placed bugged, so be extra careful what you say."

"Well that ain't going to be a problem, 'cause I won't be there. Who told you the meeting was going to be in La Costa?"

"Well we just assumed that because that's where you said all the secret meetings are held."

"Look, you'll be wasting your time. In fact, this meeting is so important they didn't announce its location until today. But don't worry about it. As soon as I learn the particulars, I'll fill you in on what you need to know."

"Jackie, please, I need to have a few more details."

"Okay, here's something you can put in your field report. You tell your superiors that The Tailor has taken matters into his own hands. You couldn't take care of business, so I took care of it for you."

"Are you saying you know what this secret meeting is all about?"

"What I'm telling you is that Jackie Presser takes care of business."

"My career is coming real close to reaching critical mass. You can't believe the amount of pressure that's coming down. Now I've helped you every way I can. It's now time for you to reciprocate."

"All right, all right. Christ, all I need is another cry-baby in my life. The meeting you've picked up on involves all the vice-presidents of the International. It's going to be held the day after tomorrow in New Mexico."

"That's a pretty big state. Any idea where in New Mexico?"

"It's going to be held in a special meeting place near Masclao called the Inn Of The Mountain Of The Gods. Now that's all I know."

"Maybe you can record the special meeting on your key-chain recorder?" Friedrick suggested.

"No, 'cause I wasn't invited. And neither was Roy Williams. It's just for the king makers."

"Any guesses on what the 'king makers' might discuss?" Friedrick pressed.

"Hmm. Don't quote me on this, but my guess is they're going to pick Williams' replacement. I've already relayed my sentiments to the organization."

"Thanks Jackie. You've literally saved my ass by coming through for me on this one. Is there anything you think we should be watching out for?"

"Yeah, ... if I were you guys, I'd stay a hundred miles away from that meeting. If any of those guys spot agents hanging around, they'll cancel the meeting in a New York minute. So do us both a favor."

"What's that?"

"Let 'em take care of business."

◆

BY THE TIME Agent Friedrick filed his written field report, the Phoenix FBI office had less than a day to scurry to Masclao and set up an advance surveillance system in time to monitor the otherwise secret meeting. Special agents managed to sneak out the backdoor just as 14 of the International's vice presidents were arriving. The group had gathered to hear Sammy Provenzano cover the primary topic of conversation.

"I think everyone present knows why we're here," Sammy announced. "Just to make sure there's no misunderstanding, we've got to decide on what we want to do about Roy Williams."

"If it's decided he has to step down as president of the Teamsters, who's gonna take his place?"

"The general consensus seems to be that Jackie Presser should take Williams' place."

"Not as far as I'm concerned, it isn't," Andy Anderson objected.

"I think the first thing we have to do is to carefully explore all options," another vice president announced.

"Yeah, we've at least a half-dozen guys we can install. Jackie isn't my first choice, either."

"Okay, but which of those guys is as tight with the Reagan administration as Jackie? None of them have his influence with the President," Sammy offered in rebuttal.

"Yeah, some influence," Anderson retorted. "He didn't get the Secretary of Labor position. So what kinda influence are we talking about?"

"We're talking about the fact that he's going to be appointed Special Advisor to the President on Labor Affairs. That means we'll have a voice speaking on our behalf, directly into the ear of the President of these United States."

"Good point," one of the other vice presidents replied.

"But how do we know we can trust or control Jackie? Let's face facts. Jackie is no Big Bill Presser. Half the Syndicate members deserted his organization after Big Bill died. Even his own Uncle Allen has deserted him." The board members began shifting in their seats and grumbling, and the meeting was on the verge of turmoil.

Sammy held up his hand to quiet the discontent, "Okay, I'll tell you why we can trust Jackie ..." He paused long enough to make sure he had everyone's attention before continuing.

The two FBI agents gasped as Sammy continued. They could discern from the silence of the group that the audience at the other end was equally in shock.

Only Andy Anderson, the Eleventh Vice President from Los Angeles, continued to voice opposition, "I still don't like the idea. Rumors have cropped up that he's an FBI informant. What if that's true?"

"Maishe Rockman has checked out those rumors from beginning to end. Some guy by the name of Harry Haler got all that started, and Skippy Felice simply picked up on it to get back at Jackie."

Again, the general consensus around the room was that Maishe's judgment was sufficient. Anderson, however, was not persuaded, "I still say we pick someone else. Besides, suppose Williams wants to put up a fight? Suppose friendly persuasion doesn't work?"

Anderson's inquiry brought a second hush of silence.

"If any of our other options are not possible, other arrangements will have to be made to ensure that Williams does not complete his term in office," Sammy offered.

Hearing no further objections, there was mutual consensus by silence.

At the other end of the monitoring equipment, however, FBI agents listening and recording every word were outraged. What the two agents did not realize, however, was that the man being discussed was The Tailor, the Bureau's most valuable informant. Furthermore, what they did not understand was that the Reagan administration would have its own man calling the shots and controlling the largest labor organization in the world. Those political considerations were far more important to the administration than Jackie Presser's criminal duplicity.

◆

Following that meeting, Jackie' personality changed. Like the caterpillar emerging from the cocoon, Jackie experienced a transformation, a metamorphous that afforded him the luxury of arrogance.

Boasting, "I'm in. You're now talking to the next General President of the International Brotherhood of Teamsters."

"Don't you have to be elected by the Teamster membership to make it official?" Friedrick asked.

"That's bullshit. The official decision's been made. All I got to do now is have a sit-down in New York with the five crime families making up the Commission. They'll probably want to go over some of the details."

"What about the local Mafia? Who will be representing them?" Friedrick inquired.

"They ain't invited. They ain't even going to be consulted."

"We want you to be careful. Treasury boys have been coming in hot and heavy."

"Well they ain't got nothin' on General President Presser."

"Excuse me Mister President."

"Okay, you're excused."

"That's very good," Friedrick smiled.

"Is there something else you wanted to discuss?"

"No, I just thought I should bring something else to your attention."

"You meant to say, 'to your attention, sir.'"

"Yes sir, to 'your attention.'"

"What is it?"

"I suppose you've noticed the articles appearing in newspapers and magazines lately on your predecessor, Jimmy Hoffa."

"I ain't got time for reading shit like that. I'm too busy now. After this, I'm ordering you not to mention his name in my presence."

"Yes sir."

"Go on," Jackie invited.

"It happened exactly seven years ago today. This marks his ..."

"Anniversary?" Jackie inserted. "He's dead. It makes no difference to me if he's dead or officially dead. So why are you bringing this to my attention? Are you going to start a serious investigation?"

"Not hardly. Everyone who was involved had an air-tight alibi."

"What do you mean by that wisecrack?"

"I'm sorry sir. I didn't mean for it to come out that way," Friedrick surrendered "Lately, we've had a lot of media inquires, especially under the Freedom of Information Act. My guess is that the Bureau will most likely recycle the cover stories and rumors that have circulated since day one."

Jackie finished the thought, "You have to hand it old J. Edgar ... he certainly had the media trained good. I heard he had guys like Walter Winchell, Ed Sullivan and Walt Disney doing some of his dirty work. By the way, about the media, John was wondering if anyone could find out about me or him through that Information Act. I want our names kept out of the newspapers and television unless it's totally positive."

"Yes sir."

"In case you haven't heard, I'm going to be appointed Special Adviser to the President. So, what are you doing to protect me?"

"With regard to the Freedom of Information Act, you're fully protected. No one outside the FBI will acknowledge your identity or know which file to ask for."

"What about federal judges?" Jackie inquired.

"Including federal judges. Besides that, Jackie, we've assigned several code names that have been changed over the years. As an added precaution, we've given you a middle initial."

"Oh? What initial is that?"

"We've assigned a 'B' to your name. If any individual outside the Bureau wants to see what we have with your name on it, they would have to specifically ask for Jackie *B*. Presser. If they don't know to specify your name in that exact manner, they'll come up empty handed."

"Hmm? All presidents have middle initials. ... Good work. ... Maybe I should get a presidential portrait of myself painted."

"We're only trying to keep you happy."

"And you're sure this middle initial thing will protect me?"

"Even federal judges can't find out anything, unless they specifically ask for Jackie B. Presser."

"Not bad. ... I like that."

"If all this media coverage stirs up any new information, we'd still like to be informed. That way, we can head-off any potentially damaging inquiries."

"I want you to throw the media off the track."

"Yes sir."

"You're doing such a good job, I got something new for you. Why don't you check out North American Van Lines?"

"Okay. What's the story?" Friedrick asked.

"Them drivers are members of Local 392. They've been operating without a contract, and have been, ever since you-know-who set it up. It goes back something like twenty-five years."

"That long? Have you told anyone about this before, sir?"

"No. I just thought of it. You can't expect me to remember everything. Besides, I got a lot on my mind."

"How did you-know-who fit into this?"

"Like I said, he set the whole thing up right from the beginning. That Local doesn't have a labor contract. They get no benefits for their union dues."

"I'll make a note on this sir, but I have to tell you, this amounts to slim pickings. If you would have thought of this ten years ago, we could have used the information more productively."

"Okay, I just thought of something else. Remember how I keep telling you to keep the heat on Williams?" Jackie reiterated.

"The Labor and Justice Departments are doing that. The only reason we haven't stepped in, is because we feel we can use our manpower more productively by targeting Dorfman."

"They've just tapped the Pension Fund for something like forty or fifty million," Jackie revealed.

"Who are 'they' sir?" Friedrick asked.

Jackie took a long drag from his cigarette, "The money is part of a deal with that U.S. Senator who wants to help Roy Williams with his federal indictment."

"Anyone involved?"

"A guy by the name of George Lehr and some attorney by the name of Tom Wadden. Bottom line is this. They are the ones who are supposedly responsible for setting up the deal."

"Any idea how they are able to pull this off?"

"Let's see," Jackie replied scratching his chin. "If I'm not mistaken, Williams' son-in-law, Amos Massa, his son and daughter, his wife and his assistant, I think his name is Thomas O'Malley, are all on the Pension Fund payroll." Jackie took another puff from his cigarette before switching to a facetious tone and rising. "You know, now that you mention it, I haven't the slightest idea how he's able to pull this shit off."

Friedrick laughed to show his appreciation of Jackie's twisted sense of humor. "That's choice."

♦

FOR SEVEN YEARS, the U.S. Treasury, the Secret Service, the U.S. Marshal's Service and the OIG Section of the Department of Labor had confronted one bureaucratic obstacle after another when it came to inquiring about Jackie's criminal activities. Request after request for the FBI to supply vital information on Jackie or Big Bill went unanswered or were simply ignored.

Occasionally, a persistent government agency would be disquietly informed that national security and foreign governments were involved, and therefore, no information would be forthcoming.

The two special undercover agents with the Department of Labor, however, were becoming suspicious, not of Jackie Presser whom they knew was deeply involved in an endless assortment of criminal activity, but with the FBI. On the morning of October 8th, the two undercover agents from the Office of the Inspector General were standing outside Jackie's office with secretly issued search warrants when his secretary, Gail George, arrived at 8 AM.

Their investigation caught the FBI flatfooted. The Bureau's ego was bruised as it learned about the investigation-in-progress from local radio news broadcasts. Within minutes of the announcement, the Bureau's secured telephone lines began lighting up, followed by a hastily scheduled emergency meeting.

"What the hell is going on?" Friedrick demanded to know. "What are these two guys trying to pull?"

"Let's get some calls out and see if we can keep a lid on this thing before things get any further out of hand," Agent Foran commanded.

After a half dozen calls to various agencies, one name came up that Foran recognized as he replaced the telephone receiver. "Well, I think I found out what happened. I just got off the line with Steven Olah. Does anyone remember a guy we had IRS target?"

"Hell, there's been so many. Do we get to have a clue?" one agent fielded.

"You're not going to believe this, but remember a guy by the name of Harry Haler." A wave of groans circled the room. "He finally got someone to listen to him. Thomas and Simmons with the Special Strike Force actually believed the shit Haler fed them."

"I thought the IRS clamped a lid on that guy. Didn't we send him up the river on some federal wrap for using stolen bonds or something like that?"

"Yes, but these two tracked him down. It looks like Haler finally got his revenge against Jackie for cutting him out of the action. According to Olah, he has just advised me that they are proceeding against Jackie under Title 29, USC Section 501, subsection 'c,' for embezzling union funds."

Special Agent Friedrick jumped up, "We have to stop them! Now! Christ, these two are going to screw-up everything."

One agent turned to another and whispered, "God, if the White House finds out about this, I don't want to be the one having to answer their questions."

"You're not alone," another agent groaned.

"Okay, here's the emergency game plan. We're going to tell these two clowns that national security is involved. That will allow us to take over jurisdiction of their investigation, whether they like it or not." Foran turned to Friedrick, "In the meantime, I want you to set up a real quiet meeting with Alpro. They'll be watching him very close, so inform him that he has to take special precautions."

ON THE MORNING of October 20th, 1982, Special Agents Foran and Friedrick waited for Jackie to arrive. "You think this is really going to work?" Friedrick asked.

"Beats the shit out of me. I know one thing, ... if it don't, we can kiss both our careers good bye." Looking out the window, Foran spotted Jackie getting out of his car. "Here he is. Christ, he drove his own vehicle. You'd think he would have enough brains to switch cars."

"I'll check to see if he was followed," Friedrick volunteered.

Foran took the initiative. "Hi Jackie. It's been a while."

"Cut the crap. You bastards were supposed to be protecting me against shit like this. I got agents swarming over my ass like pack of hungry buzzards."

"The state of your ass is the least of our worries for the moment. This is serious shit. This time we've got to cover our own asses. So sit down and start answering some questions," Foran ordered.

Jackie took the closest available chair. He padded his pockets to feel for an extra pack of cigarettes.

Foran kicked a chair around to sit down, "What's this shit about you having the President of the United States in your pocket?"

"I don't know what you're talking about."

"Oh? It has just recently come to our attention, or at least to my attention, that you've been playing us for a bunch of suckers. We've just discovered a half zillion items that you seem to have absentmindedly forgot to tell us about."

"Like what? I've been straight-up with you guys. You've been listening to too many of your own rumors."

"I don't think so. What's this shit about you financing special projects for the President? We hear that you've been funneling money to some guy at the White House. In turn, he's promised you special access to the President. Your name has cropped up on a list of special donors, and it has been rumored that you've been in direct contact with the Israeli, South Korean and Japanese governments. Shall I go on, or am I still drawing you a clouded picture?"

"Okay, so maybe I forgot to mention a few things.... But this ain't got nothing to do with our arrangement. You want details—fine, but you got to do something for me in return."

Turning to Friedrick, "How do you like this shit!" Then back to Jackie, "I'll say this much, you sure got balls! Here, we've gone out on a limb to cover your ass, kill a major criminal investigation, let you make ... what? Twenty or thirty million in tax-free income—not to mention all the money we've paid you. We've even helped you get yourself appointed General President of the International Brotherhood of Teamsters, and you want us to do you more special favors. All I can say is that, you got a brass set of balls!"

"Hey, I got competition. Besides, I got a lot of expenses, not to mention a whole lot of risk. I don't see any of you guys sticking your fuckin' necks out. I'm the one who's life is on the damn line!"

Whispering into Foran's ear, Friedrick suggested, "You know, he's got a point. Maybe you ought to lighten up a little."

Turning toward Friedrick, "Get-out-of-my-face," Foran whispered back. Returning to Jackie, "No! No promises. I'll hear what you have, and that's all. If it's too risky a situation, you're on your own. But first, no more holding back. These scams you've been running for the past eight years are going to stop. You want favors? We want trust. You start spilling the beans, or I'm personally going to see that you get cut loose."

Slowly, Jackie began outlining his history with Harry Haler and how Watergate began. For more than three hours, he recited as many details as he could remember, given the stress of the moment. The only thing he managed to successfully avoid mentioning was how much money he had stolen. He felt that if they thought it was only thirty million, that was a nice round figure to leave on the table. As his self-confession wound down, he changed the subject.

"... So that's where it stands at this time. I'm close to landing the presidency of the International, but like I said, it ain't a totally done deal."

"What's the problem?"

"It's this guy by the name of Rolan M. Lee. He's been operating out of St. Petersbury, Missouri, and he's beating my action."

"How so?" Foran's interest was waning.

"Don't you see. He's competing for the same Teamster dollars that I need. He's drawing off funds that should be available for us ... I mean, the President's special programs. As it stands, the funds in the form of kickbacks are going to organized crime families in Chicago and Kansas City. I can hardly get my hands on a damn nickel of that bread. You guys have gotta do something about shutting down that Missouri operation for me."

"At the risk of opening another can of worms, what do you suggest?" Foran inquired.

"You guys can go after Ed Wheeler for me. He's the attorney for the International. Put enough heat on him, and there's a good chance he'll resign."

"Won't they simply put someone else in to take his place?" It all sounded a little bizarre to Foran, but in light of these new revelations, nothing Jackie said surprised him.

"No, it ain't that easy. It's got to be some attorney the outfits think they can really trust. They'll be asking me for my recommendation."

Amusingly, "Oh? And who do you have in mind to take his place?"

"My attorney, John Climaco, of course."

Foran turned to Friedrick only to catch each mirroring the other's smile. "What makes you think you can pull this off?"

"Let me level with you," Jackie suggested.

"No! Let me level with you," Foran countered. "You either tell it to us straight or I'm cutting you loose."

"You'll probably find it out soon enough with all these other guys hanging over my shoulder. ... God, I got to have rocks in my head for saying this stuff."

"Would you rather we find it out on our own?" Foran snapped back.

"... Maishe Rockman's my contact. He's the prime liaison with the various crime families. I might have mentioned it to Friedrick off the record, but the reason I didn't want that known is because you might have wanted me to start pressuring him for information. You wouldn't understand."

"Try me."

"You don't understand. You can't do that with Maishe. I can't be asking him anything directly. The guy's not stupid. I have to just wait until he tells me something on his own. I ask him the wrong question, and ..."

"We're familiar with him traveling to Las Vegas and things like that, but I don't see what the big deal is."

"You don't see the big picture. I ain't told you all the stuff that perhaps like maybe I should have. You guys just wouldn't understand."

"Is there something else involved in all this?" Foran wanted to know.

"Yeah. You see, Maishe's the main man. He controls the information between organized crime families.

Not just here, but all over. He handles everything between Chicago and New York and from Detroit to Pittsburgh, sometimes even to Kansas City. But you got to promise me you won't mess with him. He's got to be left alone. If I lose Maishe, I got no contacts, no information. —Understand?"

"We get the picture," Foran responded.

"So, is that it?" Jackie was anxious to leave, and started to get up.

"Yes, I think that will wrap it up. Get out of here." Foran was not happy about the amount of information Jackie had been withholding from the Bureau. He felt that had he stayed on him, Jackie would never have been able to get away with this much duplicity. He let Jackie reach the door before firing his last question, "One more thing before you leave." He waited for Jackie to turn around.

"What's that?" Jackie responded.

"I was just thinking about Jimmy Hoffa. You know those two brothers on the east coast by the name of Sammy and Tony Provenzano?" Foran and Jackie's eyes came into direct contact with one another. "Seeing as how you know the go-between so well, I was just wondering, after Maishe took the money to the airport locker, did he ever tell you what Provenzano's hit men, Sal, Gabe and Tom, did with Jimmy Hoffa's body?"

The look on Jackie's face answered Agent Foran's poignant question.

"I wouldn't know nothin' about that."

"Bullshit. An answer like that could get your special privileges canceled, and that's the only thing between you and federal prison."

"Don't quote me or nothing like that but ..."

"Go on," Foran ordered.

"I may have heard stuff, but I got nothin' to prove it."

"Stop wasting my time. What did you hear?"

"I heard that they may have duped Chuckie O'Brien into picking up Hoffa and driving him to some scheduling meeting place."

"Duped? You think O'Brien was duped?"

"I don't think they let him in on their plans or nothin' like that. Hoffa wasn't no dummy, for Christ sake. He wouldn't have gotten into just any car."

"Okay, so O'Brien may have been used as the patsy to get Hoffa in the car. Then what?"

"After they got him into the meeting house, one of them guys you mentioned put a couple rounds in the back of his head when Hoffa wasn't lookin'."

"Tom?"

"What difference does it make?"

"That's not an answer to my question. I want to know what happened to his body?"

"I heard they removed and burned his clothes and belongings. ... They may have put him in the trunk of some old car."

"Then what?"

"Well, you know."

"No, I don't know. What?"

"The Provenzanos are in the trash compacting business. I suppose he got pressed into a cube and recycled. ... Listen, I'd really appreciate it if you'd keep that information real quite for the next fifty years."

"Why's that?"

"If this stuff gets out, they'll whack me for sure. Besides that, it might not look so good if people found out you guys had all these deals and didn't do nothin'."

It wasn't necessary for Agent Foran to clarify who the *they* might be; he knew who *they* were.

## *Chapter 15*

## Lamentations & Machinations

ON THE AFTERNOON of January 20th, 1983, the man the FBI had been targeting for special investigation left the Hyatt Hotel in downtown Chicago. He had been having lunch with a business associate. Now he had a personal errand to run, and he headed toward a short alley. He turned the corner and made it almost half way when a car pulled in behind him and stopped. With the sound vehicle's motor still running, the 60-year-old Allen Dorfman glanced over his shoulder. He saw two young men step out of the car. They drew weapons. A hail of bullets were emptied in his direction. He took a few steps then fell down.

Dorfman's blood began painting the alley.

The gangland-style hit alarmed the Chicago Teamsters and the Chicago SAC office immediately telexed the FBI in Cleveland for Alpro's assistance. They wanted to know if he could furnish the Bureau with any new leads.

SLIDING into Jackie's front seat Special Agent Friedrick asked, "I suppose by now you've heard the news about Dorfman being hit?"

"I heard. Is that what this is about?"

"Our Chicago office wants to know if Alpro has any information?" Friedrick replied.

"Word has it that his hit originated on Dorfman's own turf." Jackie fought to hold back a smile, "I can't begin to tell you how broken up I am over the whole matter."

"Foran said you'd be broken up. I was asked to see if you knew any particulars or had any leads?"

"Leads, let's see. ... Anderson probably had a hand in it," Jackie offered.

"But Anderson is out of Los Angeles," Friedrick fired back.

*Whoops!* "I know that, but what you don't realize is that Anderson's tight with Joey Auippa, and Auippa's out of Chicago."

"So you think Auippa had something to do with the hit?" Friedrick logically concluded.

"I didn't say no such thing. Goddamn-it, stop putting words in my mouth. All I know is that after the Treasury nailed Dorfman, he announced that he wasn't gonna do no jail for fifty years."

"So you think that the Chicago mob perceived this as a threat?"

"Yeah, something like that," Jackie abstractly responded.

"And they took that as a sign Dorfman would talk?" Friedrick asked.

"Right. Listen, I know I can say this to you without you mentioning it to Foran, but what are the possibilities of taking out Joe Morgan for me?"

"Sure. What's the situation?"

"Morgan is the seventh vice president with the Teamsters. He's in charge of the Southern Conference."

"What's on your mind?"

"I got this presidency thing just about locked up. Now that Dorfman's out of the way, he's the only one left. All you got to do is put some federal heat on him, and he'll back off from running against me. ... Hey, I got an idea. What if his name started cropping up in that Amalgamated case the government is working on?" Jackie suggested.

"How will that help you?" Friedrick inquired.

"Morgan's really worried about his name appearing on any of the records the feds seized. Just let him know, or think that his name's all over the place. Morgan will jump right out of his skin. He might even leave the country. Either way, that'll take him out of action."

"Speaking of Amalgamated, that reminds me, ... during our Strawman investigation, we confiscated a bunch of records and notes from a Carl Deluna out of Kansas City. We think he goes by the nickname of Tuffy."

"I don't know too much about Tuffy's operation."

"Did you make him any loans?" Friedrick inquired.

"Why would I do anything like that? Look, just tell me what you have."

"We came up with a term we know nothing about. Does the name or word 'Fireplug' mean anything to you?" Friedrick asked.

Jackie knew that was the nickname Hoffa used in reference to his father. "Nah, I can't say that rings any kind of bell with me. Is that all you've got?"

"What about the code name, Argent?" Friedrick inquired. "It was referenced in regard to the purchase of Recrion through the Pension Fund."

"Nah, again I can't help you. But I'll tell you what ... I'll see if my attorney has anything on Recrion. He handles most of our major investments."

"Please Mister Presser, I need to file something in my field report. Surely you can think of something interesting. It's going to look like I'm not doing my job. Besides, how would it look if I reported that Alpro was of no assistance?"

"Okay, here's an item. Williams has just appointed Walter Shea to serve on the Central States Pension. Shea's in way over his head. Besides that, he's a weak-minded boozer. But I suppose Williams could have appointed someone worse."

"Oh? Such as?"

"Such as Jimmy Hoffa's old ally, Harold Gibbons. He would be a whole lot worse. That s-o-b is nothing but a batch of trouble as far as John and me are concerned. Shea is about the only appointment we support."

Within a week of Jackie's last meeting with Special Agent Friedrick, Trerotola called Jackie to inform him that he was withdrawing his support. He was going to throw his endorsement to Joe Morgan due to a prior commitment.

"Damn, Tony. I knew if they moved too slow on this, something like this was going to happen."

"You think someone got to him?" Tony surmised.

"You know damn-well someone got to him, but who?"

"Don't get yourself worked up over this. I don't think Morgan can pull it off. Besides, he don't have your White House connections."

Gail's voice came over the intercom, "John Joyce is on the line."

"Find out what he wants, then tell him I'll call him back."

Gail continued, "Your daughter is on the line. What do you want me to tell her?"

"Tell her I'm tied up with my attorney."

"Maishe called before you arrived and wanted to discuss something about peanuts. He said you'd know what that meant. I told him you'd contact him."

"That it?"

"For the moment," Gail signed off.

"Where were we?" Jackie asked.

"You were telling me about Trerotola withdrawing his support," Tony reminded.

"Okay, if this is the way Morgan and Trerotola want to play politics, I'm going to teach 'em guys a few lessons."

"I don't like it when you talk that way, Jackie. I hope you ain't got something crazy on your mind."

"Crazy? You think I'm crazy?"

"That's not what I meant."

"Foran thinks I'm crazy. Everyone I know thinks I'm crazy, but I don't give a damn what anyone thinks. I want the general presidency's position and I aim to have it one way or the other."

"That's how John Nardi used to talk and look where it got him. You can live without being general president of the Teamsters. Besides, you got the real power with your presidential connections and position on the Central States Pension. God knows you got all the money and women you'll ever need. What more you want?"

"It's not the money, damn-it. I deserve it. I want the same respect that Hoffa had, and the only way I'm going to get that type of respect is by having Hoffa's old job."

JACKIE REACHED for the telephone to page Friedrick, punching in a special five-digit sequence of code numbers that would signal Friedrick to meet him on March 18, 1983.

"I got some real interesting stuff for Big Brother. Turn on your tape recorder."

Friedrick did not have to be told twice, "Ready."

"Okay, here's the up-to-the-minute low down on what's really going down. I met with Maishe last week. I also met with a guy by the name of Johnny Tronolone. He goes by the name of Peanuts."

"What did your meeting with Maishe involve?"

"I may have forgotten to mention this to you before, but Maishe is one of the top financial advisors for the Mafia and the Syndicate."

"Oh? ... How long has that been?"

"It must have just skipped my mind, that's all. You can't expect me to remember every damn little thing. Besides, I got a lot on my mind. Anyway, as I was about to say, part of his responsibility is to keep me informed of important financial decisions."

"And this other guy, Johnny Peanuts... who's he? Does he work with Maishe?" Friedrick asked.

"There you go again. You're getting everything screwed up. Let me think how I want to say this ..."

"Just tell me who he is," Friedrick pleaded.

"Look, maybe we shouldn't be talking about Peanuts. He's too high up in the organization."

"In what way?" Friedrick inquired.

"Goddamn-it, don't you understand, Peanuts works directly for the crime Commission in New York. He's the fucking *consigliere* for Christ sake."

"I'll check our files to see if the Bureau has any background information on his Peanuts guy."

"Fat chance. Like I told Foran once, you guys are in over your heads when it comes to the serious stuff."

"Maybe our New York office has a file on him."

"Yeah, sure. In a pig's ass they'll have something. If they do, it's probably all bullshit."

"Please, Mister Presser. You know we'll help you anyway we can, but you have play it straight. If you know something important about this guy, you have to share it with us. Otherwise, how are we going to protect you?"

"Okay. This guy Peanuts ain't stupid. ... The reason you guys ain't been able to keep tabs on him is because he lives in Florida and travels back and forth to take care of important Mafia business."

Jackie took out another cigarette before continuing, "I may have forgotten to mention it before, but it was Peanuts who informed me that Roy Williams was finished as president of the International."

"What you're telling me is that this guy Peanuts delivered you the official message," Friedrick clarified.

"Yeah. Peanuts also told me that I got the support I need from the five crime families that make up the New York Commission."

"Will that be enough for you to become the next General President of the International?" Friedrick queried.

Crushing out his cigarette, "Yeah."

"What about Joe Morgan supporters?"

"I don't have to worry about Morgan any longer."

"Then that's it?"

"Yeah ... no, not exactly. There's a hitch to all this stuff I'm telling you."

"What kind of hitch?"

"Peanuts told me I got to start doing favors for each of the various crime families that support me, and all their requests will be coming directly through him."

Silence filled the room. Something was obviously bothering Jackie, and Friedrick took the opportunity to check his pocket for a spare tape.

"... Me and Peanuts had a little discussion."

"You want to tell me about it?"

"... I may have gotten into a discussion about him going around Maishe. He got a little hot under the collar. He told me he knew Maishe's role and that he was canceling that arrangement."

"How did you respond?"

"I told him I needed that kind of buffer between me and the various crime families, and that's when Peanuts informed me that I'd be taking all my orders from him."

"What does that mean?"

"That means exactly what it sounds like, damn-it. That means that after they make me president, I got to start dealing directly with the major Mafia dons. They don't want no middlemen in the picture, 'cause that way, something might get misunderstood or their orders not communicated just right." Jackie leaned forward, "Is any of this making any sense to you?"

Friedrick slowly bobbed his head, while maintaining eye contact. He mentally began taking an inventory of all the names Jackie had furnished the Bureau in the last 13 years. He could not recall any occasion where

Jackie had referenced this individual. Perhaps there were others, he thought. Perhaps Foran was right. Perhaps Jackie had a totally separate agenda from that of the FBI.

"Anyway, as I was saying, Peanuts said he would contact Maishe and set him straight on a few things, and how things are going to be handled from now on between me and the Mafia. He said if I had to contact him for any reason, I'm to call the Peter Pan Travel Agency in Miami. He ordered me not to call him direct, but contact Tony Rockman, that's Maishe's son. He would then place the call. But if it was some kind of emergency, and I have to get word to him right away, I'm to use the code name 'Pasquale,' the same one my ol' man had me used when I first contacted Nixon at the White House." Suddenly, Jackie stopped talking and looked down at the tape recorder, "Shut that damn thing off."

Friedrick pressed the stop button, "Sure. Something wrong?"

"... I got to tell you, I'm scared as shit. You guys have to help me. I didn't know what I was getting myself into."

"What do you mean?"

"In the past, I only had to deal with Maishe. He always delivered the messages. But this shit is dangerous."

"Would you like to stop someplace and have something to drink?" Friedrick asked.

"Do me a favor, leave that last part out. Say in your field report that I was 'concerned' or something like that. Say something like 'this was a significant meeting.' Say that I don't know how to, ..."

"Evaluate the situation?" Friedrick suggested.

"Yeah. Tell them I don't know how to 'evaluate the situation' and that I need the Bureau's advice on how you guys want me to proceed ... now that I'm dealing directly with the hands of death."

"I'll fire this off to headquarters right away."

"Now I know why Fitz and Williams was always scared half out of their minds all the time. Hoffa was the only one who could handle these guys. ... Listen, I'm getting tired all of a sudden. We'll take this up again in a few days."

Agent Friedrick reached down, pressed the tape ejection button, then carefully removed the tape. He had a thousand-and-one burning questions, but not one of those questions was worth destroying this tape over. As monumental a moment as this was for Jackie Presser, it was an even bigger moment for Agent Robert Friedrick and his FBI career.

◆

ON MAY 10th, 1983, Oliver B. Revell, the Bureau's assistant deputy director made his recommendations to William French Smith, director of the FBI. One of his recommendations was that *The Tailor* and *Alpro* files be maintained in the Special File Room at FBI headquarters. Revell requested that the director personally sign-off his approval for Jackie to continue his ongoing criminal participation with *La Cosa Nostra*.

FBI Director Smith pulled the Alpro and Tailor files, which referenced dozens of taped conversations. He began to randomly select tapes that had been recorded—some legally, but most did not carry a federal authorization. He picked up one of the unauthorized tapes and began to listen. He played the tape until it reached an exchange between Andy Anderson and Sammy Provenzano that had been recorded at the Inn Of The Mountain Of The Gods in Masclao, New Mexico. He played the tape until it reached Sammy saying, *'Okay, I'll tell you why we can trust Jackie. ... Because Maishe informed me that he financed the hit on Hoffa, that's why.'*

Smith picked up a pen and began drafting a hand-written note informing Revell that he had decided not to sign Revell's request for his personal authorization. That decision would eventually make it possible for other government agencies to some day pursue criminal prosecution, should Jackie Presser ever decide to divorce himself from the FBI's control. Unbeknown to Revell, however, Smith jotted down another note, one that would remind him to personally review Special Agent Robert S. Friedrick's personnel file.

The director's decision upset Revell. He fired back a detailed memo to the director, outlining his reasons why he felt the director should personally authorize Jackie's ongoing criminal conduct. The director reaffirmed his earlier decision.

AS THE WINTER season approached, all the obstacles that had blocked Jackie's access to ultimate power had been removed. Jackie Presser, special advisor to President Ronald Reagan on Labor Affairs, and the man heralded by the FBI as its most valuable informant in U.S. history, was appointed General President of the International Brotherhood of Teamsters.

He had started out life with nothing more than a seventh-grade education. Now he had it all: Money, power and respectability. He had made an impossible transition; one that took him from abject poverty into the underworld, and from the underworld into the overworld, with all the rank and privileges presidential influence allowed. The only remaining questions were: How many special favors would he have to return? What new national alliances would be created? Who could he really trust if things got out of hand, and would the FBI allow him to continue living the life of a master criminal?

But the most important questions were the ones he silently asked himself: He wondered how long he would live to enjoy it, and like the hit team sent to assassinate Hoffa, would he be able to get away free and

... clear!

# Epilog

Upon his reelection to President of the United States in November of 1984, Ronald Reagan exercised executive privilege and issued a Executive Order, which immediately disbanded the President's Commission on Organized Crime. As a former FBI informant himself during the McCarthy era, President Reagan realized the precarious position Jackie faced. The Executive Order was issued only days before two special undercover agents, George Simmons and Jim Thomas, were closing in with their federal warrants to arrest Jackie Presser for an assortment of capital crimes. The President's Executive Order brought their seven-year RICO investigation to an abrupt halt, thus allowing the man who was totally under the control of the Mafia to continue advising the President of the United States on important labor issues.

Within weeks of the President's decision to protect the nation's highest paid and most valuable informant, the U.S. State Department and the U.S. Treasury Department fell in line. The incriminating evidence, documents and undercover field reports directly linking the Mafia and the Syndicate to Jackie, and Jackie to President Reagan were ordered destroyed.

Although Jackie Presser was officially terminated from the FBI upon his election to General President of the International Brotherhood of Teamsters, Jackie continued to gratuitously provide the Bureau with select information until his death in 1988.

Shortly after Jackie's death, **Special Agent Robert Friedrick**, who served as Jackie's third FBI handler, was arrested and convicted for his criminal involvement. Upon his release from prison, he became a licensed PI, and maintains a close rapport with Jackie's attorney, John R. Climaco.

Jackie's third wife, **Patricia Presser**, lives quietly in the suburbs on a small stipend from a trust.

Jackie's fourth wife, **Carmen Presser**, squandered her $1.2 million divorce settlement. She was last known to be working as a cashier in a gas station.

Jackie's former bookkeeper, **Cynthia Ann Jerabic**, became Jackie's fifth wife for a brief period prior to his death. She continued to dine at the White House with First Lady Barbara Bush throughout George Bush's presidency. Of the four heirs to Jackie's multi-million-dollar estate, Cynthia Ann was the big winner, next to his attorney. Upon transferring the bulk the Jackie's multi-million-dollar estate to her relatives and former husband, Cynthia declared in early 1994 that the Presser estate was bankrupt.

Jackie's two lawful children, **Bari Lynn** and **Gary Presser**, each received a token amount from Jackie's estate, even though Jackie's will specified that the estate would be divided equally three ways.

A portion of Jackie's estate went to his long-time attorney, **John R. Climaco**, to cover legal expenses in fending off a number of lawsuits filed after Jackie's death. His attorney negotiated a settlement with IRS for an undisclosed amount. Climaco currently serves as the attorney of record as outside legal counsel for Blue Cross. The FBI refuses all comment on his current or past FBI status.

**Anthony "Fat Tony" Salerno**, the former Mafia don of the Genovese crime family was replaced by Vincent Gigante. Salerno died in prison at the age of 80.

**John Joyce**, Jackie's undercover detective and former Beachwood Chief of Police, moved to Washington, DC where he manages various HUD projects.

**Anthony Liberatore** was one of the few LCN members to make the FBI's *10 Most Wanted List* after he went into hiding. He was later arrested and sent to prison in 1982 for bribing an FBI file clerk, and for masterminding the bombing death of Danny Greene in 1977. Upon his release, he was arrested and convicted on June 14, 1993, for racketeering and money laundering.

Former FBI clerk, **Geraldine Linhart,** was placed into the Witness Protection Program.

In 1986, both **Tony Hughes** and **Harold Friedman** were convicted for the ghost employees Jackie Presser placed on the Teamster payroll at the suggestion of his first FBI handler. Their questionable convictions were upheld by the Sixth Circuit Court of Appeals in 1993.

**Angelo "Big Ange" Lonardo**, the former underboss of the Cleveland Mafia, was recruited by the U.S. Treasury as a registered informant. Upon completing his testimony before the U.S. Senate's Permanent Subcommittee on Organized Crime in 1988, Lonardo was placed into the Witness Protection Program.

**Assistant Deputy Director, Oliver "Buck" Revell**, was demoted and reassigned from the FBI's Washington headquarters to Texas.

**Milton "Maishe" Rockman**, Big Bill Presser's bagman, and later, Jackie's main liaison with New York's Genovese crime family and "Fat Tony" Salerno, was convicted and later sent to prison in 1987. He was paroled in 1993 at the age of 80.

On his death bed, Jackie's **Uncle Allen Friedman** revealed his small participation in Watergate to a family relative. He died broke in 1993.

**Roy Lee Williams** went to federal prison in Kansas

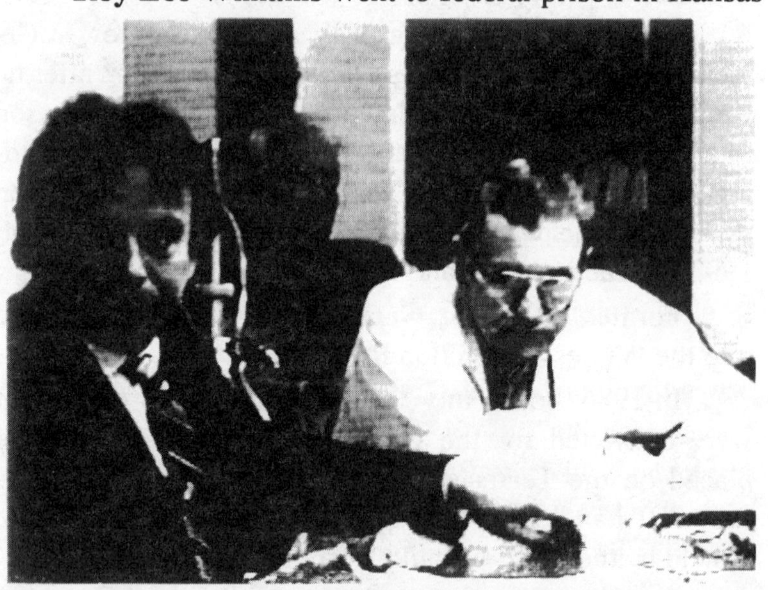

City. He is shown here being depositioned about his underworld connections. In the left foreground is the attorney representing the **Genovese** crime family.

**Jimmy "The Weasel" Fratianno** was one of the Mafia's more prolific hit men. Originally from Murray Hill, he moved to Los Angeles in the late '40s, where he subsequently became an FBI informant until 1975. He was placed into the Witness Protection Program in 1977 after being implicated in the death of Danny Greene. He died in 1993 at the age of 79.

**George "Red" Simmons**, one of the undercover agents who served on the President's Strike Force on

Organized Crime, filed suit (case # 68791) against John Climaco, et al, in 1984. He was elected Sheriff of Geauga County, Ohio, in 1993.

**Clyde Tolson**, the former Deputy Director of the FBI under J. Edgar Hoover has never been officially acknowledged as the Watergate Deep Throat.

**Richard Nixon**, the 37th President of the United States, eventually retired to California to write his memoirs. Nixon, however, forgot to mention or make reference to a few significant items, such as: his granting of Hoffa's Presidential Pardon, or the 18-minute gap on the White House tapes. And except for a brief passing reference to Hoover, he forgot to mention a signal word about his close rapport with J. Edgar, or issuing an Executive Order that no autopsy was to be performed on Hoover's body, which is the other story behind his resignation.

According to a confidential source formerly employed with the Pentagon, **John F. Kennedy** was most likely assassinated on orders of **Sam Giancana**, who was himself assassinated one month before Jimmy Hoffa. This assessment was based upon an independent investigation secretly conducted by the Pentagon, which has never been made public.

As of 1994, **Jimmy Hoffa's** FBI file remains sealed. The FBI maintains the position that Hoffa's unsolved assassination is still an open investigation, even though **Robert J. Garrity**, the sole FBI agent assigned to investigate the crime, has since retired from the Bureau after 21 years of service.

# FBI & DOL Documents

THE FOLLOWING section contains a cross-sampling of FBI and Department of Labor (DOL) field reports prepared by Special Agents (SA) with both agencies. These documents represent less than .06% of the more than 6,000 files that were carefully examined and evaluated in the preparation of this material.

Some of the highly incriminating documents not selected had to be eliminated simply because they were of poor quality, too heavily censored or lengthy.

The reader is reminded that information provided by Jackie under the FBI code names of *Alpro, Probex* and *The Tailor* does not necessarily represent objective truth. The information garnered from the Department of Labor documents, however, was secured without the informant's cooperation and consent, and therefore, may represents more accurate and objective information.

On the next two pages, a typical FBI cover sheet appears. The material was telexed to the various Station Area Commands (SAC offices) throughout the country. This information was distributed directly from the Director of the FBI. The suspected reason for the FBI using multiple code names was to avoid compliance with Freedom of Information Act requests, as well as to hide the information from other law enforcement agencies, such as the Strike Force on Organized Crime and U.S. Treasury agents, both of whom were working at cross purposes.

airtel

1 - Mr. Reutter

1/12/79

To: SACs, Albany (183-244) (Enclosure)
Anchorage (Enclosure)
Boston (183-175) (Enclosure)
Chicago (183-291) (Enclosure)
Cleveland (183-136) (Enclosure)
Detroit (183-781) (Enclosure)
Kansas City (183-105) (Enclosure)
Las Vegas (183-155) (Enclosure)
Los Angeles (183-264) (Enclosure)
Miami (183-277) (Enclosure)
Newark (183-289) (Enclosure)
New York (183-688) (Enclosure)
Philadelphia (183-323) (Enclosure)
Sacramento (Enclosure)
St. Louis (183-136) (Enclosure)
San Diego (183-93) (Enclosure)
San Francisco (183-191) (Enclosure)

From: Director, FBI (183-1099)

PROBEX

ALPRO

A highly confidential Bureau source furnished the enclosed information relative to captioned matter.

DE-111 159-4733-39

Due to the very sensitive nature of the information furnished by the source, extreme caution should be exercised in handling and use of this information. UNDER NO CIRCUMSTANCES SHOULD THE EXISTENCE OF THIS SOURCE BE DISCUSSED OUTSIDE THE BUREAU. FBI personnel should be advised on a need-to-know basis. Care should be exercised so as to not to reveal information provided by this source which might tend to reveal source's identity.

MAILED 13
JAN 15 1979
FBI

REC-50

183-1099

16 JAN 16 1979

BER:jrg (36)

Assoc. Dir.
Dep. AD Adm.
Dep. AD Inv.
Asst. Dir.:
Adm. Servs.
Crim. Inv.
Ident.
Intell.
Laboratory
Legal Coun.
Plan. & Insp.
Rec. Mgnt.
Tech. Servs.

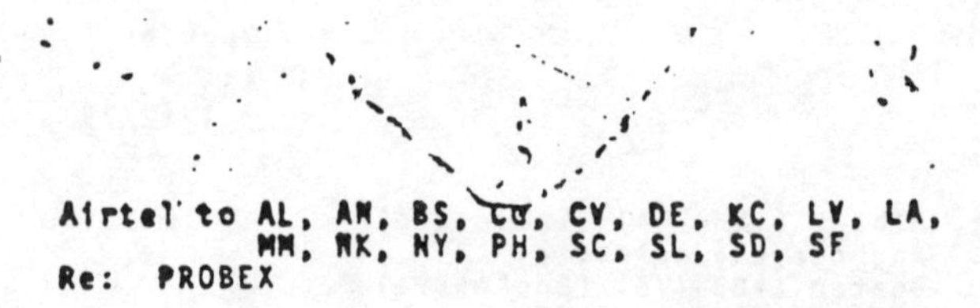

Airtel to AL, AN, BS, CO, CV, DE, KC, LV, LA,
MM, NK, NY, PH, SC, SL, SD, SF
Re: PROBEX

Should it be necessary to include portions of the information furnished by source in subsequent Bureau communications, the information should be suitably paraphrased in order to further protect the source's identity. Source should be referred to as, "a confidential Bureau source."

This information should be filed in the Probex file and maintained in a P&C secure area.

Coverage of leads provided by the enclosed information is being left to the descretion of each office.

-2-

The following two-page document is an FBI memorandum, dated 4/11/73. A few interesting items may escape the casual reader's attention. For example, "CV 882-C-TE" is the coded symbol that was used to identify the informant during the height of the Watergate era. The "CV" stands for Cleveland. The "882" is the reverse of the informant's local telephone exchange. The "-C" means that it is a confidential source. If it was a personal agent's contact, the letter "P" is used. The letters "TE" indicate the source is Top Echelon.

At the bottom of the first sheet, there are a list of names and entities. The first set of brackets are preceded by a number designation. These numbers are then used to cross-reference other material pertaining to the same subject matter. The name appearing in the second set of brackets refer to the Special Agent (SA) assigned to monitor the individual or group.

What is most significant about this particular document is that William "Big Bill" Presser, who headed up the largest crime Syndicate in the country, and Tony "Old Man" Milano, who was serving as the underboss for the local Mafia (or LCN) were not assigned to be watched by FBI agents. The reader may draw his or her own conclusions from this.

As far as the specifics contained in this memorandum, the material speaks for itself.

UNITED STATES GOVERNMENT

*Memorandum*

TO : SAC, CLEVELAND (137-3046) DATE: 4/11/73

FROM : SUPERVISOR MARTIN P. MC CANN, JR.

SUBJECT: CV 882-C-TE

Source was contacted on 3/8 and 22/73, at which time he advised as follows:

Re: PEOPLE's INDUSTRIAL CONSULTANTS
ET AL cc: LA

Source advised that he had not heard of PETER JOHN MILANO being in town at the present time or in the recent past. Source stated that JACKIE PRESSER knows PETER JOHN MILANO and has known him for a number of years as he also knows PETER JOHN's father, TONY MILANO.

Source stated at the present time JACKIE PRESSER can best be described as the one having the most potential to take over his father's position of President of Joint Council 41 in the future. Source stated that there is a lot of talk that HAROLD FRIEDMAN may be the one who takes this position, but it is the source's considered opinion that JACKIE PRESSER will ultimately take over. Source stated that in the past year in the Cleveland area BABE TRISCARO was strongly aligned with JIMMY HOFFA and was favorable toward HOFFA's return to the International Brotherhood of Teamsters (IBT). Source stated, however, that within the past three to four months, TRISCARO has seen the handwriting on the wall and has thrown in behind FITZSIMMONS. Source stated that FITZSIMMONS recently, along with the assistance of other trusted IBT officials, managed to reduce the power that HAROLD GIBBONS of St. Louis had in the IBT. Source stated that an airplane allotte for the utilization of GIBBONS was removed and that GIBBONS' main power now rests in the control of his local IBT union in the St. Louis area. Source stated that GIBBONS was closely aligned with HOFFA and it was mainly because of this alignment that he was forced out of his more powerful position on the International Board.

1 - 92-179 (TRISCARO) (SA MASTERSON)
1 - 92-178 (WM. PRESSER)
1 - 92-400 (TONY MILANO)
1 - 92-477 (CIP) (SA JUREY)
1 - 92-748 (COVERT) (LCN)
1 - 92-494 (INFLUENCE OF ORGANIZED CRIME IN LABOR)
1 - 183-12 (PEOPLES INDUSTRIAL CONSULTANTS, ET AL)
MPM:jev

70

137-3046-

SEARCHED INDEXED
SERIALIZED FILED

CV 137-3046

Source stated that "DOC" PARKER, a former FBI Agent in the Los Angeles area, has recently been hired by the Teamsters to keep a close eye on their pension and welfare fund. Source stated that this is in line with the present leadership policy of attempting to remove those who would not keep within the law in connection with their various union activities. Source stated that it is just one part of the Teamsters' attempt to brighten the image of the IBT.

Source stated that TRISCARO as mentioned above has now fallen into line and it does not appear as if he will make a play for power in the local Teamster structure. His main interest is in seeing that his son-in-law, SAM BUZZACA (ph) retains a responsible position within Joint Council 41. Source stated, however, at this time this cannot be assured because BUZZACA is considered by JACKIE PRESSER and others in the leadership position as being a poor risk, completely unreliable and untrustworthy.

Source stated that TONY MILANO, a long-time power within the Teamsters movement in the northern Ohio area, is now "out of it." Source stated that Mr. MILANO is extremely old and appears to be somewhat senile. He stated that he/continues to talk only of the "old days," and that he has practically little or no influence whatsoever within the responsible leadership of the IBT in the Cleveland area. Source stated, however, due to respect for this old gentleman, he would still be granted favors if they were within reason, mainly out of consideration for him for what he was.

Source stated that HAROLD FRIEDMAN, if it came to a vie for power within the Teamsters Union with JACKIE PRESSER, source stated there is no doubt in his mind that JACKIE PRESSER would win this power struggle, however, he does not believe that such a struggle will take place and that HAROLD FRIEDMAN is making a considerable amount of money in his various union positions and would not jeopardize this in a show-down. Source stated that the individual who would obtain additional power in the future would be SKIPPY FELICE, the son of JOHN FELICE of the Beear and Bevarage Driver's, IBT. Source stated that SKIPPY FELICE had recently been put on the Port Authority merely for the show of placing a union official within that body.

On the following page is an FBI memorandum dated 8/22/75, three weeks after Hoffa's assassination. Although the memorandum was circulated locally, it illustrates one of several attempts to link O'Brien to Hoffa's disappearance.

Throughout this memorandum, as well as several dozen other FBI memos and field reports, it should be noted that absolutely no mention is made to the Genovese crime family in New York or to the Provenzano brothers from New Jersey. If the reader remembers from the story, the local Mafia from Murray Hill reports to the Genovese family, just like Detroit reports to Chicago.

The local FBI office will not discover the direct link between the local crime family and New York until several years later. It is reasonable to draw from this that the informat intentionally pointed the FBI in directions that led the Bureau away from himself or any personal knowledge linking himself to Jimmy Hoffa.

OPTIONAL FORM NO. 10
JULY 1973 EDITION
GSA FPMR (41 CFR) 101-11.6

UNITED STATES GOVERNMENT

*Memorandum*

TO : SAC, CLEVELAND (137-3046) DATE: 8/22/75

FROM : SUPERVISOR MARTIN P. MC CANN, JR.

SUBJECT: CV 882-C-TE

Source was contacted on August 18, 1975, at which time he advised as follows: <RE: HOFFA

Source stated that he understands that JACKIE PRESSER, local teamster official, as of this date, now believes that HOFFA in all likelihood is "gone." Source stated that he also believes that CHUCK O'BRIEN, HOFFA's so-called foster-son is aware of what transpired in connection with HOFFA's disappearance.

Source stated that PRESSER is currently in Boston, Massachusetts, in connection with his daughter, age approximately 20 years, concerning an operation on her arm. Source advised he understands that if the operation cannot be done in Boston, PRESSER will proceed to New York.

Source stated that he understands that CHUCK O'BRIEN was in the Cleveland area on August 4, 1975. Source stated that allegedly, this information came from SKIP FELICE who indicated that O'BRIEN was in a motel in the Strongsville area on August 4, 1975, and that O'BRIEN was attempting to set up a meeting with JACKIE PRESSER but that PRESSER wanted nothing to do with O'BRIEN and the result was that no meeting ever took place. (THIS INFORMATION SHOULD NOT BE DISSEMINTED OUTSIDE THE BUREAU IN VIEW OF THE FACT THAT THIS CONVERSATION WAS ONLY KNOWN BY A SELECT FEW AND POSSIBLY MAY DISCLOSE THE IDENTITY OF THE SOURCE.)

SERIALIZED ____ FILED ____

The following eight-page FBI report was prepared on 10/4/78. The individual preparing the report is not identified, but in all probability, especially in terms of the quality and depth of the material, it was Special Agent Patrick Foran, who was serving as Jackie's second FBI handler at the time.

Upon Hoffa's disappearance, Jackie began implicating Nick Civella, who was subsequently dubbed the code name "Strawman."

What is interesting about this report is that it is one of the earliest references to Milton "Maishe" Rockman, who served as Big Bill's bagman and chief liaison among the various crime families around the country. Upon Big Bill's retirement in 1976, Maishe then served in an identical capacity for Jackie.

The real issue, however, is that Jackie didn't bring this information to the FBI's attention for eight years. Even though Jackie had a limited formal education, his attorney kept him regularly apprised of statute of limitation issues.

In addition, it should be noted that none of the FBI reports prior to this date mention Danny J. Greene, who was assassinated the previous year. Was someone protecting Greene? If so, why? The reader may draw whatever conclusions he or she wishes as to why no information about this psychopathic killer who was deeply involved in massive criminal activity is never referenced in FBI reports.

DATE OF THIS CONTACT
WAS 10/4/78

RE: STRAWMAN
OO: Kansas City

It is to be noted that on September 29, 1978, MILTON ROCKMAN, Financial Advisor to the Cleveland LCN family, met with Kansas City LCN boss, NICK CIVELLA at Kansas City International Airport.

Source advised that during the past two weeks, MILTON ROCKMAN has made trips across the United States for the purpose of contacting LCN bosses in various cities for JAMES LICAVOLI the reputed boss of the Cleveland LCN family. Source advised that ROCKMAN contacted LCN family bosses in St. Louis, Chicago, Detroit, Kansas City and also made contact with LCN members in Las Vegas. Source advised that ROCKMAN contacted JOSEPH AIUPPA, aka., Joey O'Brien in Chicago; NICK CIVELLA and CARL TUFFY DE LUNA in Kansas City and ANTHONY GIACALONE in Detroit. Source advised source has been unable to determine with whom ROCKMAN met in St. Louis and Las Vegas.

Source advised that contact was made with AIUPPA and CIVELLA for the purpose of advising both of these individuals that JAMES LICAVOLI, boss of the Cleveland family, would continue to control JACKIE and BILL PRESSER of the International Brotherhood of Teamsters (IBT). Source advised that ROCKMAN indicated that the Cleveland family would be responsible for the

PRESSERs and that no one had the right to ask for anything from the PRESSERs without first getting the okay from JAMES LICAVOLI, MILTON ROCKMAN or ANGELO LONARDO, the reputed underboss of the Cleveland LCN family. Source advised that this point was made by ROCKMAN due to the fact that the Chicago family of the LCN had moved a trucking company into the Cleveland, Ohio, area, called Rentar and had done so without the approval of the Cleveland LCN family and further had attempted to get favorable teamster treatment for Rentar through Cleveland teamster official JOHN J. FELICE, JR., aka. "Skippy." Source advised that REntar has had nothing but trouble from both IBT locals and membership since opening business in the Cleveland, Ohio, area. Also, they felt that FELICE would be able to handle any problems they would encounter. Source advised that ROCKMAN made it quite clear to both AIUPPA and CIVELLA that LICAVOLI considered FELICE to be a nothing and that in the future LICAVOLI should be contacted and arrangements for favorable treatment of any business enterprise involving the teamsters would be handled by him through BILL or JACKIE PRESSER. Source further advised that ROCKMAN determined from NICK CIVELLA that he, CIVELLA, did not want to have personal contact with JACKIE PRESSER or FRANK FITZSIMMONS as had been rumored since his release from prison in June, 1978. Source advised that CIVELLA indicated that Kansas City LCN member SAMMY ACANO (phonetic) had not been instructed by he,

CIVELLA to take messages to FITZSIMMONS or PRESSER, that he CIVELLA wanted to see them. CIVELLA indicated that ACANO was wrong in bringing that message to FITZSIMMONS and PRESSER and was trying to show how much power and prestige he, ACANO, had and was trying to feather his own bed.

Source further advised that CIVELLA indicated to ROCKMAN that he would like to have ROY WILLIAMS made the next president of the IBT; however, he was doubtful that this could be accomplished and that in all probability, JACKIE PRESSER would be made the next IBT president in view of the fact that PRESSER is "cleaner than WILLIAMS." Source further advised that FITZSIMMONS is expected to remain president of the IBT until the convention in1980.

Source advised that during ROCKMAN's meeting with CIVELLA, he CIVELLA, requested that ROCKMAN contact JACKIE PRESSER and have him, PRESSER, get a job for a JIM STEER in the Public Relations Department of the IBT. Source advised that STEER was a news commmentator in the Kansas City area who was recently fired by his television station after it was determined that he was very close to NICK CIVELLA and further after it was determined that he had done favors for CIVELLA.

Source further advised that ROCKMAN indicated without giving any specifics that he, ROCKMAN, had traveled to all of the above described cities because the Cleveland family was having problems getting their skim money out of Las Vegas.

Source advised that the source is unaware of the exact problems the Cleveland family was having with regard to this scam.

Source advised that for years various families of the LCN have obtained skim monies from various casinos in Las Vegas. To the best of the source's knowledge, listed below are the casinos controlled by an LCN family.

| CASINO | FAMILY |
|---|---|
| Caesar's Palace | Cleveland and New York |
| Flamingo<br>This casino is presently being leased by Caesar's Palace | Cleveland and New York |
| Hacienda | Cleveland and Kansas City |
| Dunnes<br>Purportedly owned by MORRIE SHANKER and ALLEN DORFMAN | Kansas City and Chicago<br>Chicago purportedly gives Cleveland a piece of their end |
| Sands | New York |
| Circus-Circus | Chicago and Kansas City |
| Marina | Kansas City |
| Slots of Fun<br>Owned by DORFMAN | Chicago |
| Tropicana | Detroit and St. Louis |
| Aladdin | Detroit<br>Purportedly gives a piece of their skim to the Cleveland family |
| Sahara | Los Angeles |

Source advised that in the past, the Milwaukee family of the LCN receives skim money out of Las Vegas, exact casino unknown. Source advised that FRANK RANNEY, former trustee of the Central States Pension Fund (CSPF) was the courier for the Milwaukee family; however, he has gone into retirement and is presently residing in Florida.

Source advised that Kansas City family of the LCN has utilized PERRY THOMAS the head of the Stardust as their courier. (PERRY THOMAS is believed to be identical with CARL THOMAS). Source advised that the Cleveland family utilized GEORGE GORDON as a courier until his death in 1973 and it is believed that at the present time, MILTON ROCKMAN, aka., Maishe is carrying the skim for Cleveland. Source advised that JIMMY TAMMER has been utilized by the Detroit family of the LCN as a courier for the skim money. Source advised that the Chicago family has utilized SIDNEY KORCHAK, ALLEN DORFMAN and DON PETERS (former trustee of the CSPF and officer of the Amalgamated Bank, Chicago, Illinois) for carrying skim money out of Las Vegas. Source advised that in the recent past an individual named SLICKER SAM who owns a restaurant in Chicago, Illinois, has been doing a great deal of traveling between Chicago, Illinois, and Las Vegas and could very well be carrying skim between these two cities.

Source advised that in Cleveland, Ohio, the skim money is believed to have been split up between JOHN T. SCALISH, JOHN DE MARCO, JAMES LICAVOLI, and DOMINIC SOSPIRATO and further that MILTON ROCKMAN had also gotten a piece of the action. Source advised that since the death of SCALISH and DE MARCO the skim is now being split between JAMES LICAVOLI, ANGELO LONARDO, the reputed underboss of the Cleveland family and DOMINIC SOSPIRATO with MILTON ROCKMAN continuing to get a token piece of the skim.

Source explained that in most cases the upper management of the casino in Las Vegas are not active participants with LCN members in getting skim out of the casinos. Source advised that the skim is generally gotten out of the casinos through cooperation with the "pit bosses" in the casinos. The source advised that if the pit bosses in the casinos of Las Vegas were identified and it was determined which cities in the United States that the pit bosses are originally from this will generally give an indication of which family in the United States is obtaining the skim from that particular casino. For example if the pit boss at the Dunnes is from Chicago, Illinois or Kansas City the skim from the Dunnes would be going to Chicago or Kansas City.

Source advised that the money taken out of the casinos as skim for the most part does not come from the money rooms but rather comes right from the various tables in the casinos. Source advised that there is no accounting system in the casinos for chips which are sold. Therefore, an individual can be given a large sum of chips, they can sit and play with those chips for a short period of time, get up from the table, go to the windows and cash in the chips. These individuals then carry the cash back to the LCN members in the various cities in the United States. Source advised for example, if a dealer brought out $100,000 on a chip tray at the end of his shift he may turn in hypothetically $50,000 in chips and $20,000 in cash. The missing $30,000 in chips would be written off to losses at the table or the $30,000 worth of chips may still be in play at another table or casino. Source advised that the pit bosses generally are the individuals who furnish the LCN bag men with the chips that they cash in in order to get the skim money out of the casinos.

Source advised that another method of getting the skim money out of the casinos is by having a pit boss send a large amount of chips by courier from the casino to an individual's room. When the individual returns to his room he picks up the chips, takes them back to the windows and cashes them in to obtain cash which is then carried out of Las Vegas back to the LCN members. Source advised that another method of getting skim out of the casinos is by prying on high rollers who do not want their losses known to the IRS. Source advised that in some cases, legitimate business men who have large losses at the casino usually in excess of $100,000 do not want these losses recorded by the pit bosses but rather arrange to pay off their losses in cash to the pit boss. The pit boss in turn can skim this money without anyone in the casino management knowing and thus aiding the high roller by keeping his losses from IRS.

Source advised that this skim money is generally carried out in suitcases and private airplanes are utilized from Las Vegas to the city which is to receive the skim money.

Source advised that the individual who oversees the operations for the LCN families in Las Vegas is MOE DALITZ. Source advised that DALITZ makes certain that there is no cheating with regard to the skim money taken out of the casinos and further, that there is no fighting among families for the control of various casinos.

The following two pages consist of ten items of Jackie's official informant contract with the FBI. The day after he received a copy of the contract, Jackie had his attorney reviewed it for loopholes. Although the Special Agent's name has been censored, it is known through other documents that Agent Patrick Foran was assigned the responsibility of reading the contract to Jackie.

# Memorandum

TO : SAC, CLEVELAND DATE: 4/4/79

FROM : SA [redacted] b7C

SUBJECT: CV 5963-TE

Current Bureau regulations require that informants receive various instructions from their contacting Agents. These instructions, if not already given, should be given to captioned informant at the earliest possible date. The initialing of this memorandum by the contacting Agent will serve as indication captioned informant has received each of the instructions set forth below:

1) Informant has been advised his assistance is strictly voluntary.

2) Informant has been advised he is not, and cannot consider himself to be, an employee or undercover agent of the FBI.

3) Informant has been advised his relationship must be maintained in the strictest confidence and he must exercise constant care to insure this relationship is not divulged to anyone.

4) Informant has been assured that the FBI will take all possible steps to maintain full confidentiality of the informant's relationship with the FBI.

5) Informant has been instructed to report positive information as soon as obtained in order to insure the information is as accurate and complete as possible. Informant has also been instructed that this information should only be furnished to the FBI.

6) Informant has been instructed that when carrying out assignments he shall not participate in acts of violence or use unlawful techniques to obtain information for the FBI or initiate a plan to commit criminal acts.

80

b7C

SEARCHED ___ INDEXED ___
SERIALIZED ___ FILED ___
APR 4 1979

7) Informant has been instructed that when carrying out assignments, he shall not participate in criminal activities of persons under investigation except insofar as the FBI determines that such participation is necessary to obtain information needed for purposes of Federal prosecution.

8) Informant has been advised of FBI jurisdiction in criminal matters and, where applicable, domestic security matters.

9) Informant has been advised that any compensation received for his services must be reported as income when filing Federal income tax returns or other appropriate tax forms.

10) Informant has been advised of the FBI policy against the obtaining of information relating to defense plans and strategy of persons awaiting trial.

Although only four pages of the following FBI report have been selected, these pages constitute a small fraction of the material located in the famous Pendorf files. The Pendorf Operation was the largest legal operation ever conducted by the FBI, with the exception of the Lindbergh kidnapping case of the '30s.

Jackie had informed the FBI that Allen Dorfman had taken over organized crime activity from Jimmy Hoffa and was "now running the show." Therefore, the Bureau logically concluded that Allen Dorfman and his Chicago insurance operation had to be targeted for special investigation. It was during this investigation that the FBI discovered the direct link between Nevada's Senator Howard Cannon and organized crime.

RE: ALLEN DORFMAN

Senator TED KENNEDY recently proposed legislation to deregulate the trucking industry. It is felt by the Executive body of the International Brotherhood of Teamsters (IBT) that this would be detrimental to the Teamsters if this legislation were to pass. IBT Vice-President ROY WILLIAMS of Kansas City, Missouri, determined that this bill would end up in a Senate Committee whose chairman was Senator CANNON of Nevada. Therefore, WILLIAMS made contact with Senator CANNON, through an attorney in Washington, D.C., First Name Unknown [redacted] WILLIAMS requested that Senator CANNON hold hearings with regard to Senator KENNEDY's deregulation bill and attempt, through these hearings, to kill the bill and have it die in Committee. According to WILLIAMS, Senator CANNON agreed and in return requested that WILLIAMS handle a land deal for him, Senator CANNON, with the trustees of the Central States Pension Fund. Purportedly, Senator CANNON owns a parcel of land in Nevada, exact location unknown; and adjoining this parcel of land is a parcel of land which is owned by the Central States Pension Fund.

Senator CANNON, through his son-in-law, had attempted to purchase the parcel of land owned by the Central States Pension Fund (CSPF); however, this purchase was denied in that Senator CANNON's son-in-law's bid was considered too low by the Fund. Senator CANNON therefore, asked ROY WILLIAMS to get the trustees of the CSPF to sell this parcel of land to his, CANNON's son-in-law and in return, he, CANNON would take care of Senator KENNEDY's deregulation bill. The parcel of land in which Senator CANNON was interested has been sold by the CSPF trustees to CANNON's son-in-law for in excess of one-half million dollars less than the actual appraised value. Senator CANNON is going to use this property to build a condominium and golf course.

Following the meeting between ROY WILLIAMS and Senator CANNON, the source advised that WILLIAMS determined that CANNON was closely associated with ALLEN DORFMAN. WILLIAMS had contact with DORFMAN and DORFMAN advised him, when hearing of WILLIAMS contact with CANNON, that they should have come to him, DORFMAN, if they needed anything from Senator CANNON in that Dorfman had recently given Senator

CANNON $300,000 in a land deal in Nevada. The source did not have any specifics with regard to this deal, other than the fact that the DORFMAN deal with Senator CANNON was completely separate from the deal Senator CANNON had with ROY WILLIAMS.

ALLEN DORFMAN is involved in several deals at the present time. In particular, DORFMAN is presently negotiating with DON JO MEDLAVINE (phonetic). MEDLAVINE owns numerous theaters throughout the United States including the Circle Star Theater in Chicago. MEDLAVINE is originally from Chicago, Illinois, has [redacted] and presently resides in Los Angeles, California. In the recent past, MEDLAVINE purchased the Sunrise Theater located outside Miami, Florida, and is fronting this purchase for ALLEN DORFMAN. It is DORFMAN and MEDLAVINE's plans to book big name acts into the Sunrise Theater and skim the ticket money in much the same fashion that was done at the Westchester Theater in New York.

DORFMAN, in the recent past, is also engaged in a land deal with HY GREENE from New York. GREENE is a major land developer in the New York area and that he and DORFMAN have been very close throughout the years.

RE: SAMMY PROVENZANO

Since mid-December 1978, PROVENZANO has remained in the Miami, Florida, area and since the institution of negotiations with regard to the Master Freight Agreement in Miami, PROVENZANO has attended every day. SAMMY PROVENZANO was spending a great deal of time following the negotiations at either Gulfstream or Hialeah Racetracks, which ever one is open. SAMMY PROVENZANO has indicated that his brother, TONY PROVENZANO, has been moved from Attica State Prison to a prison located closer to his home in New Jersey. SAMMY PROVENZANO has located hey have a judge" who will get TONY PROVENZANO out of jail for a price.

After President Jimmy Carter formed the President's Strike Force on Organized Crime, the new agency began zeroing in on Jackie's vast criminal empire, which dated back to his early days as an FBI informant.

The criminal activity appearing in DOL field reports is generally absent from FBI files. The primary reason for this discrepancy is because each criminal investigation agency was working with two separate agendas. The Bureau wanted to protect its most valuable informant at all cost, while the Strike Force wanted to convict him.

There is of course, another explanation: The FBI's most valuable and trusted informant didn't go out of his way to reveal the full extent of his criminal participation. If that is not the case, then the FBI was encouraging him so that he could maintain his "cover," which allowed him to exponentially quadruple his tax-free wealth.

Reply to the Attention of

7C

DATE: March 9, 1981

SUBJECT: Aladdin Hotel and Casino
Continental Corporation
IBT Central States SE and SW Areas
Pension Fund (CSPF)
Jackie Presser

TO: b2

In approximately mid December, 1980, LMSA Chicago, mentioned in a meeting with Strike Force Chief and the writer that information had been received from LMSA Cleveland of a press report alleging that JACKIE PRESSER received a six million dollar finders fee in connection with the acquisition of the ALADDIN HOTEL AND CASINO by the CONTINENTAL CORPORATION. PRESSER is a Vice President of the International as well as an officer of the Cleveland Area Joint Council and a local union. PRESSER also is a former Trustee of the CSPF. The CSPF provided the original financing for construction of the ALADDIN and currently holds the mortgage on the property and buildings.

7C

In response to follow up questions by the writer, supplied the attached photocopy of a letter from LMSA Chicago Area Administrator to setting forth all information relative to the allegation. stated that LMSA was evaluating the information to determine if an investigation of possible fiduciary violations is warranted.

7C

On December 23, 1980, OOCR - Washington, D.C., instructed the writer to conduct a preliminary inquiry for purposes of evaluating the validity of the information. advised that Chief, Strike Force 18, had received the same information from LMSA concerning the finders fee and was interested in pursuing an investigation with OOCR if the information was valid.

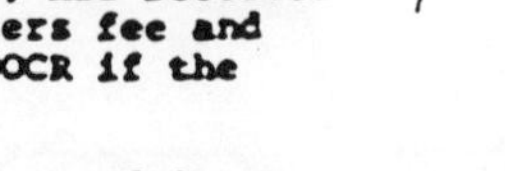

7C

Inquiry by the writer disclosed that the information and its source,

b2

-2-

as originally furnished, was partially erroneous. The original, correct information is that PRESSER received a three million dollar finders fee in connection with the sale of the ALADDIN. The information originated from a known reliable media source; however, there have never been any reports in the press of any kind to that effect.

7d
b5

Excerpts of the Investment Management Report to the Equitable Life Assurance Society of the United States and the Trustees of the Central States SE and SW Areas Pension Fund for the months of July and August, 1980, prepared by VICTOR PALMIERI AND CO., INC., setting forth the status of the ALADDIN HOTEL CORPORATION financing negotiations, have been reviewed and are attached. The reports reflect that negotiations for sale to were continuing, that gaming operations were suspended in July due to the inability of the shareholders to provide large amounts of additional working capital as demanded by the Nevada Gaming Commission, and also, that a Notice of Default was delivered to the borrower on July 13 and the Notice of Breach was recorded on July 28, 1980. The August report reflects that an agreement in principle had been reached between the ALADDIN shareholders and and the Valley Bank as Trustee The agreement was made subject to consent by the Fund and provided that a company owned jointly by and the Trust would buy all of the ALADDIN stock for $85 million less an estimated $45 million in liabilities at closing. Valley Bank would control the equity jointly with and will act as

7C

7C

As to the financing arrangements by the CSPF, the buyers would be permitted to assume the existing loans at an increased interest rate of 12% retroactive to July 1, 1980. A payment schedule was to be formulated providing for amortization of the consolidated loans to the original maturity date of January 1, 1977. Buyers would also reimburse the Fund for all expenses incurred by the Fund in previous negotiations and for the costs in connection with the

-3-

forbearance and foreclosure.

The proposed agreement also required that all documents prepared in connection with it be examined and approved by Fund counsel and NPCO.

Of possible significance, according to the report the proposed deal would provide the selling shareholders with a net of $40 million as compared to $55 to $60 million under previously submitted deals.

On January 15, 1981, [redacted] Area Administrator, Chicago LMSA, advised [redacted] agency intended no action based on the above information. [redacted] questioned the validity of the information stating that three million dollars appeared to be very high on a $12 million deal. 7C

On January 23, 1981, [redacted] Special Attorney, New Haven, Connecticut, Strike Force, contacted the writer telephonically and advised that the scope of [redacted] investigation concerning the acquisition of the ALADDIN HOTEL AND CASINO involves [redacted] as a possible Hobbs Act victim within the context of [redacted] acquisition of the hotel and casino. [redacted] is interested in any associations, ties, contacts, money exchanges involving [redacted] and [redacted] partner [redacted] and LA OC figure [redacted] stated that [redacted] does not have any information on the receipt of a finders fee and/or kickback by JACKIE PRESSER in connection with the ALADDIN. 7C

Contact with [redacted] Special Attorney, Las Vegas, Nevada, Strike Force, disclosed that there is a lot of general street talk in Las Vegas on who made money on the ALADDIN deal but nothing of specific value. [redacted] stated that $3 million to $6 million on what [redacted] understands was a $40 million plus deal does not sound unreasonable. [redacted] understands that several offers were made for the ALADDIN by other investors who purportedly would have put more cash up front than [redacted] group did. 7C

On February 27, 1981, information was received by the writer that word is going around the IBT Cleveland Joint Council that PRESSER is moving substantial amounts of money. Money is reportedly being moved into or out of unknown business investments of PRESSER in York Penn.

| | | G. R. Simmons |
|---|---|---|
| | | AT: Cleveland, Ohio |
| | | STATUS: |

Onsite field investigation: From: G. R. Simmons To: File

SYNOPSIS:

For the past several weeks the Cleveland Field Office has been conducting an investigation of allegations that Jackie Presser, a Vice President of the International Brotherhood of Teamsters, was the recipient of large sums of money from a public relations and consulting firm which had a contract with the International Brotherhood of Teamsters. This report is a summary of that investigation to date as well as a compilation and listing of undeveloped leads.

Details:

On August 23, 24, and 25, 1981, the Cleveland Plain Dealer published a series of copyrighted stories alleging that Jackie Presser, Secretary-Treasurer of Teamsters Local 507 at Cleveland, Ohio, President of Joint Council #41 of the International Brotherhood of Teamsters, as well as an International Vice President of the International Brotherhood of Teamsters, was the recipient of approximately $300,000.00 in illegal kickbacks from Hoover-Gorin and Associates, Inc. during the time frame August, 1972 through June, 1974.

b7C b7D

The monthly payments to Presser were allegedly made in cash by

DISTRIBUTION:

APPROVAL: GROUP LEADER James F. Thomas

APPROVAL: OPERATIONS

APPROVAL: DIRECTOR

This document is the property of the Office of the Secretary, OIG. Its contents are not to be disclosed to unauthorized persons.

OIG 104 (11/78)

| | VIOLATION(S): | November 4, 1981 |
|---|---|---|
| JACKIE PRESSER, ET AL. | | BY: J. F. Thomas |
| | | AT: Cleveland, Ohio |
| | | STATUS: |

Onsite field investigation: From: J. F. Thomas To: File

SYNOPSIS:

Information has been received that [redacted] is very closely aligned with Jackie Presser. [redacted] has attended numerous ground breaking ceremonies with Presser and recently announced that the teamsters in Columbus, Ohio have received the first HUD grant under the Reagan Administration in the amount of $3.6 million.

[redacted]

b6 7C

b7C b6

| U.S. DEPARTMENT OF LABOR<br>Office of the Secretary<br>Office of Inspector General | REPORT OF INVESTIGATION | FILE NO.: [redacted] 62 |
|---|---|---|
| SUBJECT: | PROGRAM: | DATE: November 4, 1981 |
| JACKIE PRESSER, ET AL. | VIOLATION(S): | BY: J. F. Thomas |
| | | AT: Cleveland, Ohio |

Date of Interview January 27, 1982

b7D

This Report of Interview with ████ was conducted on ████ ████

b7C

According to the Source, ████ has dental plans operating in seven Ohio Local Unions. Six are located in Cleveland, i.e. five Teamster Locals which are headquartered in the Joint Council #41 building and the Cleveland Trash Haulers Local located elsewhere. The Source could not remember the Local Union numbers. One Teamster Local (636?) is located in Zainesville.

b7C

The Source also stated that he understood the kickback arrangement with ████ on these dental plans to be 4% of the gross to the Local Union official and 6% to Jackie Presser.

The Source said that the "word" is that Jackie Presser will not be prosecuted for any wrongdoing by the Federal Government. It is said Jackie has been promised, from the highest levels of Government, that any investigations of him would not be followed through.

By ████ b7C

At Cleveland, Ohio

Date Dictated 1/28/82

Date Transcribed 1/29/82

File No. ████ b2



OIG 103 (11.78)

| Subject | Violation Character | File No |
|---|---|---|
| JACKIE PRESSER, ET AL. | | [redacted] b2 |
| | | Report Type: Memorandum |
| | | By: S/A James F. Thomas |
| | | At: Cleveland, Ohio |
| | | Date: April 22, 1982 |

[redacted] advised b7D
the following:

JACKIE PRESSER is acting very cocky and is telling everybody that he will beat any investigation of him because he has everything going for him. PRESSER said that the female judge handling his case is a complete fool and that she knows nothing about labor laws. He also said that the two federal agents working the case have recently got themselves in a lot of trouble with the Justice Department for embarrassing members of the PRESSER family. He stated that the agents served [redacted] in a way that caused them great embarrassment. He said that he has contacts in high places within the Government and that he is not afraid of this or any other investigation. b3 b6

| Distribution | Page 1 of 1 | Approved By |
|---|---|---|

| Subject | Violation Character | File No |
|---|---|---|
| JACKIE PRESSER, ET AL. | | [redacted] b2 |
| | | Report Type: Memorandum |
| | | By: S/A JAMES F. THOMAS |
| | | At: Cleveland, Ohio |
| | | Date: October 1, 1982 |

On [redacted] contacted Special Agent James F. Thomas and advised the following: b7D

JACKIE PRESSER is telling people that he has the "government on the run". PRESSER told him that he has everyone's telephone tapped in an effort to find out who is "snitching" on him. PRESSER said that he has had five detective agencies investigating the Federal Agents working the case. PRESSER said the Cleveland Plain Dealer is going to print a retraction and pay him two million dollars.

PRESSER further said that he has been able to quash everything on the investigation except for the trouble being caused him by his own family, most specifically ALLEN and HARRY FRIEDMAN, his two uncles.

| Distribution | Page 1 of 1 | Approved By |
|---|---|---|
| | | [signature] |

# CALENDAR OF EVENTS

**1957** Big Bill Presser nominates Jimmy Hoffa to serve ss IBT's General President. Bobby Kennedy is appointed to serve as General Legal Counsel for the McClellan Committee to investigate IBT. The Mafia chieftains meet in upstate New York. To avoid high-profile gatherings, all future meetings would be held in La Costa.

**1961** John F. Kennedy becomes the 35th U.S. President, and appoints his brother (Bobby) to serve as U.S. Attorney General. Jackie Presser opens the Eastgate Coliseum (Jan 25) with Sammy Davis, Jr. and a loan ($850,000) from the Central States Pension Fund (CSPF). The new Attorney General orders J. Edgar Hoover to target Hoffa instead of the Pressers.

**1962** Bobby Kennedy orders the Justice Department to indict Hoffa for violating the Taft-Hartley Act, which fails.

**1963** The FBI coerce a witness into giving false testimony in connection with Hoffa federal trail. Joe Valachi (New York), reveals on camera that he is a hit-man for a secret organization known as *La Cosa Nostra*. Kennedy assassinated (Nov 22).

**1964** Hoffa's federal trial in Tennessee drags on. The FBI begins secretly compiling psychological profiles on prospective jurors to secure Hoffa's conviction.

**1965** Hoover reaches the mandatory age of retirement. President Johnson refuses to order his retirement. Upon discovery of Hoover's plan to frame Hoffa, Herbert J. Miller, Jr., Assistant Attorney General informs Hoover by memo that further investigation by the Criminal Division of Hoffa is not necessary and that criminal proceedings will not be instituted. The memo is ignored.

**1966** Hoffa is convicted of witness tampering and sentenced to Lewisburg Federal Prison for 18 years. While Hoffa is en route to prison, Big Bill forms Local 507 with the approval of Frank Fitzsimmons. Big Bill assigns 15,000 members from other Locals to get the project financially off the ground.

**1967** "Babe" Triscaro (Big Bill's second in command) holds a testimonial diner for Big Bill. The testimonial is attended by state and local politicians, as well as 41 judges who are fearful of offending the most powerful Syndicate crime boss in the country.

**1968** Jackie retains the legal services of John R. Climaco to handle his divorce from his third wife (Patricia). Danny Greene, a small time hoodlum, becomes involved with the Pressers in gunning down Pete DiGravio. Big Bill throws his financial support behind Richard Nixon's Presidential candidacy.

**1969** Richard M. Nixon becomes the 37th U.S. President.

**1970** White House secrets begin appearing in Joseph Kraft's newspaper column Jackie is recruited by the FBI to become a registered informant, known as *The Tailor*.

**1971** Jackie is given his first important FBI assignment to track down a White House leak. The Pressers begin pouring cash donations into CREEP. U.S. Attorney General John Mitchell is in regular contract with both Jackie and Big Bill. Danny Greene's power is on the rise with the bombing death of Arthur Sneperger (Oct 31). The following month (Nov 26), Greene guns down Michael Frato in broad daylight. Hoffa is pardoned by Nixon and released from Lewisburg (Dec 23).

**1972** Greene has Joseph Brancato killed (Jan, 1). Hoover is discovered dead by his housekeeper (May 2). Nixon issues an Executive Order that Hoover's body is not to be autopsied. Big Bill is contacted by Mitchell for money. Within 48 hours, Jackie flies to Washington, and using the words "Pasquale has a delivery for the President." He meets with Mitchell and Nixon (Jun 20) and a gift of cufflinks. Jackie replaces Harry Haler with Duke Zeller, and awards Zeller with a $10 million advertising contract. A major portion of the money is earmarked for the Committee to Reelect the President (CREEP).

**1973** Haler approaches the Chicago IRS for a finders fee, and reports Jackie and Big Bill's money laundering scheme to Nixon. When IRS discovers that Teamster money is involved, IRS agents contact Attorney General Mitchell. Instead of investigating the Pressers, Haler is indicted for using stolen bonds. Jackie is offered one-third interest in a multi-million Front Row Theater project for less than $40,000. Jackie will use this investment to launder millions of dollars in cash.

**1974** The Front Row Theatre (TFRT) opens with Sammy Davis, Jr. (Jul 5). Nixon resigns his presidency (Aug 9) over the Watergate scandal, fearing the exposure of his lies to Big Bill's crime Syndicate. Jackie meets with Allen Glick (Las Vegas) and Delbert Coleman (Chicago) to structure a $62 million loan from the Central States Pension Fund (CSPF). For his cooperation is structuring the loan, Jackie receives ownership in both The Stardust and Frement Hotels in Las Vegas. Jackie's attorney (Climaco) begins constructing a labyrinth of various holding companies to conceal Jackie's secret ownership in various business ventures. Seaway Acceptance Corp. is used to avoid compliance with the Bank Secrecy Act.

**1975** Jackie's $40,000 investment in TFRT is now generating $1 million laundered, capital gains profits. His union salary is $900,000 annually, making him the highest paid union official in the country. Greene has Shonder Birns killed (Mar 29). Greene is recruited by John Nardi to form a new crime consortium to complete with the Mafia. Jackie serves as a stand-in recipient for his father to receive two of Israel's highest awards. Hoffa comes to Cleveland (Jun 22) to line up support for his bid to recapture the IBT General Presidency. Jackie meets with Maishe Rockman (mid-July) to pick up $25,000 from Jackie. The money will be used to finance Hoffa's hit. Greene learns from Babe Triscaro about Hoffa's scheduled assassination and tips off the FBI. Hoffa is reported missing by his family (Jul 30). Jackie sells his interest in TFRT to Seeburg Industries for $1 million, which is resold to Xcor, in which Jackie is a major stockholder. For his assistance in structuring this convoluted financial transaction, Jackie appoints Climaco to replace Robert Rotatori, and serve as general counsel for all Ohio Teamsters. With his excess funds, Jackie purchases a $1 million estate for his mistress.

**1976** The Cleveland Mafia don (Scalish) passes away in the presence of Maishe (May 26). Maishe reveals that Jack Licavoli is to be the next Mafia don. Big Bill announces his retirement (Jun 26). Eugene Ciasullo is injured by a bomb built by Greene. Frank Percio is killed (Sept 24) by a bomb built by Greene. Leo Moceri disappears (Aug 22), and Greene is the prime suspect after he publicly avowed to have "all the Jews and Italians" assassinated. Jackie makes the decision to support the Mafia (Aug 22) in its war against Greene. Jimmy "The Weasel" Fratianno flies in from Los Angeles to induct four new Mafia members (Sept 5), which takes place the following month. Attempt to assassinate John Nardi fails (Sept 10). Liberatore reveals to Fratianno that he as developed a snitch inside the FBI. At the national Teamster convention (Las Vegas), Jackie delivers his famous anti-Communist speech.

**1977** Jimmy Carter is elected 39th U.S. President in the wake of the Watergate scandal. Liberatore obtains a list of FBI informants from an FBI file clerk (Feb 2). Jackie's FBI handler retires (Feb 6), and Jackie is assigned a new code name (Alpro). The FBI opens its *Operation Strawman* investigation to target the Kansas City Mafia. Greene kills Enos Crnic (Apr 5). The Mafia eliminates Greene's alli, John Nardi (May 17). A new RICO investigation is initiated with the renewed interest in Hoffa's disappearance (Jun). Greene is assassinated (Oct 4) in an operation planned by Liberatore and Fratianno.

**1978** The FBI initiates its largest investigation since the Lindbergh Kidnapping case against Allen Dorfman (Aug). The secret investigation will become known as *The Pendorf Operation*.

**1979** Nevada Senator Cannon, Dorfman, Roy Williams and Ed Wheeler meet in Las Vegas (Jan 10) to discuss the acquisition of 5.8 acres from the Teamsters. Maishe will present their deal to Jackie. Senator Kennedy introduces the Trucking Deregulation Bill in Congress (Jan 22). Senator Cannon puts the Bill into his Commerce Committee where the Bill dies. The FBI obtains federal authorization to install 13 telephone tapes on Dorfman (Jan 29), based upon Jackie's information. Dorfman meets with Nick Civella to discuss how to take control of the $2 billion CSPF. Jackie receives a written copy of his formal FBI contract (Apr 4). Civella summons Williams to Kansas City (Apr 23) to meet with Dorfman and Sam Arcona. They want Williams to turn over the CSPF to them. Jackie informs the FBI of the details. Jackie also informs the FBI about Cannon's efforts to sabotage the Deregulation Bill in an effort to make Carter and Kennedy appear foolish before the next election. Agent Foran introduces Jackie to Robert S. Friedrick, Jackie's third FBI handler (Aug 7).

**1980** Treasury Agent Steven Wells pays Jackie an unofficial visit to inform him of an assassination attempt on his life by Joseph DeRosa, Jr. (Jul 3). Jackie financially backs Reagan's candidacy.

**1981** Ronald Reagan becomes the 40th U.S. President. Reagan attempts to appoint Jackie to Secretary of Labor, but the effort is defeated. Jackie's Uncle Allen is arrested by the Strike Force for embezzlement union funds under the RICO Act (Jan 20). DeRosa, the individual who was scheduled to assassinate Jackie, is found murdered in his car (Apr, 17).

**1982** The Strike Force seizes Jackie's financial records (Mar 1). Hoffa is officially declared dead (Jul 30). Jackie's attorney (Climaco) is officially notified that the Justice Department has closed its investigation of Jackie in relationship to his participation in funneling secret cash donations to Nixon (Oct 4). Ten agents with the office of Labor Racketeering seal off Jackie's Local (Oct 8). In addition to records, agents seize porno tapes and a large stash of gold coins. FBI agents Foran and Friedrick meet with Jackie to discretely discuss the Labor Racketeering investigation, and review what steps could be taken to kill or stall the criminal investigation (Oct 20).

**1983** Allen Dorfman is assassinated (Jan 20). Agent Friedrick meets with Jackie to discuss possible leads on who assassinated Dorfman (Jan 21). Jackie meets with Friedrick and reveals his contact with Johnny "Peanuts" Tronolone, the *consigliere* with the Genovese crime family (Mar 18). Assistant FBI Deputy Director Oliver Revell meets with FBI Director Smith and recommends that the FBI continue to protect Jackie (May 10). Jackie is appointed to serve as IBT's General President with the approval of the Genovese crime family. The following month, President Reagan appoints Jackie to serve as Special Advisor to the President on Labor Affairs. The appointment does not require Senate conformation.

**1984** By Executive Order, President Reagan disbands the Strike Force on Organized Crime, thus saving the President from having his tie to organized crime publicly exposed. Jackie is officially retired from being an FBI informant, but the Bureau offers to continue providing him and his attorney with Special Privileges.

Syndicate Boss, Jackie Presser, while serving as Special Advisor to President Reagan on Labor Affairs

# INDEX

*Note:* Names, companies and agencies appearing in Calendar of Events and the various FBI and DOL documents have not been included in this index.

## Footnotes



## Photos